THE ESSENTIAL BOOK OF
HORSE TACK
& EQUIPMENT

THE ESSENTIAL BOOK OF
HORSE TACK
& EQUIPMENT

SUSAN McBANE

David & Charles

In memory of little Sam, a puppy till the day he died and very much missed

Susan McBane has a lifelong experience of riding and looking after all types of horses and ponies. She has an HNC in Equine Science and Management, is a Shiatsu for Horses Level 2 therapist and is the author of over 40 equestrian books. She was co-founder with the late Dr Moyra Williams of The Equine Behaviour Forum and is the Editor and Membership Secretary. A teacher of classical riding, she holds The Classical Riding Club's Gold Star award and is listed in its Trainers Directory. She also currently runs her own internet magazine at www.susanmcbane.com

636.1
McBane

A DAVID & CHARLES BOOK

Hardback edition first published in the UK in 2000
Paperback edition first published in the UK in 2000
This edition first published in the UK in 2002

A catalogue record for this book is available from the British Library.

ISBN 0 7153 1389 4

Printed in Hong Kong by Dai Nippon
for David & Charles
Brunel House   Newton Abbot   Devon

CONTENTS

CONTENTS

PREFACE

Tack seems to hold a never-ending fascination for horse enthusiasts. However, there is such a profusion of tack and other equipment now in circulation that the range is truly confusing. Although there is no shortage of information about it, horse magazines still receive frequent enquiries about it: how to use it, what sort to get, how to tell good from bad, where can a reader buy this or that, can the editor explain the bitting arrangement on last month's front cover, and why is a certain horse still not going well despite the owner having tried over two dozen bits?!

There are many other colourful guides around which catalogue what is available in the tack shops. But this is much more than a catalogue. I want the reader to start thinking about *why* he or she has chosen a particular piece of tack and to think about *how* it will affect the horse. I explain – mainly in Chapter 1, but with references elsewhere – how the horse's body works, also how he should move and carry himself when he is working correctly and in the most effective way to carry a rider; and how anything we fasten to his body and then manipulate will affect his movement and overall well-being.

Clothing affects a horse much more than many people ever imagine, and this is discussed and explained in Chapter 6. You will learn about the dressage horse whose turnout rug ruined his performance in the arena, and the three-day-eventer who died because his New Zealand rug was fitted incorrectly. You will also read about the legendary steeplechaser and his famous jockey who won the Prix d'Auteuil on the browband because the bit had snapped in two.

Stable and yard equipment is also discussed, and even this can directly affect a horse's health and behaviour. For example, you will discover how feeding your horse from a haynet can cause problems when he is ridden, how a favourite family hack was permanently lamed by an unsuitable feed bucket, and how a Grade A showjumper nearly died from colic because his manger was fixed too high.

Finally, I do hope that the information given in this book will help you to realise that the choosing of good quality tack and equipment which is right for both you and your horse need not be nearly so complicated as at first it seems.

SUSAN MCBANE

June 2000

1 HOW THE HORSE MOVES

The sight of a supple, healthy and happy horse in movement, especially at liberty, is one which warms the heart of any ardent horse lover. However, we rarely stop to consider more closely the immense intricacy and split-second co-ordination of the bones, muscles, nerves, tendons and ligaments, and the system that contains them and enables this movement to take place. We just drink in the spectacle of one of nature's finest athletes revelling in the capabilities of his body – his strength, his lightning reactions, his speed, agility and sheer athleticism.

Most animals easily outclass humans as athletes, but the horse is unique in his attraction to man because of his size, strength, speed and beauty, and lastly but far from least, his willingness (in general) to associate with us and to do as we wish – his trainability.

But what happens to the horse's freedom of movement as described above once a human gets on his back? If the person is a good rider who goes with the movements of the horse's body, and who rides without anything on the horse's back or head(!), not a lot of deterioration will be seen in his ability to perform – but once people start fixing 'things' to his body with fairly tight (sometimes very tight) straps or ropes – blankets, saddles, headgear such as halters and bridles – and putting what we now call bits in his mouth, made of anything from wood, horn and bone to metal, rubber and, nowadays, various poly-whatever materials, then the picture changes immediately.

Although the horse is a far more efficient athlete than the human, the similarities in the physique of a staying steeplechaser and a marathon runner are apparent. Both mammals have lean, spare physiques with tuned-up, slow-twitch muscles

9

Even the presence of these items on his body will change the horse's direction of thought from forwards (where he is going) to here (his head where his thoughts come from) or backwards (where most of his body is). Any tack on his body can obviously be felt, and the added weight of even a good rider will certainly compromise his inclination towards the free, forward movement that we all seek – but provided he does not feel discomfort or pain, his mind will not be distracted, nor his natural movement impeded too much.

If, on the other hand, all this gear is poorly fitted, badly adjusted, misused and, insult of insults, operated by a bad rider, then the horse will experience unacceptable pressure or friction, irritation and discomfort, all certainly enough to cause restriction of his natural movement and his will to co-operate. And once pain enters the scene, then the picture described in the first paragraph is ruined. The horse will start changing the way he moves in an attempt to get away from these sensations, weighting and over-stressing his body in a manner it was neither designed nor equipped to cope with – and further pain, and 'mysterious', unidentified injuries can be the result. His natural movement will be changed for the worse, maybe permanently as it becomes a habit. Badly fitting rugs (which are worn for many hours at a time) can cause as many problems as ill-fitting saddles, and so can headcollars.

Above: The horse at liberty (left) shows his full expression in movement. Caught at exactly the same moment in the stride (right) the same horse as in the picture on the left, although ridden by a competent rider, is visibly less expressive and free in his way of going

Below: Severe overbending like this serves no useful purpose and can cause tearing of the nuchal ligament in the poll area with subsequent pain, tension, possible development of head-shyness and reluctance to work and move freely

A great many riding problems can ultimately be traced to physical trauma caused by us. Moreover not many of us would be prepared to strap tight, uncomfortable contraptions to our own body, put a significantly heavy, unstable and demanding animal on our back, and then go running and jumping where it tells us – nor would we want to haul it round the lanes in a vehicle – therefore we will never have any real idea of how the horse must feel. We can only use our imagination, and recall what it is like to wear a pair of shoes that really hurts, or clothes that infuriate us because they are so uncomfortable, or are forced to do some kind of physical work or exercise that we don't want to do, or are pushed around or bullied by someone we don't want to know, or even worse, thought we could trust to treat us well.

Below: This horse is going in exactly the opposite way to that required of a riding horse. Well 'above the bit', the horse's poll, neck, back and loins are tense and contracted, the spine if sagging and the hindquarters and legs are not engaged

This must be something like the experience that many horses are obliged to tolerate every day. I know of few humans who would put up with this, or could experience it and remain mentally and physically unchanged, so it is no wonder that there are so many soured, distrustful, resigned or rebellious horses around.

Well fitting, properly adjusted tack in good condition will do the least damage to the horse's body and movement, particularly if combined with an empathetic rider who really knows how to move with the horse. It is therefore essential that the rider learns, firstly, how to move so as not to

11

restrict the horse's natural move-ment: this is passivity, which is really active non-interference, and not the same thing at all as 'sitting still' which we are often exhorted to do in lessons. Secondly and later, he or she must learn how to move his or her body to influence the horse's mind and movement: this is active influence. (The subject of learning how to ride in this way is well outside the scope of this book, so if it sounds new to you I recommend respectfully that you read *Enlightened Equitation* by Heather Moffett [David & Charles], a book which may well change your riding life.)

We will now consider more closely tack and clothing, and how they affect a horse's movement and well-being.

THE SKELETON

The horse's body is founded on his bony skeleton, an intricate marvel of living, hard but non-rigid bone, plus gristly cartilage with more 'give' in it. The bones are bound and lashed together and supported by tough, fibrous tissue called ligament which can take the form of large, flat sheets, narrower, flat 'straps' or rope-like cords.

Ligament is very strong, but only very slightly elastic; it is also very sensitive, and can certainly be injured by over-stress (usually tension). Unfortunately it does not heal well, and never returns to its previous state after an injury because the tissue produced to repair and replace the injured tissue is not as strong as the original. Each subsequent injury in the same spot weakens the repair tissue (known as 'scar' tissue) even more, so that a horse who keeps sustaining injury to a particular part is constantly taking one step forwards (as he heals) and two steps back, because the part becomes weaker and more susceptible to injury each time, particularly if the horse's people keep recreating the circumstances which caused the original injury. This is why so many racehorses and eventers, for example, which sustain serious tendon or ligament injuries rarely reappear in their original sport, and if they do, they don't last long because they can't withstand the original level of stress any more.

Left: The photograph shows clearly how much the back dips and the hip comes forwards on the side on which a hindleg is moving forwards

Right: A short section of the vertebral column showing the upright (spinous) and sideways (traverse) processes or extensions

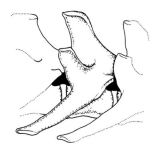

This repair phenomenon applies to all soft (non-bone) tissue – muscles and tendons as well as ligaments and other general connective tissue.

The bones of the skeleton can also repair themselves after injury, probably better than any other tissue in the horse's body. The skeleton has approximately 210 bones; these consist of living cells and minerals and are supplied with blood, with lymph which supports and assists the blood system, and also with nerves. The bones of the spinal cord (the vertebrae in their vertebral column) are complex. Each is hollow through the middle, and with the bones lying end to end as they do, this forms a tunnel down which the spinal cord runs from the brain. This cord is made of the same sort of vulnerable nervous tissue as the brain itself, and is

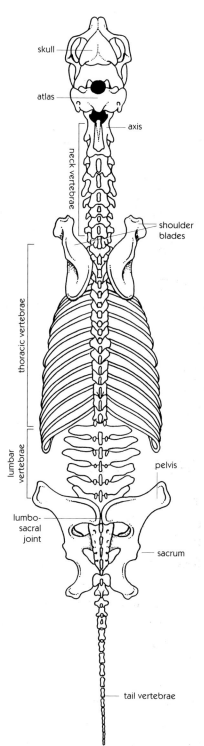

The skeleton from above

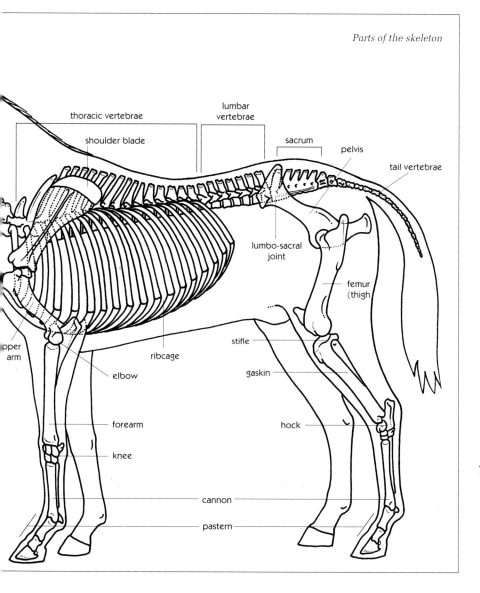

Parts of the skeleton

HOW THE HORSE MOVES

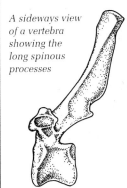

A sideways view of a vertebra showing the long spinous processes

responsible for receiving information and sending messages via the nerves which pass out between the vertebrae to most parts of the body.

The individual vertebrae have bony projections called processes: those that protrude from their tops are called the spinous processes, and those at the sides the transverse processes (to which are attached the ribs in the chest and back areas). These act as attachment points for muscles, ligaments and tendons. The spinous processes in the fore part of the vertebral column (see diagram) slope backwards towards the tail, gradually becoming more upright. Those in the hind part of the column slope towards the head likewise, and one vertebra, the anticlinal vertebra, has an upright spinous process. This area is capable of the most movement – although this in itself is only slight – and so it is the weakest part of the horse's back: unfortunately for him, it is right under where the saddle goes and where the rider sits. The implications of this are obvious.

THE VERTEBRAL BOW

Further back in the spine, in the croup area which forms a 'ceiling' to the bony ring of the pelvis, are five vertebrae which are fused together to form a single bone known as the sacrum; the sacrum itself forms very tight joints with the ilia of the pelvis (see diagrams). The joint between the front end of the sacrum and the vertebra in front of it (the last of the lumbar

Far right: The large muscles attached underneath the loin area and pelvis and to the femur (thigh bone) contract to flex the lumbosacral joint, tilt the pelvis under and bring the thigh, and therefore, the hind leg forwards

A diagrammatic representation of the vertebral bow. The solid line indicates an undesirably sharp flexion of the poll, a neck which tends towards lowering (kinking) at the base in front of the rider's hands, and a back which is sagging, with hindquarters not really engaging (coming under). The dotted line indicates a smoother, more rounded flexion and neck raised from the base, raised back and engaged hindquarters

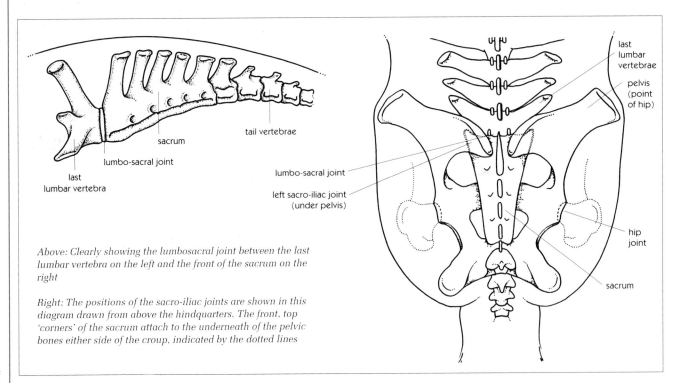

Above: Clearly showing the lumbosacral joint between the last lumbar vertebra on the left and the front of the sacrum on the right

Right: The positions of the sacro-iliac joints are shown in this diagram drawn from above the hindquarters. The front, top 'corners' of the sacrum attach to the underneath of the pelvic bones either side of the croup, indicated by the dotted lines

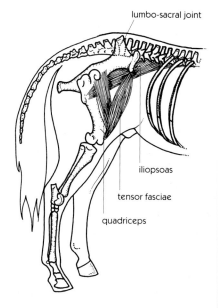

vertebrae in the loin area) is called the lumbosacral joint; it is the flexion of this joint which is essential if the horse is to be able to 'bring his hindlegs under him', or to 'engage his hindquarters'.

This engagement is brought about by the contraction of, among others, the iliopsoas muscles under the loin and hindquarter part of the vertebral column (attached to the lumbar vertebrae and part of the pelvis at one end, and to the femur or thigh bone at the other) and by the abdominal muscles, or rectus abdominis muscles (attached to the back part of the sternum or breastbone at one end and to the pelvis at the other). The shortening by contraction of mainly these muscles tilts the lower part of the pelvis forwards and helps to advance the femur or thigh bone. Obviously this is another forward influence on the hindlegs since they are attached to the pelvis at the hip joints, helping to bring them under the hindquarters as the horse 'tucks his bottom under'.

To achieve engaged hindquarters, and hindleg joints that are slightly flexed when weight-bearing, is something that all good riders and trainers aim for in their horse; however, it is only a part of the whole functioning of the horse which increases to a small degree the natural, slight, upward bow or arch to the vertebral column, thereby creating a strengthened back posture.

The vertebrae of the neck are usually described as being formed in the shape of a letter S which is tipping towards the horse's head (and reversed if you are looking at the horse's left side). The skull joins at the poll to the top vertebra of the neck, the atlas, which permits up-and-down movement of the head. The atlas is followed by the axis which permits side-to-side movement of the head, and the remaining neck (cervical) vertebrae follow on down the S, terminating just in front of the scapulae (shoulder blades) where the thoracic vertebrae (those of the chest or thorax) take over. These, in turn, lead to the lumbar vertebrae of the loins and quarters, the sacrum already described, and finally, to the coccygeal (tail) vertebrae.

Below left: The 'ring of muscles' in a correctly moving horse, showing a smooth, gently stretched and rounded topline, the neck being raised from underneath its base, the hindquarters and hindlegs engaging and the abdominal muscles contracting to provide 'lift' and support from below

Below right: Here the 'ring' is not at work. The neck, back and quarters are tense, shortening the topline and allowing the back to sag. The neck is dipping at the base, the hindlegs are trailing and the abdominal muscles stretched – exactly the opposite functioning to that required

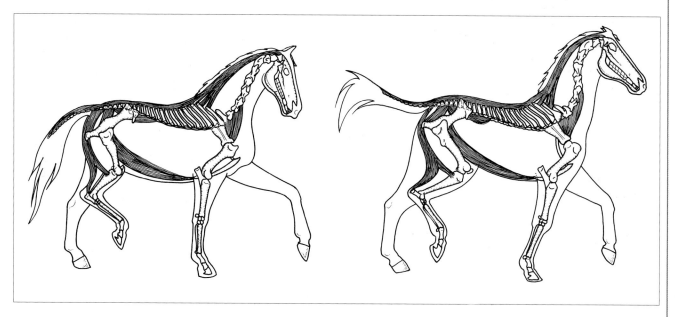

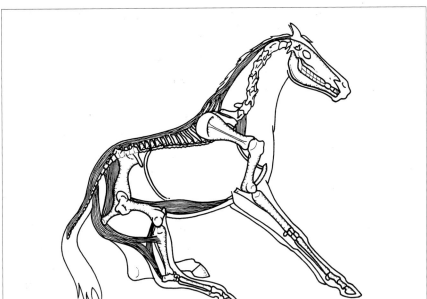

Left: Ultimate engagement of the back and hindquarters with contracted, supporting abdominal muscles and balancing head and neck are shown in the diagram of the sliding stop of a stock horse, a movement often used when working cattle

Under the lowest, downward curve of the neck's S-bend, towards each side and attached to the cervical vertebrae, are the scalenus muscles: these are crucial to correct head and neck carriage and, therefore, to the continuation of the rounded outline (begun by the engagement of the hindquarters) and self-carriage of the well trained, correctly balanced and freely moving riding horse. When the scaleni contract, they cause the base of the neck to rise, slightly flattening the lower S-curve upwards and pushing the neck and head forwards.

This action should be initiated by the horse himself and maintained by him, with other muscles, as self-carriage on a comfortably light rein/bit

Right: Diagrammatic representation of the effect on a horse of draw-reins where the horse's head is pulled back and in: the stress is shown on the muscles beneath the neck vertebrae and in the poll area as the horse tenses to avoid the pressure caused by a forced posture

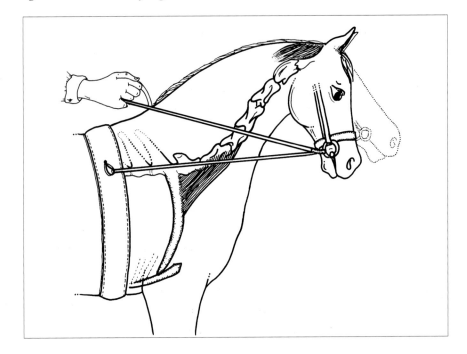

contact: this is the only strong, safe and correct functioning of the head and neck. Any technique employed by the rider to force the position of the head and neck, such as harsh, pulling hands, or the incorrect use of various schooling aids will result in false flexion and incorrect muscle use, because the horse will use the 'wrong' muscles to avoid the discomfort and pain and so those muscles will develop at the expense of the 'right' ones.

In addition, the tensioned vertebral bow which protects the horse's back against the weight of the rider will not be maintained under saddle, and so the back will sag and become over-stressed, weakened and possibly injured, adversely affecting not only the horse's movement but his comfort, well-being and physical functioning.

The head and neck act as the horse's balancing pole: the large nuchal ligament that attaches to the poll area runs down the crest of the neck and then attaches in the area of the withers, allowing the horse to rest effortlessly with his head about level with his withers. Sheets of ligamentous tissue run down from the nuchal ligament; these attach to the neck vertebrae, helping to support and stabilise them. The nuchal ligament continues down the back over the spine as the supraspinous ligament, attaching to the spinous processes in the loins and hindquarters. It helps to limit excessive spinal flexion.

The complex arrangement of the various back muscles, particularly the latissimus dorsi, attached all along and around the horse's spine and linking and supporting his two ends, helps him to brace his back during movement; these muscles become more and more tensioned the faster the horse goes, thus protecting the spine against excessive flexion at speed which could cause injury in such a big, heavy animal. They tense and relax alternately, allowing normal blood circulation through them which promotes health and development. Any adverse influence may cause them to become actually stiff: this might be incorrect work, or forcing a head carriage, or it might be as a self-protective mechanism against pain from a badly fitting saddle, a lumpy saddle pad, bad riding or inappropriate schooling aids – anything, in fact, which prevents their natural functioning: in these circumstances they become hard, wiry, stringy and flat, and underdeveloped because constant stiffness and over-tension disrupts the normal flow of blood through them.

JOINTS

The bones of the skeleton have various types of joint between them which are 'padded' by gristly cartilage so the bones can move without causing pain (from bone rubbing against bone). Some joints are freely movable, some can only move forwards and back, whereas others can move slightly sideways as well. Others are actually fixed, such as the sacrum and those between the many bones of the skull, even though there may still be a thin layer of fibrous tissue or cartilage between them.

THINGS MAY NOT BE WHAT THEY SEEM

As we have seen, the spinal cord runs inside its bony tunnel some inches down inside the horse's back, and is relatively well protected by bone and surrounding elastic muscle and other soft tissue. It takes quite a significant injury to affect it – but the spinous processes are a different matter.

When you run your fingers down your horse's spine it is the tops of the spinous processes that you feel, not the bodies of the vertebrae themselves. These tops are covered by a thin layer of skin, ligament and other soft-tissue structures, and are very susceptible to pressure and over-stress, as are the sensitive, elastic muscles of the back. A saddle which presses on the tops of these processes, a numnah which is pushed down onto them by the saddle, a rug which presses on them (nearly always at the withers) and/or a bad rider who thumps and twists on top of these processes and on the muscles at the sides: all these can cause intense pain and injury.

Readers interested in complementary therapies may be interested to know that the back is the site of many acupuncture/acupressure points which are constantly stimulated by the saddle, with all sorts of wide-ranging, far-reaching effects. Too much pressure, and the wrong sort of pressure in the wrong places – due to bad fit, bad riding, lumpy stuffing, uneven or wrinkled saddle pads and so on – can cause all sorts of physical and behavioural problems.

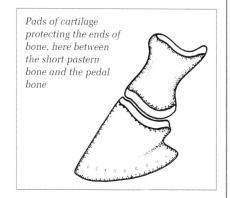

Pads of cartilage protecting the ends of bone, here between the short pastern bone and the pedal bone

MUSCLES

Muscles are integral to the body structure in that the bones cannot move, or rather be moved, without their influence. Muscle tissue is the meaty part of an animal, as opposed to the fat, skin or gristle; it is soft and elastic, and profusely served by blood and nerves. There are three types of muscle, only one of which, skeletal muscle, concerns us in relation to tack. (There is also smooth or visceral muscle, found in the walls of the hollow organs of the body such as the digestive tract, the arteries and the uterus; and cardiac muscle, found only in the walls of the heart.)

Most skeletal muscles are powerful, sensitive structures that operate in specific groups to move or stabilise specific parts of the body – for instance, the hindquarters, the forehand and so on. Muscle consists of cells (like any other tissue) which in this case take the form of long fibres controlled by the nervous system. Muscles work their influence by contracting or shortening; however, they cannot stretch themselves, but must be stretched by the action of opposing muscles in their group.

Work and exercise cause muscles to increase in size and strength – to develop – whereas lack of work causes them to atrophy or shrink in size and strength. From the point of view of riding, training, tack fitting and tack use, this is a fundamental premise.

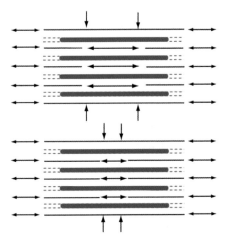

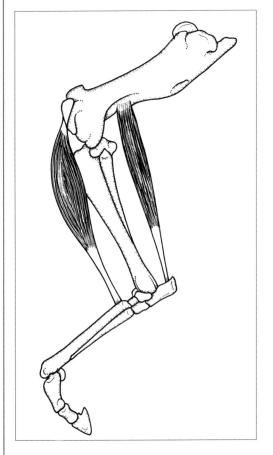

Above right: The shortening effect on a muscle as different types of muscle fibres (cells) contract the muscle by sliding over each other. The top diagram shows an uncontracted muscle and the lower one a contracted muscle

Left: The contracting and stretching of opposing muscles. The muscle in front of the hindleg is shortening and 'fattening', pulling on its lower tendon (attached to the cannon bone) and forcing it to lift, so flexing the hindleg, whilst the muscle behind the leg is passively stretched. When that muscle contracts, it will straighten or extend the leg and the muscle in front of the leg will be stretched

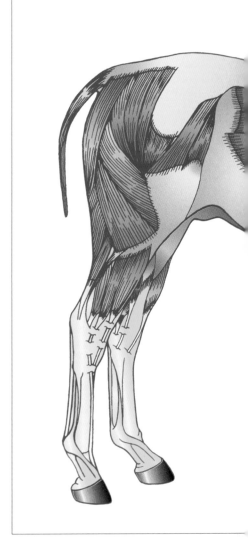

Skeletal muscles are attached to one bone at one end, and to a different bone at the other, and they are attached by means of strong, slightly elastic, modified muscle tissue called a tendon. In between the two ends of the muscle is a joint. When a nerve message reaches the muscle fibres, the muscle contracts or shortens, pulling on the tendon and so moving the bone to which it is attached, and thus flexing or rotating the joint in between.

For example, certain muscles attached to the rear of the shoulder and the forearm bones contract to bring a foreleg backwards. Then an opposing set attached to the front of the bones contracts whilst the first set relaxes, thus bringing the leg forwards again – and so each step is taken.

These opposing muscle groups also maintain a slight antagonistic tension, or tone, which helps control the movement of their partners and normally prevents over-extension of, and distress to, the joints. This

The musculature of the horse

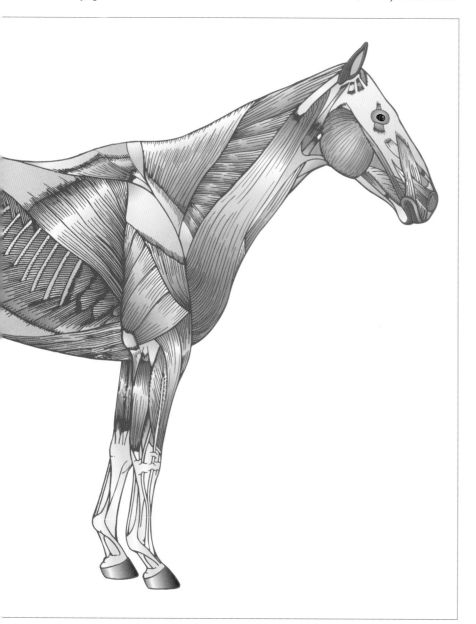

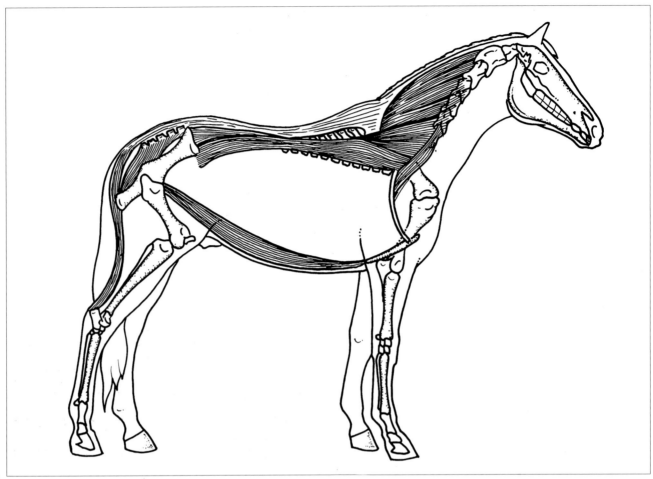

muscle tone, with its counter-balancing effect, helps the horse to keep his balance and stay upright when standing, for instance, and is also important in his sense of place and body posture, or proprioception, during movement and positioning, from galloping to lying down.

THE RING OF MUSCLES

The correct contraction and relaxation of these main muscles (with others) results in several favourable things: it shortens the horse's underline (abdomen or belly); it flexes the joints of the hindlegs; it stretches, relaxes and lengthens the muscles and ligaments of the horse's topline; and it develops the appropriate muscles of the neck, forehand, upper legs, back, loins and hindquarters, thereby encouraging a strong, bowed shape and proper physical function throughout the whole body, so that it will support the rider easily (his or her weight permitting).

If the rider holds the horse's head up and/or in by means of the bit and reins or various gadgets, it may look to the uninitiated as though he is moving correctly, but in fact the result will be a stiff neck which dips at the base; development of the wrong muscles; a sagging, weakened back;

The 'ring of muscles' in a standing horse. The full action of all the muscles involved (which are not shown) is very complex but it is only necessary to understand their basic effects as described in the text to see how they are hampered by discomfort and pain from tack or by poor riding. The muscles 'topline' attaches to and around the whole vertebral column and to the pelvis and hindlimbs. The abdominal muscles attach to the breastbone and pelvis; when they contract in correct movement the belly-line is shortened and the topline encouraged to round and stretch more. Basically the horse should go with a downward influence on head and hindquarters and an upward one on belly and back

and faulty leg action front and back, the forelegs flipping out instead of arcing elegantly and the hindlegs trailing. This way of going also over-stresses the back, neck and limbs.

To the knowledgeable trainer or rider, the way in which a horse's different muscle groups have developed, or not, are a clear indication as to whether that horse has had good or bad training, or been well ridden and managed; they won't even need to see him in action. Such an expert will be able to predict how the horse will go, and maybe even what tack has been used on him.

These various muscles and their associated soft tissues have come to be called 'the ring of muscles' or just 'the ring'. They must all work together as described, and they must also be in healthy working order for the horse to be able to move correctly with the least risk of over-stress and associated injury.

IRRESISTIBLE REFLEX ACTIONS

Skeletal muscles are often called 'voluntary' muscles because it is assumed that the horse has their control under his will and decides whether or not to move. However, many movements are involuntary or automatic (such as the horse's muscles constantly twitching to help him keep his balance, or contracting sharply to move him away from pain), in that they are caused by nerve cells called receptor cells all over the body which detect sensations and send information messages about them to the nervous system, which then sends instruction messages back along other nerves: the result is a reflex action. This happens so quickly, and sometimes countless times a second, that the horse is not even aware of the process until he has moved.

Imagine a sudden pain in the mouth from the bit: a lightning message goes to the central nervous system and one comes back equally quickly, so that the horse changes the position

Socking the horse in the mouth for whatever reason causes a reflex action due to the pain which his instincts tell him to avoid. His head comes up, his neck kinks downwards, his back tenses and drops, his hindquarters and hindlegs trail and his belly drops

of his head in such a way as to avoid the pain – he perhaps throws up his head, and in doing so probably also alters the position of his body to keep his balance, and so his whole outline and movement changes. The pain will also have frightened him so his mental 'equilibrium', co-operation and maybe trust are also severely compromised – all in a split second, but an experience which may take very much more time to overcome.

ENERGY AND TOXINS

Muscles store energy as the nutrient glycogen (a form of glucose extracted from food and delivered by the blood); waste products or toxins resulting from the 'burning up' of glycogen are also present. The most usual waste product is carbon dioxide which is produced by the using up of glycogen in the presence of oxygen to provide energy for work – even the tiniest, quickest movement of a muscle demands energy. Lactic acid is another, more toxic waste product produced when muscles have to produce energy with little or no oxygen.

Blood supplies nutrients and oxygen, and it also removes these waste products. However, sometimes the supply of oxygen is too slow for the rate at which certain muscles are using it: this can happen, for example, during fast work such as sprinting; during excessively sustained work or tension, such as when a horse has to constantly brace his hindquarters during forward-facing travel in order to keep his balance; or through being made to hold a particular outline during training; or by being made to work for too long without a break. In these circumstances energy is supplied anaerobically (without oxygen), and waste products build up more quickly in the muscles: this causes pain, stiffness, fatigue and eventual loss of function, even muscle damage.

Muscles which are intended to work by means of a quick, alternate contract-and-relax function quickly become fatigued, poisoned and stiff by being forced to maintain tension (contraction) for too long. Muscles in this condition do not, in fact, develop as the trainer may wish and expect, but become thin, hard and stringy; this is because their chemically imbalanced internal environment prevents them functioning properly and their hardened condition makes it difficult for the blood to circulate through them. However, adequate rest and relaxation, alternating with contraction and tension, will enable the blood and lymph to keep passing through and to remove waste products, thus promoting healthy function and development.

Dr Sharon Cregier, equine transport specialist, was probably the first to point out the stressful effect on the back, loins, hindquarter and hindleg muscles when horses are transported facing the direction of movement – forwards. The horse needs to brace (contract) the muscles of his topline and keep his head raised for long periods just to keep his balance in an erratically moving vehicle which throws his weight onto his hindquarters. This greatly stresses the muscles and can result in the production of lactic acid and other toxins which can actually cause muscle damage by the end of the journey – just when the horse is expected to work. Rear-face transport, perhaps herringbone, allows the horse to take the weight more naturally on his forehand, balancing with his head down. A lowered head is also needed for the respiratory drainage necessary to help avoid shipping

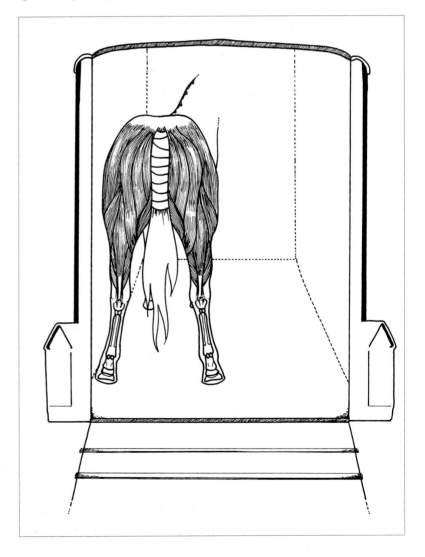

REINFORCEMENT

Many skeletal muscles are reinforced by strips of tendon, ligament and other soft tissue called connective tissue running through them, sometimes linking one end of a muscle with the other and blending with the tendinous tissue at each end. Some muscles have a good deal of this reinforcing tissue, and are strong enough to act as supports and shock-absorbers when muscles have to brace to bear weight, such as when a horse shifts his weight to his hindquarters, or rears, or works in collection, or jumps. The hamstring group of muscles down the back of the horse's quarters and thighs is structured like this.

WORKING TOGETHER

As well as such muscles being themselves reinforced within by linking lengths of supportive tissue, many are also linked to each other because they receive fibres from neighbouring muscles and other soft tissues; in this way, all the muscle groups of the horse's body are linked. The natural reaction of the horse, or any creature, on feeling discomfort or pain is to cringe away from it (sudden pain, as described, results in a rapid reflex action); so in the context of the horse's muscle groups being interlinked, let us see what might happen if he experiences pain or discomfort in his back due to a badly fitting saddle.

The hindquarter and hindleg muscles which contract suddenly to produce the force needed in jumping

His instinctive reaction will be to drop his back down (in the opposite direction of the upward ventral bow) and to stiffen his back muscles against the pain. Dropping his back stretches the ligament running underneath the vertebral column (the infraspinous ligament), and at once puts the spinous processes at risk of rubbing against each other and of severely pressuring and tearing the soft tissues attached to and surrounding them. The bones themselves may even be damaged in some cases. This can all be extremely painful and debilitating, depending on degree, as anyone who has had any sort of back injury will know.

The stiffened back muscles, being linked to the muscles of the hindquarters and forehand, will pull on these neighbouring muscles and they will stiffen, too. The muscles of the neck are similarly affected, so whatever self-carriage has been achieved here will be completely lost, and the neck will also lose its correctly curved upper outline. The muscles around the poll and jaw will clamp up, the horse will cease to flex or to accept the bit kindly and his head will go up, his muzzle out and his neck will drop at the base. The shoulder and chest muscles will also be affected, and so will not initiate that swinging, sweeping movement of the

forelegs which every trainer strives to establish – indeed, the action will become shorter and more 'proppy'.

Behind the saddle, a similar chain of events occurs. The muscles of the loins, hindquarters and hindlegs will all stiffen and so the action will deteriorate: the lumbosacral joint does not flex, and the hindlegs stiffen and trail as the joints are unable to flex and absorb weight under the horse. The abdominal muscles will drop and stiffen, rather than relaxing and contracting to lift the belly, and the horse will start to look more like a hammock slung between weak, unstable fore and aft supports, rather than like a strong, braced suspension bridge.

Pain in the mouth from a badly fitted or harshly used bit; a bit of the wrong design for the particular horse; a tight, restricting noseband; pain or discomfort in the jowl region due to forced or incorrect flexion caused by the rider pulling back on the reins or by unsuitable gadgets: all these will cause the horse to stiffen the muscles in the poll region. And because of the soft tissue connections between muscles and muscle groups, this stiffness will run on down the neck to the forehand, the back, the loins, quarters and hindlegs, with ultimately the same results as back pain.

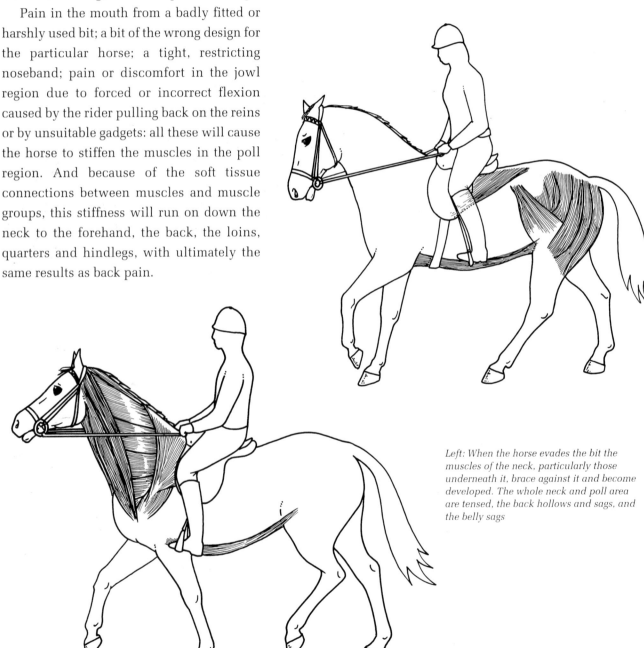

Below: Muscles affected when the rider moves harshly and stiffly in even a well fitting saddle, not blending with the natural movements of the horse's back. The back muscles are compressed which tenses them, the back is shortened and dropped, the abdominal muscles sag and the hindquarter muscles are stressed as the horse tries to push forwards despite his awkward posture

Left: When the horse evades the bit the muscles of the neck, particularly those underneath it, brace against it and become developed. The whole neck and poll area are tensed, the back hollows and sags, and the belly sags

24

The same process occurs when the horse is caused discomfort or pain by any item of tack which is badly designed, incorrectly used, poorly fitted or in hard, dirty condition. Physically he will tense up, stiffening and hardening his muscles. If his tack and the way it is used imprisons him in a particular posture or outline from which he feels he cannot escape, he will try to relieve the pain in his muscles and other structures by adopting other postures within the framework imposed upon him: coming behind, over or above the bit, carrying his head up and out and cringing down the bottom part of his neck, sinking his back, trailing his hindlegs and so on, all in an effort to relieve the ache and escape the pain. As well as adopting 'the hammock position', he will go crookedly, unevenly, take short, pottery steps or begin to play up by napping, bucking, rearing, bolting and so on.

Mentally, his trust in humans will undoubtedly be severely dented. Pain also causes fear, and a frightened horse soon reverts to the wild animal with its flight-or-fight response to danger, one which still simmers beneath the surface of every domesticated horse or pony.

Below: This illustration shows a rider with an appalling posture in sitting trot; the low, 'set' hands induce the horse to poke his nose, tense the upper neck muscles and stretch those underneath the neck and in the chest. The rider, bumping up and down on the horse's back instead of absorbing his movement through the hips, pelvis and spine, is banging about on the trapezius muscles and the latissimus dorsi behind the withers and beneath the saddle and, beneath the latissimus dorsi, the longissimus dorsi muscle of the back

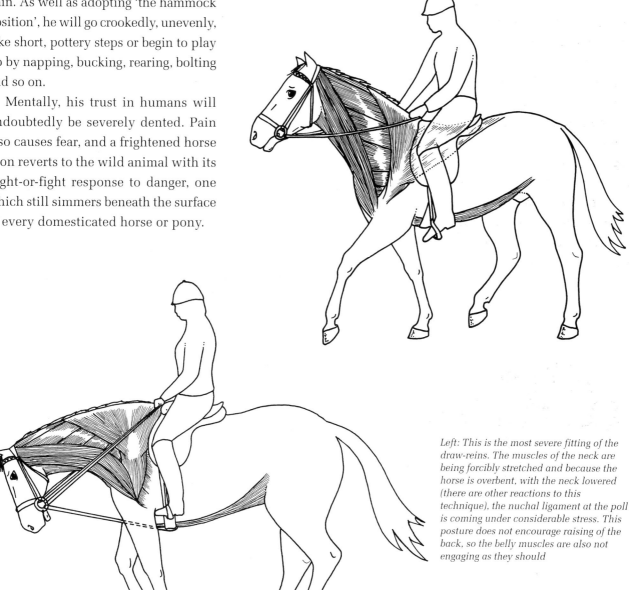

Left: This is the most severe fitting of the draw-reins. The muscles of the neck are being forcibly stretched and because the horse is overbent, with the neck lowered (there are other reactions to this technique), the nuchal ligament at the poll is coming under considerable stress. This posture does not encourage raising of the back, so the belly muscles are also not engaging as they should

25

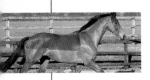

SKIN AND COAT

The skin and coat are subjected to a good deal of stress from tack and clothing, due to pressure and friction. In winter the hairy coat that covers most of the body cushions and protects the skin to a certain degree – unless we clip it off. A clipped coat or a short, summer coat offers only limited protection, and is fairly easily worn away if subjected to very regular friction; and pressure will cause bruising, at the very least.

The skin consists of two main layers, the thin top layer of which (the epidermis) is composed of dead skin cells which are continually sloughing off. Being insensitive, this offers some protection to the layer below, the dermis with its many highly sensitive nerve endings that detect not only heat and cold but also pressure, friction and pain. This layer is also well supplied with the blood vessels and capillaries that are necessary to keep this life-maintaining, elastic organ in good health.

If the epidermis is subjected to enough friction, it does wear away exposing the dermis so that the horse has a raw and very painful sore. We all know how painful a burst blister or raw patch can be, due to shoes or other equipment which has rubbed us. Riding in underwear with seams in the wrong places can produce really painful, even raw saddle sores, just as jodhpurs or breeches with any kind of unevenness or roughness in the internal fabric or stitching can cause similar sores on the rider's legs. This sort of pain is exactly like that experienced by a horse suffering from girth galls, for instance, or any other friction sore caused by his tack. When such skin injuries heal, the hair may never regrow, or if it does, it will probably grow back white – a sure testament to previously badly fitting tack or rugs.

Bruising is caused by excessive and maybe uneven pressure, again

PROBLEMS IN THE GIRTH AREA

The girth area also has many acupressure points, as well as being richly supplied with nerves; however, in my opinion it is often grievously abused these days by incredibly tight over-girthing, a pernicious current trend, the effects of which are greatly underestimated in my experience – not to mention the sheer physical pain, discomfort, mental distress and restriction of movement and breathing that is caused by a very tight girth around the ribcage.

This is a common sight – the shoulders have been rubbed bare (and possibly bruised) by pressure from a rug which is too large in the neckline and has slipped back. The withers are also probably affected as the rug will have slipped on to or even behind them

often from rugs at the withers and, of course, from saddles, pads or numnahs and girths which dig in, press the skin hard enough to injure its cells and cause inflammation with its classic symptoms of pain, swelling, redness and heat. The microscopically fine capillaries transporting blood in the skin are flattened, and the circulation to the pressured area is greatly reduced or actually cut off, resulting in damaged skin. In repeated or severe injury, the skin and underlying tissues can actually die, forming a hard patch of dead tissue (called a 'sitfast' by horsemen) which will have to be surgically removed and will take a long time to heal.

It is now considered that horses with a high, 'sharp' wither may actually be suffering from muscle atrophy (due to a restricted blood supply) in the area just behind and below the withers, caused by pressure from the tree points and stirrup bars (see Chapter 2) of a too-narrow saddle pressing hard under a rider's weight over months or years and causing visible hollows.

The hair provides a neat insulation system. The roots in the dermis each have a tiny erector muscle which contracts to pull the hair outwards when the horse feels cold and relaxes to allow it to flatten when he warms up. In addition the hairs are hollow. This dual quality creates an adjustable, warm-air layer next to the skin particularly effective in winter due to the greater overlap of the longer hairs, creating a thick duvet

The skin is weaker and softer when wet from sweat or rain and so is more susceptible to, in particular, friction. Sweat does contain a degree of body oil, however, and so is believed by some to actually act as a lubricant. My experience is that horses fitted with saddle pads and girths of modern permeable materials which allow moisture to pass away from the skin do stay drier underneath, and this must be a good thing. However, it is true that in the days when leather saddles were used straight on the horse's back (not so usual these days) and were kept clean and soft, with even flocking that was not allowed to become hard and lumpy, horses did not suffer so much from sore backs. Neither did they suffer from girth galls when leather girths were the norm and were kept clean and soft by frequent oiling. Many horses and ponies are, of course, still equipped in this way today, and are fine – so there may well be something in the lubricant theory.

2 SADDLES and ACCESSORIES

The saddle is the most expensive single item of tack a horse owner is likely to buy, and one that has an absolutely crucial effect on how the rider rides and how the horse goes; it is therefore amazing that more care is not taken over the suitability, fit and actual putting on of the saddle, and that more thought is not given to what it does whilst on the horse's back.

HOW WE GOT WHERE WE ARE

Although there are various specialist saddles for different disciplines, I imagine that most readers will engage in what is termed in the USA and Australia 'English' riding, which means as opposed to Western, saddle seat or stock seat. This type of riding would include hacking out, dressage, cross-country competing, hunting, showjumping, showing, riding club events and that sort of thing, and there is a range of saddles which are mainly modifications of a basic design. That basic design still stems from the English hunting saddle with its 'plate' seat and revolutionary tree or framework around which the padding, leatherwork and so on were fitted.

The English hunting saddle began its development during the eighteenth century when the lovers of mounted hunting started to chase the fast and straight-running fox as a quarry. Deer had become scarce since the Civil War, when populations were decimated for food, and hare-hunting,

Below: Portrait of The Byerley Turk by John Wootton showing the typical sort of saddle, with its high pommel and cantle, used before the advent of foxhunting

Left: The fast galloping and jumping sport of foxhunting necessitated a saddle without the interference of a high pommel and cantle so that fences could be more comfortably and effectively negotiated. Most horses up to about the middle of the twentieth century were hunted in double bridles which were regarded as the mark of an educated horse and rider. The middle horse here is wearing a running martingale fitted to the curb rein, again a fairly normal practice felt to emphasise the flexing, head-lowering effect of the Weymouth or curb bit

29

although it did still continue, was circuitous and not terribly fast. In an effort to find something more challenging to hunt, the fox was selected, and its pursuers very soon found that the high-pommelled, high-cantled saddles then the norm were useless for sustained fast galloping and for jumping significant fences, hedges and ditches, more or less necessary if you were to follow the fox's line and be in at the kill. The call was out for something less cumbersome, neater and lighter, which did not hamper the movements of the rider in this new, fast pursuit – although the saddle that evolved did not help him, either, as anyone who remembers them will know. (Racing saddles were really the only exception to the traditional saddle and were, at this time, still evolving into the virtual postage stamps used today.)

PREDECESSORS

Before the appearance of the hunting saddle, the type used and often still seen today in Iberia and in eastern Europe – not to mention at the Spanish Riding School in Vienna – had a high pommel and cantle and was designed to support the rider and help him stay on in war, when bullfighting, and when working cattle (depending on where he lived); it was also intended for use on long journeys on horseback over rough, natural country and when travelling the appalling 'roads' or other commonly used travel routes which had barely received maintenance since the demise of the Roman empire. Such saddles were also normal equipment for Haute Ecole riding.

A Portuguese classical horse and rider in traditional eighteenth-century turnout. Classical saddles with high pommels and cantles are still used in this type of riding today

Saddles used by early civilisations were little more than relatively soft, treeless pads of leather or textiles stuffed with animal hair, sometimes beautifully decorated; however, the advent of armoured knights in mediaeval warfare demanded something stronger, bigger and more supportive. This type of saddle became lighter subsequently, and was the one that was used – because there wasn't anything else – during what came to be called Haute Ecole or High School riding, the movements of which originated from battlefield and bull-ring manoeuvres. The eighteenth century was notable for the equestrian renaissance – not an era marked by non-horsey historians, but a milestone in equestrianism – its participants including royalty, aristocracy, gentry, army officers (particularly of cavalry and hussar regiments), and wealthier merchants and the general well-to-do; and High School riding was regarded as an essential part of a young man's education (only the more daring young women being allowed to take part, purely as a pastime and a means of 'healthful exercise'). The saddles they used were made on a rigid, wooden frame with the high pommel and cantle already

mentioned. They were padded with sheep's wool, horsehair and the like, covered not only with leather but also with textiles and felts, and often ornately decorated with embroidery and inlays of precious metals and even stones, depending on the owner's purse and status. But for the increasingly cut-and-thrust new sport of fox-hunting they were useless – in particular a high pommel was, to put it mildly, uncomfortable when jumping, and a high cantle prevented the rider leaning back when landing over a fence, a practice which was considered necessary to 'lighten the horse's forehand' and save his forelegs. Enterprising saddlers therefore created the hunting saddle in response to market demand of the time.

I remember learning to ride on this type of saddle (which could be found easily up to and during the 1960s) with its broad tree (giving excellent weight-bearing and spread of pressure over the horse's back), its wide waist or twist (desperately painful for riders with arthritic or less-than-supple hips) and protruding stirrup bars – and, therefore, buckles which also inflicted pain and bruising. I don't actually remember feeling particularly discontent at being uncomfortable, because we did not know any better; we were told that if the saddle hurt us it was because we were not riding properly – or were told not to be soft, little girl status notwithstanding!

This type of saddle came to be used all over Europe and in the USA, and was modified by different countries, along with other designs, to suit their requirements. Although many European countries no longer hunt, the basic design has remained, to be modernised and adapted for present-day requirements.

This painting clearly shows that the English hunting saddle went to the opposite extreme to its predecessor with a very flat seat, slightly forward cut flap and stirrup leather placed well forwards, making it extremely difficult for the rider to ride with his heels beneath his seat. The horse is wearing the normal double bridle minus noseband, often considered pointless

FOR BETTER – OR WORSE?

That saddle remained the standard until the post-World War II burgeoning of the leisure and competition horse, when the twentieth-century western (note the small 'w') equestrian revolution in showjumping and eventing created another demand: for forward-cut panels and flaps to accommodate the shorter stirrup then brought in for jumping by such innovative instructors as Santini, Caprilli and Toptani (who each had their own saddle designs). The new, forward jumping position or 'half-seat' was difficult to maintain with an old-style broad-waisted tree and rather straight-cut flap, and so saddlers began to make forward-cut flaps, recessed stirrup bars and narrow waists.

However, there seems to have been no apparent thought for what these narrow waists were doing to the horse's back, whereby the same amount of weight and pressure was distributed over a much smaller area. Moreover the increasingly preferred narrow waists became translated, very unfortunately for the horse, into 'narrow tree' and most horses have suffered as a result because of the pinching pressure of the tree points (see diagram in Saddle Fitting) just behind and below the withers, sometimes to the point of atrophied, deformed musculature. (This and other points will be elaborated upon when discussing saddle fitting.)

The forward-cut panels and flaps of the new design, incorporating blocked knee rolls for added rider security (depending on the exact saddle and the conformation of its wearer), tended – indeed, still tend – to interfere with the backward movement of the top of the shoulder blade when the horse extends his forelegs or lifts them over a jump. I find that most of my students and clients use saddles which are cut unnecessarily far forward for their needs – and they also put them on slightly too far forward, so that interference with shoulder blade action and, therefore, foreleg extension too, is far more common than people realise, even if the tree is wide enough for the horse.

Until recently, it had not been fathomed out how to incorporate a narrow enough waist for the rider but with a broad enough panel/weight-bearing area for the horse's comfort. As will be seen in this book, this problem can now be solved – but many saddles made and bought are still much too narrow for the horse because this fashion has, in its turn, come to be the accepted norm, only starting to change as we enter the twenty-first century.

Below: An early effort at the new, more forward Caprilli jumping style in forward-cut saddle and with a thick numnah underneath, believed to help the horse round over the fence. Note that the horse is wearing a simple snaffle bit, noseband and no martingale

Bottom: This horse, tacked up for a cross-country competition, will be significantly hindered by his saddle being much too far forward. The forward-cut panel and knee

rolls are coming well over the tops of his shoulder blades so when he tries to extend his forelegs, for maximum scope, the tops of the shoulder blades will come back and be blocked by the saddle, resulting in a shortened stride

VARIATIONS ON THE THEME

By far the most commonly bought modification is the general purpose (GP) saddle. It is unfortunately named because it gives the impression that it is suitable for more or less everything, whereas in practice many are only suitable for jumping, and certainly do not encourage, or make it easy for, the rider to sit deep and maintain a balanced seat on the flat. Over the last decade or so, the 'very slightly dressage' (VSD) cut or design of saddle has become more popular: this is less forward cut than a GP saddle (which is, in turn, less forward cut than a pure showjumping saddle), and is probably the best choice for general riding today, depending on three things: that (a) it fits the horse; (b) it is balanced when on his back so that the deepest part of the seat is mid-way between pommel and cantle; and (c) the stirrup bars are placed sufficiently far back to enable the stirrup leathers to hang vertically when the rider is in a balanced position (so that his or her leg is not pulled forward because this, in turn, will tip the rider's seat back).

Below: The saddle on the left is a Fieldhouse 2000 Range 'all purpose riding saddle' with a fairly forward-cut flap, intended largely for eventing. The saddle on the right from the same range is the VSD (very slightly dressage) saddle, having a flap cut much less forward than a normal event or general purpose saddle and therefore suitable for all-purpose riding where serious fences will not be encountered

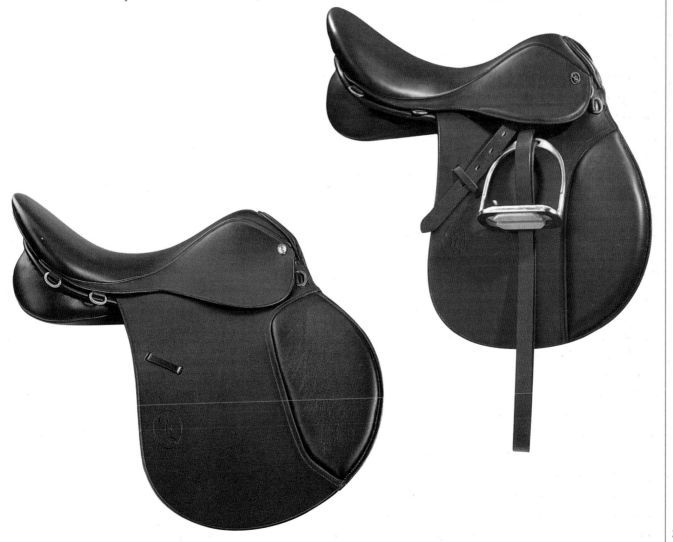

THE MAKE-UP OF A SADDLE

THE TREE

The tree or frame on which the saddle is constructed determines the shape of the saddle, and therefore the purpose or discipline for which it is to be used. The accompanying illustrations show a saddle tree and a complete saddle, naming the significant parts. Traditionally, trees have been made of laminated beechwood (though sometimes other woods are used). The parts are heated and pressed into the required shape, then joined together and covered by muslin scrim fabric. Metal is used to strengthen the head (the pommel) and the rear arch (the cantle), and for the stirrup bars. Metal strips are also added from pommel to cantle underneath the tree for strength.

STIRRUP BARS

The stirrup bars of a good saddle are made of forged steel, again for maximum strength, because it is these which very often support the entire weight of the rider, compounded by the force of movement – a rider bouncing up and down, however skillfully, is heavier than a static one. On the end of each bar is a little metal catch which is meant to be left in the 'up' position to keep the stirrup bar on during normal riding; however, kept well oiled it would move down if any untoward pressure were put on it from a backward movement of the stirrup bar, as during a fall, so that the leather

SPRING TREE OR RIGID?

Another innovation of the 1960s was the 'spring tree', in which two light blades of metal are built in on each side of the seat from pommel to cantle. This technique gives a comfortable, moderately springy feel to the seat in action, and most saddles have it incorporated. However, there is a school of thought which maintains that it causes the panel under the seat to move too much on the horse's back, and also that the springiness absorbs the rider's seat aids too much so that the horse cannot feel them. Given a choice, however, most riders would certainly opt for a spring rather than a rigid tree, even though spring trees are more expensive than rigid ones (this is probably why they are rarely incorporated into children's saddles).

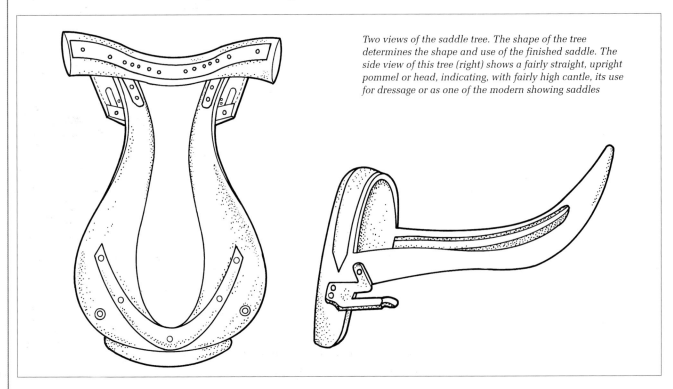

Two views of the saddle tree. The shape of the tree determines the shape and use of the finished saddle. The side view of this tree (right) shows a fairly straight, upright pommel or head, indicating, with fairly high cantle, its use for dressage or as one of the modern showing saddles

would come off the bar and the rider would not be dragged. Nowadays we are always exhorted to ride with the catch down, 'just in case'. As modern bars are recessed and the surrounding leather of the panel helps keep the leather on the bar, and also as the bar may be angled very slightly upwards towards the rear, there is little chance of the leather sliding off during normal riding. Certainly I have never known this happen.

THE SEAT AND GIRTH STRAPS

The saddle seat is set up by tacking pre-strained canvas strips under strips of leather to the tree. In a traditional leather saddle the seat itself is either of sueded leather if you want a little 'stickability' (particularly if you also wear 'sticky seat' jodhpurs or breeches), or of plain leather, most economically cow hide like the rest of the saddle, or doeskin or occasionally pigskin.

The stuffing under the seat in the panel can still be of flocking (wool), but many leather saddles now have synthetic stuffing materials for economy and because they do not become hard and lumpy like flock. The earlier problems of the material squashing or even breaking down, resulting in a lowered saddle and a baggy panel beneath the seat, have largely been overcome today in better quality saddles.

The two webs to which the two rear girth tabs or straps are fastened are fixed over the waist of the tree, and the front one is stitched to a web which may be wound round the two sides of the tree or fastened over it. This arrangement helps to stabilise the saddle, and it also means that should one web give way you will have one, quite independent of the broken one, to keep your girth fastened – most girths fasten with two buckles (occasionally three) on each end, usually to the front and back tabs leaving the middle one free. Some saddles have the hindmost girth strap fixed further back than normal and angled forward towards the others: this provides greater stability of the saddle on the horse's back, and helps prevent the back half of the saddle lifting in action and continually slapping down or moving too much.

You can use different girth straps to help keep your saddle in position, according to your horse's conformation or condition, although if your horse or pony has no natural girth groove you may need other help such as a breastplate (to keep it forward) or a crupper (to keep it back), although the latter are very rarely seen on riding animals these days.

To help keep the saddle back, fasten the girth to the two front straps: to help keep it forwards, fasten it to the two rear straps.

THE PANEL

The panel under the seat and flaps in most saddles is gusseted today for a more level fit and stability (originally this idea was only found in

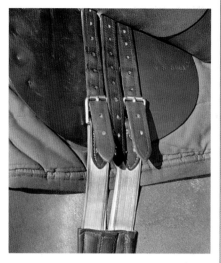
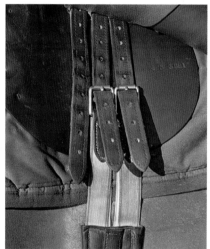
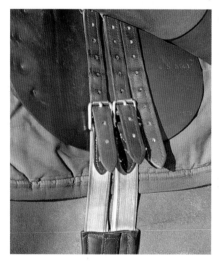

Fastening the girth to the first and third straps (top) is normal for a horse on whom the saddle stays in place; fastening the girth on the last two straps (centre) helps to keep the saddle forward and on the first two straps (bottom) helps to keep the saddle back

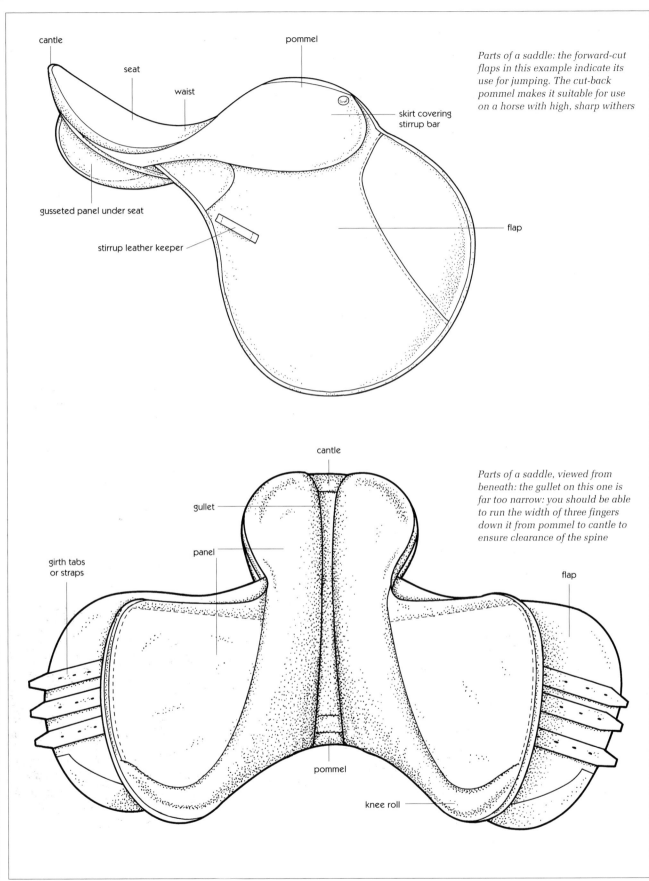

cantle

seat

waist

pommel

skirt covering
stirrup bar

gusseted panel under seat

stirrup leather keeper

flap

*Parts of a saddle: the forward-cut
flaps in this example indicate its
use for jumping. The cut-back
pommel makes it suitable for use
on a horse with high, sharp withers*

cantle

gullet

panel

girth tabs
or straps

flap

pommel

knee roll

*Parts of a saddle, viewed from
beneath: the gullet on this one is
far too narrow: you should be able
to run the width of three fingers
down it from pommel to cantle to
ensure clearance of the spine*

dressage saddles). Little leather pockets are sewn onto the panel, and the points of the tree fitted into them; the panel is then stapled or stitched into place. In my experience it is the tree points that cause more problems in modern saddles than any other part, despite being over the padding in the front part of the saddle. Most people are aware that the pommel, gullet and cantle must amply clear the spine, but they are quite oblivious of the pressure that is caused to bear down through the padding by the points of a too-narrow tree. Pressure from weight on the nearby stirrup bars often compounds this problem.

The panels must be very carefully and evenly stuffed whatever the material used, because lumpy, uneven stuffing can throw the best designed tree out of balance, and easily cause pressure points and a sore, bruised back. Stuffing and panel fit must be checked frequently by the rider (every time you tack up, ideally) and if found wanting, the faults rectified – ideally by its maker or at least by a qualified saddler – before the saddle is used again. If it is over-stuffed, the panels will take on a rounded shape quite unlikely to conform with any horse's back, concentrating most of the pressure along two thin areas down each side of the spine and resulting in significant discomfort, bruising and pain. If newly done, too, the stuffing may be too hard. This can be modified by turning the saddle onto its seat and beating the panel under the seat with two

Hard, lumpy stuffing like this will surely create discomfort and pressure bruising on the horse's back

stout sticks to break down the stuffing; fortunately nowadays, with improved knowledge of the effects of a saddle on a horse's back, this sort of elementary error in restuffing saddles is much less common than it used to be.

Another error used to be that too much stuffing was put into the front half of the saddle, which tipped the whole thing backwards – including the rider – thus concentrating weight and pressure under its rear half, and perilously near the horse's loins.

Most saddles today, except some showing saddles and a very few others, have full panels not half panels which finish half way up under the flap. These necessitate a flap of stiff leather called a sweat flap being fitted to protect the more absorbent underside of the flap from the horse's sweat. It is redundant on a full-panel saddle, and should be removed, if present, as it is one extra thickness the rider can do without.

This photograph, from the Balance organisation, shows a saddle with uneven stuffing, and, therefore, different depth panels which will make it impossible for it to sit level on the horse's back

Right: The general purpose version of the Balance Soft Option saddle

TREELESS SADDLES

Generations ago, toddlers, even little more than babies, started off their riding careers in what were known as 'basket saddles'. These were made of natural basketweave, and supported the child's wobbly little body on both sides and at its back, and sometimes in front, too. There would be a (waterproof!) cushion inside (this was in the days before leakproof nappies), and the 'rider's' chubby little legs stuck out of holes. The whole effect was of a miniature howdah.

A child progressed from the basket saddle to a felt pad saddle. These were of thick, stiff, usually green felt about 1in (2cm) thick and with no metal tree, with tough leather loops for the stirrup leathers, and a stiff, raised leather 'bar' or handle over the front part for the child to hold. They obviously afforded the child no support of any kind whatsoever (so you went from one extreme to the other), but were firm favourites with parents, grooms, teachers or whoever did not have to ride on them because it was felt that they taught the child to really feel its pony's back beneath it, and so develop 'natural horsemanship' – and they were cheap. They may still be found in old tackrooms somewhere, but I haven't seen one for many years.

These saddles would appear to have been foolproof: they had a wide girth sewn into the lower part of the 'flaps', with buckle adjustments as normal, and they fitted virtually every pony of any make or shape without the possibility of back injury (although girth galls could occur); however, they still

Below: This saddle, the Balance Soft Option dressage saddle, has only the front half of the saddle tree and appears to be extremely comfortable for the horse

tended to slip, slide and twist about, despite being used with a crupper. A more secure, 'feeling' seat was doubtless obtained by riding with a blanket-and-surcingle arrangement, with no stirrups – this was marginally more comfortable than riding bareback on certain ponies with 'backbones', and it certainly saved you from getting all sweaty from the pony. However, I always preferred going bareback when I could – a lot less time to tack up, and a lot less tack to clean! Of course, I was accused of being lazy!

Today, soft and half-tree saddles are being developed again but mainly for adults this time. I have ridden on a Balance Soft Option saddle (with a half-tree – the front end) and although it felt unusual it did not disconcert me. The seat is thick and shaped and offers more support than the old felt saddles. I understand other companies are developing a similar idea. It has been suggested that they cannot offer enough support to amateur, 'working' riders who cannot become as 'riding fit' as those able to ride for several hours a day but I feel much will depend on the rider's natural posture and seat.

BALANCE ... the way forward ...

THE BALANCE SADDLING SYSTEM

The Balance Saddling System has evolved over ten years using the experiences gained by riding and closely observing many hundreds of horses in their way of going and their reactions to different saddles.

Balance was formed by Carol Brett, Lesley Ann Taylor and Maureen Bartlett. They have found that very many horses appear to have been ridden in saddles which are too narrow for them, among other faults, and they have developed a method of assessing the horse in movement as well as when stationary in order to supply one of their own-design saddles to take both his conformation and action into account.

Their system has now been refined, and a team of Balance-trained saddle consultants covers the UK; it is also possible for non-UK horse owners to buy Balance saddles.

When a saddle tree is too narrow for the horse, the main pressure is just behind and below the withers and over time horses frequently develop hollows in this area, giving the impression that they have what are usually described as 'high, sharp withers'. After remedial groundwork advised by Balance and correct work in a saddle which is wide enough for the horse, used with appropriate padding and numnahs for the horse's stage of redevelopment and which takes into account his individual conformation and action, the correct muscle development becomes apparent, the hollows fill out and horse invariably move more freely and willingly.

SYNTHETIC MATERIALS

The main reason most people choose synthetic saddles – synthetic bridles seem to be less favoured, although they are common in endurance riding – is because they are much cheaper than traditional materials. Another big plus for busy owners, grooms and employers with an eye on labour is that they are much easier and quicker to clean than leather, which has to be washed and saddle-soaped and occasionally dressed or oiled, depending on preference and use. Newer cleaning products claim to be all-in-one, doing away with washing and drying off, the laborious rubbing-in of soap, and the need for regular dressing: however, not all of them work well in practice. A final good reason for using synthetic materials is that if your saddle gets a real soaking it will dry out in a trice compared to leather and wool flocking.

When synthetic materials were first introduced for saddles in the 1980s, there were undoubted problems with them, even though it was claimed they had been 'fully tested' for wearing qualities. Some of them split and cracked fairly easily (as many synthetic boots still do); saddle trees twisted, spread or 'gave' alarmingly, putting the saddles well out

The Thorowgood's synthetic Maxam Pony Dressage saddle, with long girth tabs and suede-effect saddle to help the rider maintain position. An economical solution when introducing children to dressage

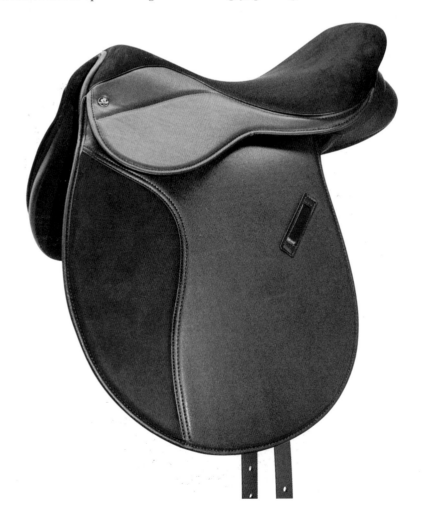

Left: The Thorowgood synthetic version of the Heather Moffett GP saddle. The stirrup bars are in the same position as on the Heather Moffett dressage saddle so that each leather falls perpendicularly under the rider's thigh. It has knee rolls attached by Velcro to the panel under the flaps and Heather has designed the dressage knee roll so that it supports the rider's thigh, keeping the knee deep. The knee rolls are interchangeable so that the same saddle can be used for both purposes. There is also a wider seat for extra rider comfort

Far right: This saddle, the Thorowgood Griffin general purpose saddle, won the Your Horse *magazine Reader Award for four years running. Described as having a 'well balanced, medium-sweep tree', it is claimed to have a roomy seat to allow movement and has adjustable knee and calf blocks to help the rider maintain leg position*

of shape and ruining their fit; and a common problem was the flattening and even breaking down of the padding in the panel beneath the seat, again causing bad fit and saddle injuries to the horse. From the rider's point of view, the saddle seat soon appeared to go out of shape and lose its resilience.

Nowadays synthetic saddles are much more reliable and of higher quality, made of vastly improved materials and padding, not to mention design. Some famous and popular makes of saddle now have their synthetic 'working' counterparts, and some riders keep their leather tack for best. Furthermore the synthetic saddles are said to 'break in' and 'bed down' more easily than leather ones, certainly an advantage provided the process does not continue indefinitely! Although synthetics still do not last as long as traditional materials, because they continue to be relatively cheap they can, at least, be replaced without breaking the bank.

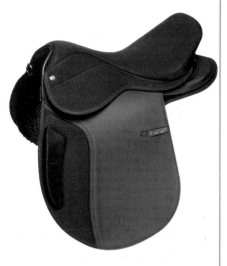

Above: The Thorowgood's synthetic Maxam Trekka saddle which is lightweight, has fleece-covered panels and a wide bearing surface for good spread of pressure on an animal carrying weight for long periods. The surface-mounted knee blocks are claimed to offer extra security when riding downhill

The materials used range from plastics, polymers, gel seat in-fills, 'sueded' materials for seat and flaps and more conventional-looking leather lookalikes. Impact-resistant foams have been taken from the aerospace industry (often the sort used in pilots' ejector seats), and the medical profession has contributed with plastics and shock-absorbing materials, too. Admittedly synthetic saddles sometimes do look cheap and cheerful, but many are now indistinguishable from a leather one from a short distance away. The designs as far as shape, knee rolls, balance and so on can be just as good and correct as in saddles or traditional materials, and so you can have an upmarket design for a fraction of the price. Some items are guaranteed for a given number of years or even for the lifetime of the original purchaser, which is most reassuring.

The girth straps – so vital in their function – may be of similar synthetic materials to the saddle flaps, or of synthetic webbing with reinforced holes. The early saddles commonly fell down badly in this department, with reports of straps snapping, holes wearing and fabric fraying. These defects do not occur with the improved synthetics.

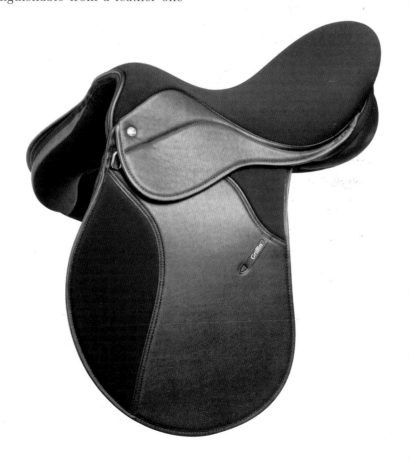

SADDLES FOR DIFFERENT DISCIPLINES

Before looking at the different design details for various disciplines, I'd like to mention two vital points regarding saddle design which have not received enough attention until recent years: these are the extent of the bearing area (on the horse's back) of the panel under the seat, and the position of the stirrup bars. A consequence of this is that there are still many saddles around which leave a lot to be desired in these areas.

BEARING AREA

The principle of spreading pressure over large or small areas respectively to lessen or increase its effects can best be appreciated by trying a simple experiment. Press a sharp needle into your hand gently and it will hurt; press a blunt pencil into your hand with the same pressure and it will not hurt at all. This is because with the needle, the weight is concentrated into a much smaller area (the point), whereas with a blunt pencil lead, the pressure is more spread out and is, therefore, easier to bear, each tiny area of skin having to bear less pressure.

On the same principle, the wider the waist or twist of a saddle, the greater the bearing surface of the panel on the horse's back, and the more easily the horse can bear a rider's weight. With a narrow waist, the same amount of weight is transferred onto a smaller area, so each square inch or centimetre of the horse's back must bear more weight, and will therefore feel more pressure. An excessively wide waist, though, forces the rider's thighs apart and the rider up in the saddle, and this can be very uncomfortable. Most modern saddles are more carefully designed, and this applies to any discipline, but particularly those for endurance riding and dressage at present; they are made to have flatter, less over-stuffed panels (and so an even bearing surface), with a wider but carefully shaped waist so that the rider's thighs are not forced apart. Saddles are also now available with separate, flexible panels attached to the underside of the seat, which give a large bearing surface with a comfortably narrow waist for the rider in the seat itself.

THE STIRRUP BARS

The positioning of the stirrup bars is also a crucial factor in the rider's ability to maintain, fairly easily, a balanced seat on the flat or over fences. Most riders are familiar with the basic classical position, which should be taught as a fundamental principle to all novices: that there should be a straight, vertical line running down from the rider's ear through the shoulder (and some would include the elbow), the hip and down the back of the heel. This line becomes diagonal in the jumping position as far as the hip,

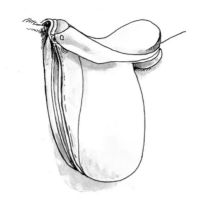

Saddle much too low on the withers and will probably bruise and injure the top of the withers

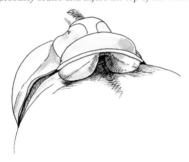

Saddle with panels overstuffed creating a rounded shape to the bearing surface which will concentrate the pressure in two narrow strips along each side of the spine

Above: Saddle placed too far forward which, along with the forward cut flap, will interfere with the backward movement of the shoulder blade when the foreleg extends, hampering the horse's action

Far left: Conventional general purpose saddle with the stirrup bar placed too far forward in relation to the centre of the seat

Left: Here, the rider's leg is pulled too far forward by the forward position of the stirrup bar

with the leg position remaining unchanged, except possibly when landing from a cross-country drop fence when it may come forwards.

Whilst the horse is stationary, this position is easy to maintain. In walk it should be similarly easy to hold, but once a rider starts sitting to the trot and cantering, it becomes progressively more difficult to keep the heel under the seat or hip if the stirrup bar is too far forward. This causes a natural tendency to pull the leg forward, which destroys the balance and makes a correct seat very difficult to keep.

The stirrup bars should be placed sufficiently far back that when the stirrups and leathers are hanging naturally vertically from the bars, the ball of the rider's foot is on the base of the stirrup, and the heel is comfortably directly below the hip. Most stirrup bars, even now, are placed too far forward, even in some very expensive dressage saddles which claim to 'place the rider in the correct position'. This is not a matter of rider conformation, either. If the deepest part of the saddle seat is in its centre mid-way between cantle and pommel, and the stirrup bar is set slightly in front of the dip – not so far as in most saddles – the stirrup leather must hang down vertically just in front of an imaginary line dropped from the deepest part of the seat. Therefore the rider's foot can rest on its ball in the stirrup and the heel must be right under the hip.

The angle at which the stirrup leather should hang to enable the rider to sit in ear/shoulder/hip/heel balance

This placement will also make it easy for a rider in the jumping position to adopt the diagonally forward line of shoulder/hip and will, therefore, not encourage him or her to be too far forward, a common fault which weakens the seat and reduces security in the saddle – not something you want over fences.

These two points are vital for any design of saddle for any discipline.

Far left: The bulge in front of the stirrup bar is the end of the point of the tree. With the stirrup bar so far forward, it is easy to see how pressure is concentrated just below and behind the withers each time the rider rises in the stirrups

GENERAL PURPOSE/EVENT SADDLE

A logical starting point is the general purpose saddle mentioned above, as it is still the design that most 'ordinary' riders choose. Although, as stated, many of these saddles (also called event saddles) are cut too far forward to assist with a correct seat on the flat, if you can find one of the less-forward-cut designs you may well end up with a saddle which really is suitable for more or less everything you want to do, provided the stirrup bar is correctly positioned, as described above.

In the GP saddle the pommel is sloped back at a 45° angle to allow for a moderately cut panel and flap to be fitted to the tree. Stuffed pads down the front edge of the panel under the flap and sometimes on the flap itself – knee rolls – give support to the knee and, therefore, the leg position when riding over uneven country, landing from a jump or during fast gaits, and they certainly help keep you secure when riding a 'stopper'.

Most saddles are, understandably, made for the average rider, although he/she seems to be getting taller and taller. Therefore, if you have fairly short legs you will probably find that, on most saddles, when your stirrups are adjusted comfortably for jumping or faster work, your knees do not actually come into contact with the knee rolls and they are consequently useless. Some firms do make saddles in size ranges to suit the rider as well as the horse, and this is a point you must check if you want the saddle to do its job for you personally. Of course, if you have very long legs, you will also need to be sure that the flaps are long enough, and the knee rolls low and deep enough to accommodate your knees.

Because GP saddles are intended for flatwork as well as jumping, it is important that they have the dip in the seat placed centrally between the cantle and the pommel, and these days, most astute purchasers want saddles in which the cantle and pommel are the same height. A common fault in earlier forward-cut saddles was that the cantle was too high, which despite a central, dipped seat, in effect pushed the rider too far forward. A central, dipped seat with pommel and cantle the same height undoubtedly helps the rider sit correctly and in a balanced way in the deepest part of the saddle; also it doesn't hamper him or her

THIGH ROLLS

Thigh rolls ostensibly to help support the thigh underneath are usually a waste of time. They are often, strangely, fitted vertically down the rear edge of the panel where they do no good at all, and are usually very puny affairs. Some saddles (usually dressage saddles) do have thigh rolls correctly angled forwards and down, but not many, and most riders don't even think about requesting thigh rolls.

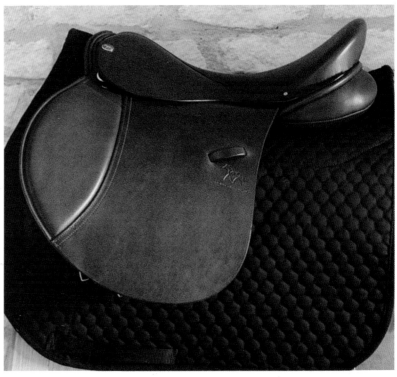

The Balance Zenith GP saddle. It shows a main feature of the Balance saddles – the flat, central dip to the seat which ensures that the rider is directed neither forwards nor backwards

This general purpose saddle has a rather more forward-cut flap than original versions. The saddle is also much too far forward on the horse and this, combined with the cut of the flap, will almost certainly significantly hamper the movement of the horse's shoulder and foreleg

Below: The Fieldhouse Extra range VSD saddle, designed to ensure freedom of movement in the horse's shoulder

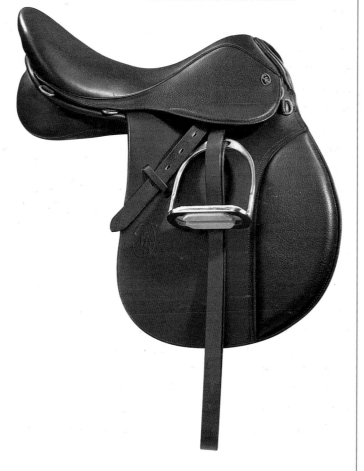

when adopting a half-seat or forward, jumping-position seat. A high pommel will cause the rider to slip back towards the horse's loins, and a high cantle will tip him or her towards the unforgiving pommel – not the most comfortable place to be. Constant readjustments of the rider's seat during riding – of the sort which should not be necessary in a well designed, balanced-seat saddle – are irritating to horse and rider alike.

THE VERY-SLIGHTLY-DRESSAGE SADDLE

Mentioned earlier, this is just like the GP/event saddle but with a flap cut less forward, falling somewhere between the fairly straight dressage saddle and the usual sort of GP type. This is really more suitable for general riding, modern GP saddles being orientated more towards cross-country jumping (with its stirrup length slightly longer than specialised showjumping) than flatwork.

THE JUMPING SADDLE

The jumping saddle is specifically intended for showjumping, and has a more forward-cut flap than the event/GP saddle to accommodate the shorter stirrup and the correspondingly more forward-placed knee. When these saddles were first brought out, a very short stirrup (although not racing length) was advised and taught for jumping fairly high fences in the show (stadium) jumping arena. Then the fashion and thinking veered towards slightly longer, more cross-country length stirrups for greater security and effectiveness – although at the time of writing, the trend is once again swinging back to a shorter length.

The main difficulty with any forward-cut flap, with its necessarily sloped-back tree-head and forward-placed knee rolls, is to avoid interfering with the backward movement of the top of the horse's shoulder blade during movement, and in particular when he tucks up his forelegs over obstacles. This point is very often ignored by purchasers as they think that, because the flap itself and the knee rolls are not made of metal, the horse's shoulder blade will not really be hampered. However, I know several horses whose action in front has improved noticeably when their saddle has been changed for one which, although still forward cut, was of a slightly different orientation and did not come into contact with the shoulder blade during movement and jumping. This was helped by the saddle being placed in the correct position on the horse's back, more or less allowed to find its own 'bed' on the back, rather than being fitted too far forward, as many people do these days.

Below: When jumping, horses need to extend their forelegs forward to their maximum which means that the top of the shoulder blade rotates back, as explained in Chapter 1. This often means that it hits the front of the saddle, bruising the top of the shoulder blade. When combined with the very forward-cut saddles usually used for specialised showjumping, this can result in significant interference with the movement of the shoulder, possible bruising and discomfort for the horse. Placing the saddle too far forward, as is usually done in the belief that

this will place the rider over the horse's centre of balance and so make the process easier, actually makes the problem even worse. It takes a skilled saddle fitter to fit a jumping saddle to a jumping horse, and an open-minded rider to place it where it ought to be

Left: The Fieldhouse close-contact jumping saddle. This has a slightly deeper and more supportive seat than most such saddles which are usually quite flat

THE DRESSAGE SADDLE

Dressage saddles are more in fashion than ever due to the greatly increased popularity of this discipline. They are also very suitable for any rider who has no desire ever to leave the ground but enjoys hacking about, schooling, having lessons and showing, too. Dressage saddles are usually very comfortable, particularly if you buy one with not-too-exaggerated knee rolls, and with short girth tabs so that you can use a normal-length, long girth. Also, they are good for showing because they do not have a forward-cut flap which will obscure the horse or pony's shoulder, and they will provide both rider and judge with a comfortable ride, always helpful to a good performance and impression.

Unlike the GP or jumping saddle, the head/pommel of a dressage saddle will be vertical, or very nearly so, to permit the straighter panel and flap used to accommodate the longer stirrup length typical of flatwork and the dressage seat. As always, the rider's seatbones should rest in the deepest, central part of the saddle seat, and should stay there without conscious effort from the rider because that is where the well designed saddle puts them.

The panel of a dressage saddle is usually gusseted under the back half to allow for a flatter bearing surface and greater stability on the horse's back; it also helps even out and spread pressure. The term 'close contact' in relation to saddles

Above: The Heather Moffett dressage saddle which is specially designed with a central and wide, comfortable seat and substantial knee rolls to offer maximum support to the rider's position, keeping the knee deep and the thigh back

Left: The correct positioning of the saddle, as shown here by Heather Moffett, riding in her Heather Moffett saddle, allows the horse full backward extension of his shoulder blade without its being blocked by the front edge of the saddle. This obviously also allows the horse full forward extension of the foreleg

is now freely bandied about, and it is a feature found more in dressage saddles than any other type, for obvious reasons. The stuffing in the panel under the seat is kept to a minimum and spread evenly over as wide an area as the design will permit for the comfort of the horse and for as much stability as possible whilst still affording the rider as little encumbrance as possible to feeling the horse's back.

Dressage saddles come with either two long girth straps to permit the fitting of a short dressage or belly girth (so that the buckles do not fall under or near the rider's leg) or with the usual three short ones, which obviously take a normal, long girth. The third strap, in the latter case, will often be fitted well back and angled forward to spread the points of 'pull' of the girth, and to help stabilise the saddle. The three-strap arrangement also allows for finer positioning of the saddle on the horse's back, as described earlier.

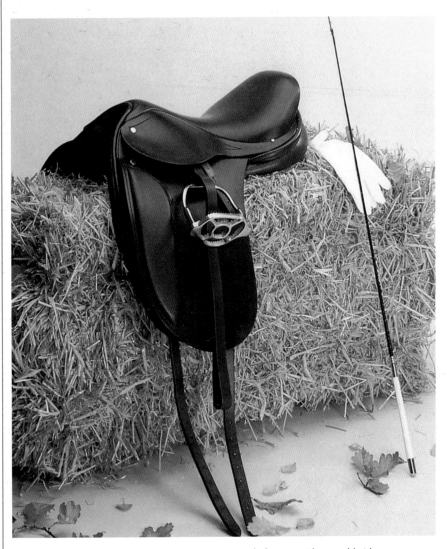

The Lauriche Dressage saddle now a firm favourite with dressage riders worldwide

LAURICHE SADDLE

With the increasing interest in Britain in true classical equitation, A.J.Foster Saddlemakers introduced the Lauriche Dressage saddle, which has, in fact, been available in the USA and Europe for many years. The seat is broad with a low pommel and cantle (unlike conventional competitive dressage saddles) so is supporting and very comfortable, but not restrictive.

The saddle panels have a wide bearing surface, fitting the horse's back well from front to rear and from side to side which gives stability with dispersed weight-bearing. There is also a wide gullet to leave the horse's spine totally free of contact. To add to the stability, balance and even pressure, the saddle has girth tabs attached to the front of the trees (at the point) and also from the swell of the tree at the back, an arrangement which takes a standard dressage girth with no problem.

The saddle is available in two models, the Intermediate and the Advanced, the difference in the seat bone to stirrup bar relationship. The Advanced saddle is intended for the advanced classical rider or the novice who aspires to that position and the Intermediate has its stirrup bar a little further forward in what Fosters describe as the 'standard dressage position'. The stirrup bar on the Advanced saddle is set a little further back to enable to rider to sit in the advanced seat and leg position unhindered by the stirrup's pulling the leg forward, as can happen on some dressage saddles. The Advanced saddle also allows for the fact that the rider's own seat shape changes from one position to the other.

Right: stirrup bar position
1 for comparison only and would be a jumper bar
2 Intermediate dressage
3 Advanced dressage

THE SHOWING SADDLE

The modern showing saddle is probably the nearest thing we still have to the original English hunting saddle. It is designed for use in the show ring and should be very discreet and close-fitting (having only a thin half or skeleton panel beneath the flap), and is cut very straight in the flap so as to show off the horse's conformation, and particularly his front, to best advantage, and not obscure his body in any way. Unfortunately most people, including many showing enthusiasts, find them not exactly painful, but certainly uncomfortable to sit in, and to sit still in. Because they are relatively flat in the seat, and never have knee or thigh rolls, you get no help at all from them; also the stirrup bars are always too far forward, although this does not matter because the traditional showing seat comprises a rather feet-forward posture which inevitably pushes the rider's bottom backwards – this is to create the illusion that perhaps the horse or pony has a bigger (longer) front (forehand) and length of rein (from mouth to withers) than he really has. This is all showmanship, of course, and harmless enough, except that long periods of riding in this way would do the animal's back no good at all.

The traditional show saddles, and particularly those made by Owens, are highly sought after, cherished by those who have one, and kept refurbished and maintained for generations! Such saddles will have a fairly straight head, or a cut-back head that goes behind, rather than over the horse's wither, and they may even have the flap cut back slightly from the vertical. These actually necessitate an extended stirrup bar so that the stirrup leather can be positioned further back, otherwise the rider's knee must come off the flap in front, which would look ridiculous, be uncomfortable, and would obscure the horse's shoulder.

Top UK showman, Robert Oliver, demonstrates the traditional showing seat in which the rider sits well back to show off the horse's form

This matter of revealing the shoulder is further emphasised by the placing of the girth. There is a point strap (a girth strap or tab fixed under the point of the tree) which, when used with the first of the two conventionally positioned girth straps, enables the saddle to be put on further back than would otherwise be possible, and holds it there, preventing it riding forward (as it would with most over-fat show animals) and so emphasising the horse's front even more.

Nowadays, however, there are slightly less extreme models of show saddle which are more comfortable, and in which it is easier to maintain a more balanced seat whilst still showing off the horse's conformation. Some even have slender knee rolls. Although the diehards in

49

any discipline will always stick to their traditional ways, as riders become (I hope) better educated in equestrianism and matters to do with conformation and action, and general equine functioning and well-being, many more forward-thinking exhibitors of all ages no longer use the feet-forward-seat-back position – nor, and this is just as important, do they show their animals as grossly fat (with a view to covering up a multitude of conformational sins) as they used to. This makes for improved riding, a better balanced way of going in the horse, and less need to keep the saddle almost forcibly back due to a fat-covered ribcage and abdomen. As mentioned, many exhibitors do now show in the more discreetly structured dressage saddles with long girths and a flap cut slightly forward of the vertical.

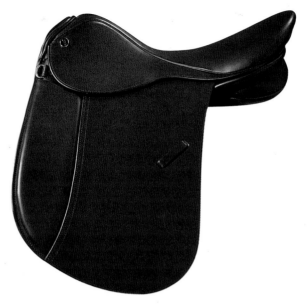

Above: The Fieldhouse Showhunter saddle from their Extra range, designed for working hunter and show riders but also claimed to be suitable for other disciplines. The moderately forward-cut shape of the panels and the modest knee rolls indicate comfort for the rider whilst still showing off the horse's front, and the low-profile cantle interferes as little as possible with the appearance of the horse's topline

THE AMERICAN SADDLE SEAT OR GAITED HORSE SADDLE

A variation of the English show saddle with a seat positioned to the rear of the saddle is extensively used in America, and to a lesser extent in Australia and the UK by enthusiasts of usually five-gaited American breeds, specifically the Morgan, the American Saddlebred, the Tennessee Walker, the Paso breeds of which the main one is the Paso Fino, and the Missouri Foxtrotter. Many Arabians are also ridden under this saddle. These breeds are often ridden in shows in what is now called the American saddle seat.

It originated in Europe, though in a less extreme form, but it died out here for a while; however, it has been reintroduced in a small way, and was taken over the Atlantic by settlers. This seat was developed by American colonists as a means not only of covering many miles daily in supervising their vast plantations, but also of showing off their beautiful,

The American Saddle Seat necessitates a flat-seated saddle with a rear-inclined seat and wide flap. The rider sits right back (here he is actually on the horse's loins), the head is often pulled back and up as here, creating a kink and tension in the base of the neck, a flattened back, trailing hindquarters and legs and a lengthened belly-line. Some saddle seat riders modify the seat towards more classical principles with considerable success

Left: Many top-level show riders today now compete in modern, discreet saddles which do not cover up the horse's shoulder yet allow the rider enough flap to make it easier to maintain a good position in comfort. This is Alistair Hood riding Champion Riding Horse, Flash Harry

51

flashy horses, specially bred as the status symbols of the day. The seat involves the rider sitting almost on the horse's loins, again to show off his front and his artificially achieved, high foreleg action.

The saddle needs a flap extended from front to back so that the rider's leg does not come off the flap at the back and become soiled by sweat or grease from the horse's coat. The head is often very cut back (called 'cow-mouthed', and usually built around a Lane Fox tree), and the saddle will have the forward-set point strap that is used on English showing saddles to keep the saddle back.

This seat, particularly in its exaggerated, modern form developed for the show ring, is even more unbalanced than the traditional English showing seat. However, its ill effects can be lessened by a rider who at least understands that, in order for the horse to function safely and with less risk of injury, particularly to his back, he must be taught and enabled to raise and extend his own neck from underneath its base and to go with his vertebral bow maintained and his quarters and hindlegs engaged beneath him using his 'ring of muscles' correctly (see Chapter 1). Although this is not easy with the rider positioned as the current saddle seat requires, it is not impossible for a talented, concerned rider.

What often happens is that the rider pulls the horse's head up and back with the reins (which are attached to a long-cheeked curb bit) and this stiffens and stresses all the 'riding' muscles, making it quite impossible for the vertebral bow to be maintained and used, or for the quarters to be brought under the horse with engaged hindlegs.

Of course, this sort of thing happens in other types of riding, too.

The late Dr Reiner Klimke competing in normal dressage turnout of double bridle and dressage saddle, the latter having been placed sufficiently far back to allow the horse freedom of shoulder movement. It also has the short girth straps favoured on the continent of Europe rather than the long ones usually preferred in the UK

Left: The Frank Baines Enduro LDR saddle. The panels extend slightly beyond the cantle to distribute the rider's weight evenly, which is fine provided a suitable size is chosen for the horse allowing both freedom of shoulder-blade movement in front and complete lack of loin contact at the back. It has a wide bearing surface and traditional wool flocking plus a cut-back pommel, a wide gullet and a deep, soft seat. There are six dees to attach trail-riding accessories and the girthing system described as a 'V rawhide' system which 'secures the saddle in position'

Endurance saddles need extra dees to carry equipment: it is interesting to note that the British Army manual, Animal Management, *stresses that under no circumstances must attachments even be allowed to touch the horse for fear of causing pressure, friction or annoyance by flopping around. Something to think about*

THE ENDURANCE SADDLE

There has probably been more development in the field of endurance saddles than in any other in recent years, as the sport has become more and more popular; as a result the effects of saddle-bearing over long periods at active gaits has become once more a matter worthy of concern. The military, of course, were very familiar with the problems involved, and the old British army manual, *Animal Management*, went into long and painstaking detail regarding saddle design and fitting, and the evils of even the slightest pressure or friction where it should not be in either pack or riding saddles – for equines and camels alike! Published in the UK by Her Majesty's Stationery Office, it is well worth trying to get hold of a copy, even an ancient one.

Most good saddlers these days have an endurance design in their range, and are also paying attention not only to horse comfort, but to rider comfort as well, incorporating quilted and/or padded seats and plenty of dees for fastening on small items of equipment which may be needed during a ride.

Some of the early endurance saddles were based on the traditional military saddle: this was designed with two broad, horizontal padded bars running down the horse's back, and the seat of leather was slung hammock-style between the front and rear arches (which obviously linked the bars front and back). These saddles completely removed pressure from the spine – although care had to be taken over the precise length, shape and padding of the bars – and the seat was heaven to sit in. These saddles are still used by the army and by some police forces.

Endurance saddle designers pioneered the use of high-tech materials for stuffing panels and spreading weight, lessening or evening out pressure and creating permeability to help disperse sweat, and many of their techniques and ideas have subsequently been incorporated into saddles of other types. Current designs of endurance saddle may have the more usual padded panels under the seat, or extended bars called 'fans' which do literally fan out under the cantle and help increase the bearing surface. They are also now made with the newer, separate or 'floating' flexible panels fixed under a conventional seat. These would seem to be particularly advantageous for endurance as a discipline in which riders habitually maintain over long distances a hovering position with their seat barely brushing the saddle and their weight, therefore, being entirely borne on the stirrups and transferred up the leathers to be concentrated on the small area of saddle beneath the bars where they attach to the tree – perilously near the tree points.

The underneath of a Reactorpanel saddle, showing the wide gullet and generous bearing surface of the 'floating' panels

It is, of course, completely erroneous for the riders to say that they are 'taking the weight off the horse's back' as a reason for adopting this position; this obviously cannot be the case unless they can magically fly along above the horse. Instead, the weight is concentrated forward over a much smaller area than if the rider sat full in the saddle, and in a conventional saddle of poor fit for the individual horse, and with insufficient padding beneath the tree points, it can cause injury (as bruising from pressure) to the muscles just below and behind the withers under the points and bars. Because such pressure will be maintained for several hours, it is obvious that the corresponding injuries can be severe. Flexible panels almost completely obviate significant pressure here.

Endurance riders are not the only ones who are in the saddle for long periods of time: those who follow hounds also subject their horses to long hours of weight-bearing, and although endurance saddles are not designed with jumping in mind, they are nevertheless equipped with knee rolls and a moderately forward-cut flap so you can certainly jump the height of fence in them that is likely to be met in the hunting field – and a good deal better than in the old English hunting saddle. (For several years I jumped – not very high, admittedly – in an early dressage saddle with knee rolls but a less-straight flap than modern ones, with no problems at all.)

A Reactorpanel saddle; one of the rear 'shock blockers' attaching the panel to the seat

One of the secrets of helping a horse through a long ride is to dismount, loosen his girth a couple of holes, and rest his back at every reasonable opportunity. You should also vary your seat and stirrup length, alternating between a full and a half seat, and putting your stirrups up and down a hole or two now and then. This changes the feel and pressures on the horse's back, which refreshes him and permits slightly varying blood circulation in the back.

Riders keen on longish, active hacks as a non-competitive leisure pursuit could do a lot worse than buy an endurance saddle: they would find it much more suitable and comfortable for this purpose for themselves and their horse than any GP saddle, and than many dressage saddles.

THE SIDE SADDLE

Once again a popular equestrian discipline, side-saddle riding is now enjoyed by ladies and gentlemen alike (being particularly suitable for those of either sex with arthritic hips), competitively and otherwise. As well as showing classes, in the UK there are dressage competitions for side-saddle riders, and there are also jumping competitions, and they can go hunting.

Only a handful of new side saddles of a standard acceptable in the UK has been made since 1939. The skills involved in making, balancing and fitting side saddles largely died as demand evaporated after World War II. In the UK, in 1996, the Society of Master Saddlers began running courses

An early side saddle, the lady riding her horse on a curb rein only and with no noseband, unlike her companion

for saddlers in refurbishing and rebuilding side saddles, with a good response. In 2000, the awards made by the Society in its saddlery competition included a new group for new or completely refurbished side saddles. No less than seven entries were exhibited, all of a high standard, one or two new. The winner of the group also won the 'Best of All Groups' prize. However, as the many would-be newcomers to side saddle riding will confirm, it is still hard to find the 'right' side saddle for both horse and rider while there are such limited numbers in circulation. In fact, The Side Saddle Association say that it is the chief factor limiting the numbers of riders coming into side saddle riding. So it is in the interest of all to look after the existing stocks of side saddles and use them correctly.

However, if you are 'into' close-contact riding, then don't bother to find out about side-saddle riding, because if there is one thing a side saddle is not, it is a close-contact saddle: you will find yourself perched what seems like a foot above your horse's back with his head an unfamiliar distance down in front of you. Although modern side saddles have much stronger, laminated and reinforced trees than the old ones, and are therefore less bulky and heavy, the seat still has to be a good few inches deep from top to bottom to provide the flat platform – usually doeskin or suede – on which the rider sits.

Nearly all side saddles are nearside ones, with the rider sitting with her or his legs on the near side of the horse. The top pommel, or fixed head, over which the rider's right leg is placed, is fixed on the left. The

SADDLING UP

The saddle should be carried with the right hand holding the fixed head, and the lining down the hip and thigh, the seat under the right arm. The girth and balance girth can be attached on the nearside and held, with the flap strap if there is one, in the left hand. The saddle is placed carefully on the horse's back a little too far forward and slid back, great care being taken to position the saddle behind the shoulder blade of the horse. This should be checked from the offside. On the nearside, the balance girth (which is sometimes referred to as a sefton girth) is buckled to the point strap and the girth to two of the three girth straps.

Next fasten the girth on the offside, from which all adjustments are made. The balance girth lies on top of the girth and must not be tighter than the girth. The overgirth strap should, likewise, be fastened no tighter than the girth and balance girth. If the horse wears a martingale, the girth, balance and overgirth strap all pass through its girth loop.

Ideally two people should saddle up the horse: one to hold the saddle in place, and the other to move around the horse carrying out the various steps involved in fitting the saddle. The girth and balance girth are finally adjusted on the offside once the rider is mounted. It is important that a full length balance strap is threaded through a keeper wihch has been stitched centrally onto the girth, and not be done up too tight, since that can cause the horse to resist.

lower pommel or leaping (jumping) head is screwed into the tree, rather than being a part of it like the fixed head, and some can be adjusted to suit the width of the rider's thigh or to accommodate either flatwork or jumping. Sometimes a saddle will have two screw-in sockets for the leaping head so that adjustments can be made easily. The thread on leaping-head sockets should always be a left-hand one, as this is safer.

The pommels do help greatly to keep the rider in place, and the fact that the thigh is across in front of the body also affords much greater protection against being unseated, particularly forwards. The first time I tried riding side saddle I must have looked a great deal more confident than I felt, because my instructress urged me to try a canter. I did one circuit of the manège in canter and was just completing it when Mirabelle, my mount, tripped and skidded along for several yards on her knees, with me lurched forwards over her neck before she regained her feet and continued in canter. My right leg across in front of me, plus the pommels, kept me on: had I been riding astride, I should probably have come off over her head and been trampled. However, had Mirabelle actually fallen, I should have been less likely to have been thrown clear than if I had been riding astride, as the pommels may have prevented it.

As mentioned, the seat of a side saddle should be quite flat, and needs to be wide enough to accommodate the rider's seat upon it, so that the

A perfectly turned out mother and daughter riding an equally well turned out brother and sister in a side saddle pairs class

A good example of how a junior side saddle rider should look. Bianca Bairstow, winning a Junior Open Equitation Championship. The girth buckles on this saddle are under the flap

outside of the right thigh is not hanging over the edge. As the rider's weight tends towards the near side, most saddles will be, or need to be, built up at the back on the nearside to keep the rider's weight correctly balanced. Imbalance in the rider is a heinous crime in side-saddle riding because it can easily give the horse a sore back and stiff (overstressed and injured) muscles as he tries to counteract his lopsided rider.

As with any saddle, the gullet must leave a clear channel of air down the horse's back, and the tree points must not interfere with shoulder movement as this can push the saddle back; nor must there be any pressure on the loins.

Side saddles have traditionally, of course, been made of leather with their panels lined with linen in the best quality ones, or serge in others. Leather is felt to be unsuitable for this purpose: some believe that it can cause a sore back due to the increased pressure from a side saddle and the fact that it is less absorbent than fabric. The panels should not, therefore, be washed or wetted when being cleaned as any water penetration is bad for the stuffing and they will take a long time to dry. Usual cleaning practice is to wipe over with a damp sponge and to brush with a stiff brush when dry.

The nearside flap must be large enough to keep the rider's right leg and foot off the horse's shoulder, so it is cut well forward and sometimes has padding underneath the front part. With the exception of the outside girthing system, there is usually an overgirth stitched to the bottom edge of the nearside flap, which is buckled onto the offside overgirth

CARE OF A SIDE SADDLE

The leather part of the saddle is cleaned in the usual way, and the doeskin or suede seat brushed. Care must be taken not to drop or misuse the saddle because of the comparatively fragile nature of most side-saddle trees. If it has to be put on the ground (it will not balance conveniently over a stable door like an astride saddle) put it down pommel first, resting on the girth. Do not leave it on the horse's back if the girths are undone. Take care not to bang the pommels against door jambs and so on, and if you are transporting the saddle in a vehicle with the horse, keep it well stacked away from the animal, and protected by other equipment so it cannot fall about. A side saddle should always be stored or transported with a cover – either custom-made or an old sheet or bedcover will do. Do not place the girths over its seat, as with other saddles, as this can leave a mark. It is well worthwhile seeking out a saddler experienced with side saddles for a yearly check, and The Society of Master Saddlers or The Sidesaddle Association should be able to help here.

Kate Lister on Champion Riding Horse Summerville, winning an Adult Newcomer's Equitation Class. This photograph shows the double girth outside the flap as discussed in the text

strap which lies over the offside girth straps under the offside panel. The offside panel will usually have a small elasticated strap with hook which attaches to the eye stitched onto the offside overgirth strap. This serves a dual purpose, firstly allowing the rider access to adjust the girth, and secondly keeping the offside panel secure.

The most suitable girth for a side saddle is a three-fold leather girth, or a Fitzwilliam. Most side saddles have three main girth straps, plus point straps. The exception is the outside girthing system which has no offside point strap, and may have either two or three girth straps visible on the outside of the panel, but usually two. A full-length balance girth is attached to the nearside point strap, passes obliquely under the horse's belly through a keeper stitched on the centre of the girth, and then buckles to the short balance strap attached to the offside rear of the saddle.

The full-length balance, or sefton girth, has two buckles, the offside buckle having two or three keepers to carry the short offside balance strap. The exception to the is the Champion & Wilton saddle which requires a balance girth that has an offside buckle with keepers and a tab with holes for the nearside. With a 'roly poly' pony, or a cob with a loaded shoulder, you can fasten the girth on the offside to the offside point strap; but with a horse with good conformation this should not be necessary. For showing or flatwork, the balance girth can be stitched to the girth on the offside; this does not keep the saddle as steady as in the previous arrangement, but it looks neater in the ring. The balance girth has a buckle and keeper at each end, one end buckling to the nearside point strap, as described, and the other to the short length stitched to the offside rear of the saddle. Sometimes the balance girth will be stitched directly to the girth on the offside. When girthing up on the offside, the front girth buckle is fastened to the offside point strap to help keep the saddle in place.

The saddle flaps usually cover the girth tabs, but there are saddles on which the offside girth attachments are visible on the outside of the flap. These are used mainly for showing, and the girths used with such saddles have high quality buckles and keepers for elegance with, often, the balance girth stitched to the girth. In either case it is important not to have the balance girth too far back or too tight, as some horses will buck against it.

There are several different methods of attaching the stirrup leather, but all must have a quick-release mechanism which should be kept well oiled – and the rider must practise using it, as they all differ. Side-saddle stirrup irons must have larger eyes than other stirrups to accommodate the adjustment hook which is an integral part of these stirrups and leathers. There will be a fitting at the top end of the leather to take its mate on the saddle, with a metal hook at the other end which threads through the eye back on itself; it can then be adjusted to the length required by means of holes in the leather near the stirrup itself. A little leather cover or sleeve protects the saddle flap and the rider's boot.

BUYING USED TACK

Purchasing used tack can save a considerable sum of money but can be quite risky.

Buying from sales is probably the most risky procedure of all. If you do not know the field well enough you should take someone with you who knows sale procedure and who can check the tack, as a good deal of faulty tack passes through sales and is offered 'as seen' with no guarantee of quality. The better auctions give some form of guarantee. In any case, you will not be able to try the tack on your horse before purchase.

Buying from private sellers may not be as 'safe' as it at first seems. They are not governed by the same consumer laws as commercial retail outlets; you have to check items offered very carefully indeed and there will, of course, be no guarantee.

The safest way to buy secondhand equipment is from a reputable saddler. Many have good stocks, can give advice on fit and suitability and offer some sort of guarantee.

Testing a used saddle for soundness of the tree by pressing the pommel towards the cantle to see if it moves or if there is a scraping, creaking noise

SADDLE FITTING

The past decade has seen a considerable increase in knowledge of just how a horse's back functions, and just what a poorly fitting or badly adjusted saddle can do to it. Chapter 1 described the natural slight bow of the horse's spine, the correct movement of the horse under saddle to enhance this bow, the results of incorrect riding and tack use, and other relevant concerns. From the horse's point of view, all that matters is that he is comfortable and can move naturally, or as best he can in response to his rider's aids, without discomfort, and without being hampered or encumbered – and certainly without pain and distress.

Riders will want to be comfortable, too; they will also want the saddle to help with the riding techniques and the seat being used, and will probably want it to make the horse look good – they will certainly not want any pain or discomfort. The one great advantage that the rider has over the horse or pony is that he or she can stop using any saddle (or other item of tack) which hurts or is uncomfortable, and can therefore relieve the pain and discomfort. The horse cannot.

Saddle fitting is much easier on a well conformed animal. It can be extremely difficult to fit any animal which has significant conformational faults; these might include being built 'downhill' (croup high); having withers which are excessively high, or very low, or rounded, or completely non-existent; having a loaded shoulder, or an exceedingly well sprung ribcage, or conversely being very slab-sided; having a roach back, or a sway back; having no natural girth groove at all – and so on, and so forth. Although it is no immediate answer, I should just like to comment that equestrianism of all sorts, including saddle fitting, would be so much easier if breeders would concentrate on line-breeding well conformed animals. At present there are just too many badly conformed animals which have to be fitted with saddles if they are to be useful to humans.

Saddle fitting is not simply a cursory glance over the saddle, checking that the pommel does not press on the withers and that's that: it is a complex procedure in which the fitter gets virtually no help from the wearer: he or she cannot ask the horse where it hurts, or whether it is comfortable or not: the fitter has to be sharp-eyed, knowledgeable, professionally trained, and concerned about the well-being of horse, pony and rider.

Buying a saddle, like buying a horse, is something not to be undertaken lightly, but requires very careful deliberation. It is also important not to be persuaded in advance by skillful advertising and marketing that a particular saddle is for you just because it is a famous make, or is endorsed by an even more famous equestrian celebrity. The bottom line is that if the saddle does not fit and is not suitable for you and for your horse, it is no good. It is also certainly not the case that the more expensive the saddle, the better it must be (the 'you get what you pay for' syndrome). Several of the best

TRADE ASSOCIATIONS

In the UK, the Society of Master Saddlers (UK) Ltd and the British Equestrian Trade Association (addresses in the Appendix) run professional-level courses for those wishing to qualify as saddle fitters, and will provide the names and addresses of fitters in particular regions of the country. Some of the better tack shops and stores will have a qualified fitter (not the same thing as a qualified saddler) on the staff to help and advise customers, and some saddlery manufacturers will have personnel specially trained to fit their own range of saddles. Many firms (makers and retailers) now have suitable premises to which customers can take their horses for fitting, or they will send a fitter out to the customer's yard for fitting.

saddles from the point of view of appropriate design for the job and fit for horse and rider are relatively reasonably priced.

Countless reams of paper have been filled with articles and other treatises on how a saddle should fit and why. Here I shall condense the plethora of available information into the basics; I also stress that it is *always* worth consulting a qualified saddle fitter when buying a saddle, new or used. A recent incident serves to demonstrate this point.

I attended the premises of a new client with a view to teaching her and did the usual tack check first. There were several things wrong with the tack and other equipment the client was using (although it was of high quality and in good condition). Most obviously, the saddle did not fit the horse and the girth was also causing discomfort.

On trying, most diplomatically, to adjust the tack to minimise discomfort to the horse and to explain why the equipment she was using would cause the horse distress and restricted movement, she said: 'Well the saddle must fit because it was made to measure for him by XYZ Saddlery' (naming a local well known and well established tack store) 'and they also recommended this girth to go with it. I think they know best.' Whoever had supplied her obviously had no idea of how the saddle was going to affect this particular horse or how he would be affected by the quite unsuitable girth supplied with it. None of my explanations persuaded her otherwise.

I have since contacted this and several similar stores and find that, in general, whilst some (by no means all) employ a qualified saddler, few employ a qualified saddle fitter. Those which do not even employ their own saddler and act simply as tack supermarkets buy in a range of branded makes and sizes and supply customers with the nearest size and fit they think will do.

This is not good enough: I recommend that, when buying from such a store, readers first establish that any saddle will be fitted to their horse by a qualified fitter, before then looking at the range on offer.

A: Shows the narrow male pubic arch, the wide female arch and how the standard pommel arch comes into contact with each

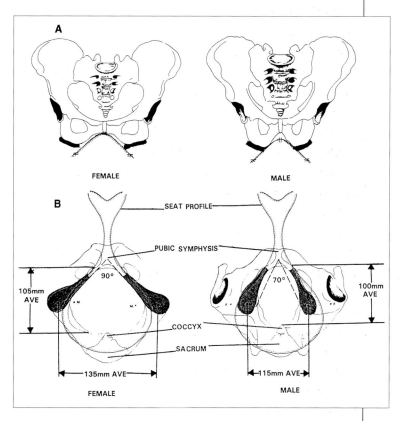

B: Each pelvis seen from below is superimposed over a standard saddle seat, demonstrating how the wider female pelvis causes the seam line to line against the inner thigh, causing great discomfort

FITTING THE RIDER

First of all, are you male or female? The reason for this question is that women have wider (from side to side) pelvises than men because of their inherent child-bearing function, and frequently find a saddle with a very narrow seat (note: seat, not particularly tree) uncomfortable and even

painful. In recent years the chiropractic and medical professions have collaborated in saddle-design testing, with the result that there are presently at least three makes of saddle in the UK specifically designed for women, with a wider seat profile; these claim to remove pressure from the tree frame, the pommel and the seams, thus enabling female riders to ride in comfort. Very often these saddles are just as comfortable for men and the advice must always be: try one and see.

Forget the misplaced Victorian values which say that a good rider can ride in any saddle, a bad workman always blames his tools, and so on. Chiropractors have found that pressure from a narrow saddle seat has caused backache, joint pains and even persistent headaches in female patients. One osteopath was referred a female patient by a four-doctor practice, each of whom had examined her; he was also a rider, and he was the only person who recognised why she suffered from recurring attacks of sciatica: he traced it back to when she changed her saddle and found that the seat seams were pressing on her seatbones and, therefore, her sciatic nerves. If you are in pain, or even uncomfortable, you cannot ride well any more than a horse in pain can work well.

The second question regarding fitting the rider might be: are you fat,

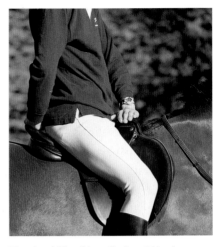

You should be able to fit the width of your hand in front and behind your seat

Far left: Riders with the typical English pear-shaped figure (meant in the nicest possible way, of course), particularly if they are also a little overweight, may find it difficult to find a saddle which fits their seat from side to side and also, if they have a smallish or short-backed horse, which is not too long for their horse's back

Left: Riders with short legs may have difficulty finding a saddle with knee rolls into which they can actually fit their knees as most cater for riders with average to long legs. The flaps are often too long and the rolls too far down

thin or in-between? This will determine how big a seat you need, not only from side to side but from front to back. Remember that you should be able to fit the width of your hand between the front of your body and the pommel, and between the back of your bottom and the cantle. You should feel no pressure or discomfort anywhere on your seat or inner thighs from anything hard or raised such as metal or stitching.

Thirdly, for what discipline do you want the saddle, and therefore what type of seat (position) are you going to adopt: a long stirrup dressage seat, a shorter stirrup jumping length, a moderate stirrup length but many hours in the saddle? Decide what you really need (with advice if necessary); do not be persuaded by what sounds glamorous or impressive!

Fourthly, how long is your leg from hip to knee? The thigh length is the crucial one for determining whether or not your knee will fit comfortably and securely into the knee rolls, or will come too far behind them, or uncomfortably over the top of them.

'Bad' behaviour under saddle such as napping, bucking, bolting and general uncooperativeness is probably caused more often by pain and discomfort than stroppiness. The horse has no other way of objecting, and if the pain is bad enough may well become desperate, as would anyone being hurt and feeling powerless to escape it. A few horses will stoically suffer, but many behave as shown here

All these points must be satisfactorily, and comfortably, taken care of as far as the rider is concerned. It is not 'soft' or selfish to insist on fit and comfort for yourself: it is the only way to go.

FITTING THE HORSE

This is much more complicated, with many points to be taken into consideration. Obviously the horse needs to feel comfortable, too, under saddle if he is to use his body in the natural way described in Chapter 1.

Imagine a horse fitted with a saddle which, in some way, does not fit him properly. He may start off by being just a little uncomfortable, a situation he may put up with stoically, as will many equines. After a while – hours, days, perhaps weeks – the discomfort becomes so unpleasant, maybe even turning into pain, that the horse starts to defend himself from it. He will probably start by lowering his back away from the pressure or pain, raising his head and dropping down the base of his neck, something most riders and trainers certainly do not want, striving as they do for the opposite outline. He will probably become stiff, short-striding and unwilling in his work, he may stop lying down, or he may even stop rolling, which most horses love.

The rider may now start to categorise the horse as difficult, and resort to any of a number of schooling aids – gadgets – aimed at persuading the horse, perhaps somewhat forcibly, to go in a 'rounder' outline with lowered head and neck, meanwhile driving him on from the hindquarters into a firmly resistant contact – all of which simply makes things worse. Furthermore, since the horse has had his primary method of pain relief taken away from him, he resorts to secondary methods such as moving unnaturally, thus putting unaccustomed stresses on limbs, shoulders, neck, hips, back, joints, muscles, ligaments and so on. The result is obviously more stress and strain, more discomfort, pain and injury, and probably what seem like problems of temperament or attitude: napping, bolting, excitability, sullenness, unco-operativeness, refusing, evading, rearing, change of temperament, bucking or otherwise trying to get the rider off, and so on.

The feet, particularly, may be affected. The horse may start moving his limbs abnormally and putting down his feet unevenly, causing unlevel wear of shoes and uneven forces on the legs and joints. In fact, a good farrier may be the first one to notice this.

In long-standing cases the topline may deteriorate and start to appear poor, and the horse develop a bigger-looking belly due to slackened abdominal muscles, and also a ewe neck, all due to constantly cringing away from the discomfort. In cases where the tree is too narrow and the points press into the muscle tissue just behind and below the withers, this pressure may cause the blood supply to be severely restricted. Tissue cannot exist without oxygen, nutrients and the removal of waste, all of which is provided by a healthy circulation of blood: the result is that the tissue dies off and atrophies so that the horse actually experiences muscle wastage, showing marked hollows in this area, and apparently developing high, sharp withers. Moreover because the horse has been unable to move correctly and naturally due to pain, discomfort and restriction, the wrong muscles have developed instead of the right ones, giving the appearance of a poor topline and condition, and even of bad conformation.

The horse may start showing intermittent, unexplained lameness; this can result in several expensive visits and investigations from the vet. He may also, or instead, show symptoms of what is still, in some quarters, called a 'cold back', a euphemism for a painful, injured back. This is actually a clear sign that the horse is suffering from pain in his back, although it is often, even today, passed off by his connections as his simply disliking the feel of cold leather on his back or, if a numnah is used, even of his simply remembering what cold leather felt like! The horse may in fact not be bothered about cold leather – but he will surely remember pain, and these habits may persist even after all pain has gone and he has a perfectly comfortable saddle.

There are various other symptoms and causes of back pain, but the above will cover most of them. Something as simple as a slide on a slippery patch on the road, or treading in a rut in the field can 'rick' a horse's back, and untreated, this can snowball into all sorts of mysterious and tricky problems. However, I am convinced that very many back injuries come from badly fitting saddles, and that the saddle should be one of the first areas of investigation if back pain is detected.

Below: The main areas which are affected by pressure or friction from badly fitting saddles or those which are put on in the wrong place, either too far forward or too far back

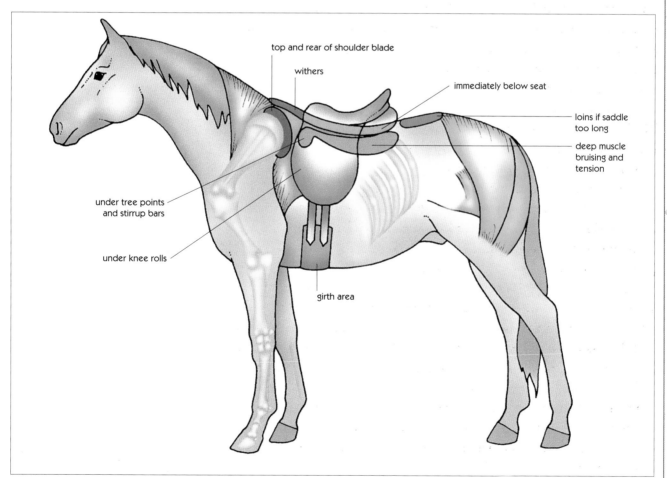

top and rear of shoulder blade

withers

immediately below seat

loins if saddle too long

deep muscle bruising and tension

under tree points and stirrup bars

under knee rolls

girth area

How Should a Saddle Fit?

We have established that the saddle must allow the horse to move fully and naturally, not only without pain and discomfort but also without restriction of movement. All the muscles in the region of the saddle (that is, around it as well as under it) must be able to maintain normal contraction/relaxation/stretching/ tension functions without hindrance. The skeleton itself, notably the spine including the neck and head, shoulder blades and forelimbs, must also be able to move naturally and without hindrance, and so must the hindlegs, which although they are nowhere near the saddle, are often restricted because of pain and discomfort: pain will make the muscles stiffen, thus preventing proper engagement of the hindquarters and hindlegs.

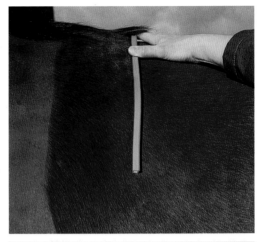

Once the muscular development of your horse – this may be a new horse or one you have had for years – has been objectively assessed by the saddle fitter or someone else who truly understands about muscle function and development in working horses, you will have some idea of how much he is likely to change shape; this may happen because his rider intends to improve his/her riding techniques (if necessary), and/or because his work/rest routine for the year is going to change to suit him better. Also, it is far safer to fit a horse with a slightly wider saddle than he seems to need than to hamper or even injure him with one that is too narrow, because suitable padding can be placed under it to take up any slight extra room. Note, however, that putting extra padding under a too-narrow saddle may make things worse because it makes the saddle fit even tighter.

Taking a wither pattern is a good way to get an initial idea of your horse's actual shape: you can then send it to the saddle fitter as a guide to the size and type of saddle to bring for a fitting and trial. This used to be done with a length of flexible lead cable, but nowadays most people, and certainly saddlers, use a Flexi-curve, available from either the tack shop or saddle fitter, or from a craft or art shop, or from a good stationer. A Flexi-curve is a length of flexible lead with vertical steel strips on either side, covered in a PVC casing. It is used for art and craft work, architectural and engineering drawing, design and so on. Mould it over your horse's withers just behind the tops of the shoulder blades where the front edge of the saddle will go, placing the centre on top of the withers and moulding it to both sides of the horse, being sure it does not move as you do so; it is a good idea to have an assistant to help hold it in place.

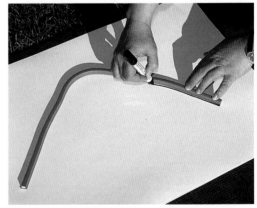

Remove it without altering its shape, and draw along its underside on a large piece of cardboard so that you have the line of your horse's body from side to side. You will later cut along the line so that you have a template from which to fit the saddle.

Some fitters require a template of the back about 6in (15cm) back from the first point (and make a note of the distance), and also one taken from along the topline from a little way in front of the withers, over them and down the horse's back. Together these templates will combine to give the saddle fitter a good idea of your horse's shape, and will enable him to bring a good selection of saddles to the fitting.

HOW DOES YOUR CURRENT SADDLE MEASURE UP?

If the templates indicate uneven development between the horse's two sides, do not assume that you have done them wrong. By all means take them again, but be aware that this discrepancy could be the first inkling you have that your horse may be 'uneven'. The fitter needs to know this, so do you, and presumably so will your teacher and maybe your vet and farrier. Something to think about!

The templates can be used to check the fit of your current saddle before they are sent to the fitter. Most people know that there should be at least three fingers' width between pommel and withers, and all the way down the gullet to the cantle. The gullet, too, should be wide enough to clear the spine at its sides – about 3in (7cm) wide all the way down is wide enough, otherwise the bearing area will actually be reduced. The rider's weight must be borne evenly on the muscles that cover the tops of the horse's ribs, from behind the shoulder blades to the last rib which can be fairly easily felt (unless the horse is much too fat). After this rib, the loin area starts, and this must never bear weight.

Having checked those points, now fit the respective 'sideways' templates in their relevant places under your saddle (while someone holds it for you at the pommel and cantle) and see whether or not they fit smoothly and evenly under the panel.

The bearing surface of the panel which goes on the horse's back should be as large as is reasonably possible, and the saddle should be symmetrical – that is, the centre of the pommel should line up with the centre of the cantle, so that were a line to be drawn between the two points it would run exactly down the middle of the gullet. Next, suspend the saddle on a rope run down the gullet, and carefully assess the appearance of the panels: you will be able to see whether the stuffing in the saddle is being compressed evenly by the horse's back. This will tell you if the horse's back is evenly developed, which in turn will indicate whether or not he is moving evenly. It is surprising how many people cannot see this in their own horse. An uneven horse will eventually

Opposite: Taking a wither pattern

(top) Mould the Flexi-curve over your horse's withers just behind the tops of the shoulder blades where the front edge of the saddle will go. You may also need to take make a similar pattern 6in (15cm) further back from this point

(centre top) Take another shape along the horse's spine, taking in withers and back

(centre below) Being careful not to change the shape of the Flexi-curve, draw along its inside edge onto a firm piece of card, labelling which part of the horse it presents

(bottom) Cut out the shape either with scissors or a craft knife

cause an uneven, twisted saddle which will obviously exacerbate the problem and nothing will ever get better. The reverse can also happen, where the saddle adversely affects the horse.

As well as being even on both sides, the stuffing should also be resilient and smooth, not hard and lumpy, and the panels should be reasonably flat, not rounded. Poor restuffing, where the flocking has been rammed in rather than adjusted with consideration for the shape of the back, will often cause the panels to be hard and rounded, and then not only will the bearing surface be actually reduced – since most of the rider's weight is being borne by the small area of the horse's back beneath the crest of the rounded part – but also the horse's back muscles will not be able to move comfortably beneath it: it will be an ungiving area of pressure that bores down on the muscles and skin.

As regards the length of a saddle, its front edge should come behind the tops of the horse's shoulder blades when the forelegs are extended to their maximum. Many saddles do not do this, although often this is because they are put on too far forwards. Put the saddle on top of the withers and slide it back with a gentle pressure of your hand so that it finds its own 'bed' on the horse's back. Keep pushing until you feel it do this, even if you think it is a little too far back: the chances are that it will in fact be in the correct position. Putting a saddle on too far forwards (illustrated top right) is a common error these days, and has the following bad effects:

1 It hampers the shoulder blades, which bang into it with every stride, lifting it first on one side and then on the other, which causes a twisting friction and pressure all the way down the horse's back to the cantle.
2 It causes the girth to lie too far forwards, with the risk of its digging in behind the elbows.
3 The tree points will be too close together, as they are on a wider part of the horse than they should be; this may cause significant discomfort and even injury, as described earlier.
4 Even if the saddle is well balanced on the horse's back when it is positioned correctly (with the cantle and pommel the same height, and the deepest part of the seat in the centre), if it is actually placed too far forwards up the withers, this tips it up at the pommel so that the cantle and centre of the seat are tilted backwards. Obviously the rider then also tips backwards (see centre right), and too much weight is placed too near the horse's loins.

5 This backward tilt also causes the stirrup leathers to hang

backwards, so when the stirrups are under pressure from the rider's feet they are actually pulled forwards, causing the feet-forward, seat-back position described earlier . It is then very difficult for the rider to maintain a balanced seat with the heels under the hips.

With the saddle pushed back an inch or two and in the right place (illustrated bottom left), it becomes once again well balanced and may be a good fit for the horse, and all these faults magically disappear; then riding becomes much easier and more comfortable for horse and rider alike (see top right). The incorrect pressures created by even a well fitting saddle that is placed too far forwards are quite enough to cause considerable discomfort in the horse – just as much as would a badly fitting saddle – with all the riding difficulties and so-called 'problem behaviour' that such discomfort provokes. And in this case, it is neither the saddle nor the horse which is at fault, but the person who put the saddle on.

There are other reasons for the shoulder blades hitting the front of the saddle: for instance, it could be that the saddle simply does not fit: it may be too long in the seat (check the back – it should not press on the loins), or the cut of the flap and the positioning of the knee rolls simply do not accord with this particular horse's make and shape. It may be the right width and length, but still just doesn't fit the horse comfortably – and carrying such a saddle your horse is unlikely to be light in hand with floating strides and extension on the flat, and free lift over obstacles.

PRACTICAL CHECK

So – put on the saddle, without a numnah or pad, in the right place, and check that it is correctly balanced as described. Next, mount up the horse's heaviest rider.

1 First check for gullet clearance with the rider leaning right forwards and then right back (see photographs centre right): there should be a clear tunnel of air all the way down the spine.

Your rider can now dismount.

2 Then, making sure that the horse is standing comfortably and reasonably square on all four feet, have someone hold each foreleg in turn behind the knee (letting the lower leg hang down) (see bottom right) and pull it forwards (as you would to smooth out the skin beneath the girth) to its fullest, comfortable extent; then check that the top of each shoulder blade is still clear of the front

edge of the saddle: it should not make contact with it, and you should be able to fit the width of the edge of your hand between the top of the shoulder blade when it is extended like this and the front of the saddle.

The reason for holding the leg behind the knee rather than lifting it straight by holding it behind the cannon or fetlock is that horses are not anatomically structured to be able to do this easily: they have to raise the leg somewhat bent, and then straighten it out once raised. Trying to make them do it the other way is the reason many horses and ponies are reluctant to bring their legs forward to stretch the skin under the girth: it hurts! If your horse is reluctant, be gentle but persistent, give him time to realise that it is not going to hurt doing it this new way, talk to him, and before long he will co-operate. When he does, reward him instantly with a sincere 'good boy' and you should find he will be quite ready to do it in future.

3 At the back, the saddle should not encroach at all on the horse's loins: there should be at least 7 or 8in (18 or 20cm) (indicated by the arrow in the photograph top right) between the back of the saddle and the horse's hip bones to avoid this. The saddle should sit on the area between the tops of the extended shoulder blades and the horse's loins (the last rib), and on this part only.

4 The width of the saddle is probably even more important than its length. You should take its width at a point about 6in (15cm) below and behind the wither, and it is this part that the tree points must fit. This is the area which develops hollows if it is subjected to pressure over a long period of time from the tree points of a saddle that is too tight or too narrow – although many horses will develop problems in their work and show discomfort long before this because of the pain and bruising. If the saddle is too narrow or tight, it will seem to perch up above the withers and to be sloping back (unless there is hardly any stuffing in the panel). If the saddle you are checking is well fitting and wide enough, it should look as though it is sitting easily with a smooth line down the front edge, with no sign of the skin being wrinkled or under pressure; you should be able to run the flat of your fingers down between the front edge of the saddle (illustrated centre right) and the horse and feel a smooth, comfortable fit with no obstructions indicating tightness and pressure points.

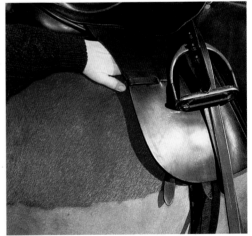

5 Once you are satisfied with the fit at the front, check that the saddle sits evenly all the way along. You should be able to slip the flat of your fingers, palm down, between the horse's back and the panel that lies behind the girth straps and below the seat (illustrated bottom right): if you run your flat hand *with* the lie of the

horse's hair, you should detect no unevenness of pressure or tightness.

6 If a saddle is too wide it will be too far down on the horse's back: the pommel will be too close to the withers and the gullet too close to the spine, and may even press on them, and the whole saddle will almost certainly rock from side to side. However, horses that have been subjected to pressure from tree points that were too narrow may well have hollows just below and behind the withers due to muscle wastage in this area, and the saddle fitter may advise you to fit the horse with a saddle which seems too wide, but which will be the correct width when his muscles are back to normal as a result of being able to move properly, and without any pressure in this area. This will be due partly, it is hoped, to correct ridden work and/or work on the lunge or long-reins, and also because the blood will be able to circulate properly through these muscles and so help to restore their structure by delivering oxygen and nutrients and removing waste products.

A slightly-too-wide saddle is therefore much safer than a narrow one, and indeed will probably be recommended if the horse has muscle wastage; any space can be filled out with layers of suitable padding (see below) which can be removed as the horse's musculature improves.

A VISIT FROM THE SADDLE FITTER

This operation is likely to take at least an hour and probably two if it is done thoroughly and if you try several saddles fairly.

The fitter will probably wear a hard hat, gloves and strong shoes or boots. He or she will observe the horse from outside his box and will almost certainly ask you a few general questions regarding his temperament, any individual likes, dislikes or habits, his age, his yearly pattern of work and rest in as much as it will affect his body condition and shape, previous relevant problems and so on, to obtain as full a picture as possible of your horse. The fitter will say 'hello' to the horse and then ask you to stand him up on a flat, hard piece of ground wearing no rugs, boots or bandages.

He or she will assess the horse's conformation and muscular development and relate them to the horse's age and work. This will give him an idea as to how much the horse is likely to change shape (as they all do) in the future: youngsters change shape as they grow, mature and develop through both age and work, and older horses are constitutionally weaker and more prone to pressure and friction sores. Also, a bad rider will have an adverse effect on the shape of any horse because he/she will promote incorrect muscular development. All these points will be taken into account by the fitter who is trained to recognise correct muscular development – and good and bad riding!

He or she will pay particular attention to the state of the horse's back,

BEFORE THE FITTER'S ARRIVAL

There are various points to which you need to attend:

* Your horse needs to be clean, not least because the sample saddles need to be kept in 'as new' condition, but also because the marks left by a saddle are a good sign as to where there are any pressure or friction points, and dirt may obscure these.

* You need an area of flat, hard standing and a level area where the horse can be trotted up. You also need somewhere where you can ride and jump freely, depending on what you are going to be doing in the saddle.

* The horse's actual rider/s need to be present because both or all people need to be fitted if at all possible. It may be necessary to compromise if the horse has several riders, such as the whole family.

* Be properly dressed for riding and with your up-to-standard hat.

* Have on hand your own girth/s, stirrup leathers and irons.

* Have on hand any saddle you wish to trade in, and make sure it is clean.

* If the horse has any infectious skin condition, is ill, or has any injury which will hamper or prevent saddle fitting or prevent him moving naturally, postpone the appointment as soon as you know about the condition so that the fitter's time is not wasted.

looking for white hair from previous saddle injuries, for lumps, sores and scabs, and feeling for tender or tight areas to which the horse will respond by 'shivering' the muscles and skin in that area and maybe by cringing away or even trying to bite in warning. Any muscular or skeletal asymmetry – and the fitter will check for this from both sides, and from front and back – will greatly affect saddle fitting. And if the horse is noticeably in pain or discomfort, the fitter will probably decline to fit him until he has recovered.

Certain flexion tests will be done, notably persuading the horse to bend neck and body by offering him a piece of carrot from around the hip area on each side. If he cannot do this on one or both sides, this will be noted and the fitter may examine him further.

The horse will next be walked and trotted up, away and back and to both sides, so the fitter can see clearly how even his gait is, any possible lameness, or stiffness in the legs, body or head and neck or in the tail carriage, if the back fails to swing, and any uneven body movement at all. The expression on the horse's face often gives a clear indication as to whether or not he is comfortable.

If there are no problems which would prevent the fitting going ahead, the fitter will now have to decide whether or not the horse is likely to change shape much, and will aim to provide a saddle which will fit him comfortably today, but will also allow for any increase or decrease in condition and development.

The fitter will have assessed any templates you sent before the visit and will have brought a selection of saddles, new or used according to your requirements, based on these, on your description and any photographs of your horse, on your own measurements, and on the job or equestrian discipline you want the saddle to do. It may be that you have

The saddle fitter will carefully observe the horse's movements coming towards and going away from her without the horse being saddled

simply asked for an assessment of your present saddle and, if necessary, how you may be able to improve any faults to make it more acceptable on a temporary basis. Whichever is the case, the basic assessment and fitting procedure is the same.

Each saddle in turn will be put on, and the horse walked and trotted up in hand so that the fitter can check for apparent fit and stability on the horse's back. A saddle which rocks and moves without a rider will still do so with one, and could be uncomfortable for the horse. When a few saddles have been short-listed, the rider will mount and they will be checked for rider-fit. The rider will need to work the horse on both reins in all gaits and over fences, if appropriate. The fitter will be assessing the rider's technique, and some may tactfully point out significant faults: poor riding can cause as many back problems as badly fitting saddles, and many riders do not want to hear about this vital aspect of looking after their horse's back! If a fault is minor or the rider does not accept the fault, the fitter may be able to select a saddle which will minimise its effects, depending on what it is.

The trained, qualified fitter will attend to all the points of basic saddle fitting detailed earlier and other finer points as well, including examining the lie of the hair and any marks or evidence of pressure or friction such as disturbed hair when each saddle is removed, as well as noting how the horse went in it.

The saddle or saddles the fitter finally recommends may still need some slight adjustment, and the possibilities of this will be explained.

Finally, the potential customer will be advised of the final cost involved, less any trade-in value of a saddle offered in part exchange. Remember, every saddle in good condition, or that can be refurbished, is worth something, even though it may be useless to you personally. Some other customer may be delighted with it, so it is always worth asking about the trade-in value of your saddle, or other tack. The price received, plus possible credit terms on a new saddle, often makes one more affordable than the initial price may suggest.

The fitter will probably also advise on the future care and maintenance of your new or replacement saddle, including future checks, restuffing and so on, and this is advice well worth following. Every rider or owner should check the fit of a horse's saddle regularly and as a matter of course. Difficulties

Below: Having seen how the horse move without any tack, the saddle fitter will then want to see the horse in movement wearing his own saddle and finally with the rider mounted using both the old and the new saddles

can arise if the horse and saddle are not yours but, whatever the case, riding a horse in a saddle which you know does not fit him and which, therefore, is probably causing him distress cannot be right and must affect his welfare and the enjoyment and effectiveness of you both.

THE SADDLE ON A MOVING HORSE

No matter how well the saddle appears to fit the horse, or how stable it seems to be on his back, it must move to some extent, be it only slightly, when the horse moves and when it is subject to slight distortion from the weight of a rider on top of it. Any movement from horse or rider will exacerbate uneven pressure or poor fit, incorrect positioning on the back, or the pressure and irritation caused by any small piece of dried-on sweat, mud or other debris which may not have been removed before saddling up. Because the horse's back swings from side to side, particularly in the slower gaits, and also flexes up and down slightly, inevitably there will be some movement of the saddle on it. Even as a horse breathes in and out, the ribs expand and contract, and therefore so too does the back on which the saddle rests, and as a horse jumps, again the back expands. The saddle must be wide enough to allow for this if bruising is not to occur.

When fitting saddles, it is often overlooked that the horse's ribs expand as it rises to a jump: for its own comfort, the saddle must be wide enough to allow this expansion without pinching or creating too much pressure. Saddles which are fitted to take into account only the stationary horse often fall short in this respect

Any movement of the saddle on the horse's back, and therefore any undue pressure and friction, can only be exacerbated by the rider's weight and movement. We want the horse to move freely, and to this end a good rider will move in the saddle as little as possible, keeping a relaxed seat and simply allowing it to follow the rhythm of the horse's paces. Even so, in the highest echelons of every single equestrian discipline, we still see riders who throw themselves around to a quite unreasonable degree, partly in their attempts to influence the horse but also in their efforts to keep their own balance on his back. I once read an interesting article by a saddler who claimed that he saw more back problems in dressage horses than in show jumpers; he considered that incorrectly performed sitting trot was responsible for this, many of the riders thudding up and down on their horses' backs because, even at the highest levels, they did not seem to know how to use their hip joints and pelvis to absorb the horses' movements.

To improve the circulation in the horse's back after removal of the saddle, gently rub the saddle and girth area with the flat of the hand. Slapping the saddle patch may cause damage to the capillaries in the skin

Every tiny movement is felt by the horse, and all affect the way the saddle feels on his back, so any small unsuitability will be magnified. Every movement of the rider is felt as weight redistribution on his back, and each one requires a counteracting movement if he is to keep himself not only in balance but physically in a position to carry out whatever movements the rider is asking for. This means he is using muscles and energy over and above those that are needed to perform the movement. Sometimes he may need to move quickly and unexpectedly to counterbalance a sudden lurch by the rider, and this may cause muscle damage as muscles contract in an unco-ordinated way. A poor rider can injure a

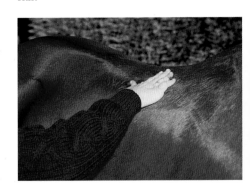

horse when riding in even the best of saddles: in a badly designed or badly fitted one, the results can be even worse.

When a horse has been under saddle for some time, the capillaries in the back will probably be squashed to some extent, and it is often advised that the saddle is not removed immediately after work but the girth loosened and the blood vessels allowed to regain their shape and 'tone' gradually. The practice of dismounting and leading the horse in hand for the last mile or so home after a hack is a good one for this reason. The saddle patch should be massaged gently after the saddle is removed, not slapped hard as is still sometimes done.

TECHNOLOGICAL AIDS TO SADDLE FITTING

Another relatively recent advance in saddle fitting is the use of mechanical, electronic and computerised pressure-testing devices. These vary in type and there will surely be other such devices and techniques developed as time goes on, but their main advantages so far are these: some can provide a shaped template of the whole saddle area; others have temperature sensors which indicate areas of the back that are warmer than normal, and therefore presumably injured by friction or bruising; and some operate by means of pressure sensors, and can show us which areas of the back are subject to the most pressure.

Ensuring as far as possible that weight is evenly distributed over the back is not easy in practice with conventional saddles. As we have already discussed, the area which usually takes the most weight is that under the points of the tree, on the muscles immediately below and behind the withers. Computerised sensor tests have shown that even when a conventional saddle appears to

In this set of scans the red areas show the points of greatest pressure. It is immediately obvious how uneven is the distribution of the rider's weight with conventional saddles. It is easy to see why the cause of so many problems can be traced to badly fitting saddles.

The two scans made from the pressure-sensitive saddle (centre and bottom right) show how it adjusts itself to distribute the weight more evenly.

It is also interesting to note that despite the commonly-held view that standing up in the stirrups helps to get the weight off the horse's back, it would appear that pressure increases just below and behind the withers, possibly inhibiting movement.

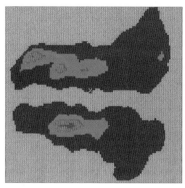
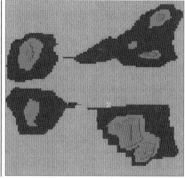

These scans show common faults with conventional saddles: (left) saddle tree too curved; (right) four-point contact

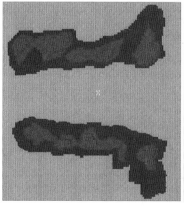
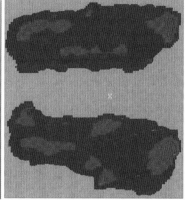

Rider sitting down in the saddle: (left) a good conventional saddle; (right) a pressure-sensitive saddle (Reactorpanel)

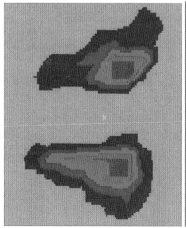
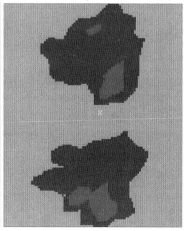

Rider standing up in the saddle: (left) a good conventional saddle; (right) a pressure-sensitive saddle (Reactorpanel)

fit well and spread pressure evenly over the back, pressure will actually be uneven, with most weight being felt on these muscles and also under the stirrup bars which are close to the tree points. I was told by one saddle fitter that 1½lb of pressure per square inch is considered acceptable if normal blood flow and tissue health is to be maintained. However, with the rider standing in the stirrups, readings for these areas of the back of 4lb of pressure per square inch were frequently recorded for conventional saddles in normal use which the owners believed fitted well, and this amount of pressure is enough to considerably flatten and actually close the capillaries – that is, completely cutting off blood supply for the time the pressure was maintained.

If you take into account the problems caused by badly fitting saddles, you can easily visualise the immense damage which can be done to a horse's back. To emphasise, 4lb or more of pressure results in complete closure of the capillaries, and it seems that this occurs with many saddles

---

'FLAIR'

Surely nothing could cause less pressure on your horse's back than air and an English company, First Thoughts (Equine) Ltd, has been developing for five years a system called Flair which can be incorporated into any style of saddle, new or used, and which exchanges the conventional flocking for air bags. To remove any 'ballooning' effect, there is a foam insert which spreads the air, providing an increased and even bearing surface on the horse's back, the panels continually and instantly adjusting to the back in movement.

The system is not a way of making a badly fitting saddle less damaging: the saddle tree must be sound and the correct width for the horse before Flair can be fitted which will be done by a trained fitter. Sensor tests using the Pliance system mentioned elsewhere in this chapter show greatly reduced and more even pressure. Riders report vastly improved action and muscle development in their horses and a much softer ride for themselves

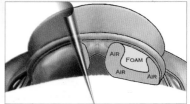

---

whenever the rider stands in the stirrups – for instance when posting to the trot, jiggling about, riding in the jumping position or just 'taking the weight off the horse's back'. This really makes you stop and think, doesn't it?

Owners who were told that their saddles were exerting dangerous amounts of pressure (according to the tests) under the tree points and stirrup bars often responded not by buying a new or different saddle, but by placing padding under the pressure area, so tilting the saddle up and back. One would be tempted to think that this would lessen the pressure, but a further test showed that this was not the case at all, but that it actually created more pressure under the cantle area.

Another interesting revelation was that inserting a riser pad under the cantle of a saddle which appeared to tilt backwards, in an understandable effort to even up the balance, did not in fact improve the situation:

what happened was that tilting the cantle upwards simply increased the pressure in front under the points and stirrup bars even more.

This research also shows that a tree which has become misshapen in use – banana-shaped or sagging, twisted, spread and so on, not to mention broken – will cause severe pressure to be exerted in other places as well; it also showed that using a conventional thick numnah or two underneath the saddle gave no less a reading. (Having said this, some remedial and therapeutic numnahs and pads do appear to make a difference, these are discussed below.)

Basically it seems that if you have a badly designed saddle, or one which does not fit to the extent that an expert saddler cannot adjust it, the only answer is to sell it or otherwise get rid of it, and to buy a better or more suitable one.

The technological aids discussed above are not widespread, and it would be as well to keep an eye on the equestrian press for further developments. Those wishing to look into it further could start by approaching the Society of Master Saddlers and the British Equestrian Trade Association in the UK (or the Australian Equestrian Trade Association in Australia, and the Saddle, Harness and Allied Trades Association in the USA) whose addresses are in the Appendix.

If buying a new saddle, or changing yours for another, try asking the

'AIR RIDE PROFESSIONAL'S CHOICE'

The Air Ride™ Suspension System is a saddle pad made up of multi-layered small air pockets which is claimed to conform to both horse and saddle, absorbing shock, staying put and 'locking down' for a more secure and comfortable ride. It is said to alleviate pressure on the most sensitive areas of a horse's back. Scientific tests showed that the pad performed better with each use. It returns to its natural shape after each use and will conform and perform just as effectively on the next horse on which it is used. The Air Ride saddle pad is available through Professional's Choice Sports Medicine Products.

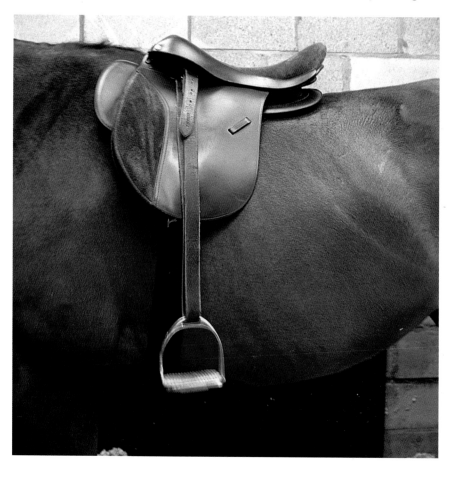

A Reactorpanel saddle in place. Actually, this one is a little too far forward. The idea is that the front of the flexible panel should come just 2.5cm (1in) onto the shoulder blade which will then lift it slightly in movement, greatly reducing pressure below and behind the withers where many conventional saddles exert their highest level of pressure

supplier if he or she could provide a computerised read-out of the pressure a well fitting saddle of their design exerts on a horse's back, and if possible, get any potential purchase tested on your own horse. Of course, there may be problems of travelling, or access to the equipment, but a conscientious owner would probably be able to overcome these. In view of the new and startling knowledge this technology provides, it seems that every effort should be made to take advantage of it.

A few conventional saddles did do well in the tests, as did the floating-panel type of design; even more important is the fact that the increasing publicity concerning these techniques of saddle testing is gradually raising public awareness for the better. So although these testing facilities are not at present widely available, perhaps we have now reached the point where it is no longer good enough to buy a conventional saddle which seems to fit all right, put a comfy-looking numnah underneath it, and ride off into the sunset thinking we have done our best. New designs of saddle continue to appear on the market, some of them specifically designed to reduce saddle pain and discomfort for both rider and horse; one advertisement actually said: 'You can ride on our saddles with a clear conscience'. There will surely be other testing techniques – and meanwhile we always have as a guide the horse's musculature, the state of his back, the way he goes physically, and the way he reacts behaviourally to work. A professional saddle fitter can always be paid to come and assess existing saddles, and we can keep up to date ourselves with technical and design developments. Furthermore, keeping a saddle in good condition will ensure that it retains a reasonable value should we wish to trade it in.

As for trading standards, wouldn't it be wonderful if, in the future, saddles which did not pass sensor tests were not allowed to be sold?

The Pliance System is a computerised system which measures the pressure distribution between the saddle and the horse's back with the help of a thin elastic sensormat. Not only saddle fit but also rider technique can be objectively assessed and corrected as areas of pressure are viewed on-screen. The pressure distribution can also be compared to time-synchronised video pictures taken during observation of horse and rider. Also, gait assymetry, possibly associated with back problems or bad saddle fit, can be assessed quantitatively. It can be connected to any PC via RS232 and works in Windows

SADDLE PADS AND NUMNAHS

I have already mentioned the point that a well fitting, leather-lined saddle in good condition should not really need a numnah or pad underneath it. These were certainly not in general use until about twenty years ago, although sheepskin numnahs were often seen on eventers and showjumpers (ostensibly to encourage them to round their backs over their fences), and the army and police often used – and still do – shabraques (ornate, shaped saddle-cloths with decorative braiding and insignia on them); but in about the 1970s the market was suddenly flooded with the now common thin, quilted cotton numnahs and thicker acrylic fleece ones as the idea spread that these would make things more comfortable for the horse. Young riders, of course, like everything colour co-ordinated, and bright, coloured numnahs with bandages and browbands to match became all the rage, whether they were needed or not. This craze confirmed their place in the market, and today's generation of riders all

WHEN TO USE A NUMNAH

1 If the horse genuinely seems to prefer it.

2 If you ride for long periods and your horse sweats a good deal, when one of the permeable textile numnahs may help to keep his back drier and, therefore, the skin more resilient (although sweat contains its own oily lubricant).

3 If you are allowing a horse to build up wasted muscle and are padding out a slightly-too-wide saddle; or

4 if you have a saddle which has been discovered to fit poorly and use one of the few remedial numnahs or pads which really do lessen pressure, purely as a temporary measure until you get a different saddle. The real solution, of course, would be to stop riding the horse in the meantime – few riding horses these days have to be ridden, most being in leisure jobs.

seem to feel that a numnah or saddle-cloth of some kind is essential.

All saddles, apart from side saddles, are lined with leather these days, and leather is a natural, breathing material. Saddlery leather is tanned and specially treated with oils and waxes and, if properly cared for, is regularly soaped, probably with glycerine saddle soap or a lubricating cream, and perhaps oiled or dressed as well, maybe with neatsfoot oil or perhaps a lanolin-based, paint-on product. Leather in this condition, provided the saddle fits the horse, will not make him sore no matter how much he sweats underneath it. Leather also soaks in moisture (including sweat) and lets moisture and other substances out. The following anecdotes illustrate its resilient qualities:

Many years ago my horse and I fell in three feet of seawater, and my saddle – leather and wool flock, of course, because there was nothing else then – was obviously completely sodden with it. Seawater, or rather the salt in it, has a reputation for rotting everything with which it comes into contact, so the girl who ran the yard where I kept my horse completely dunked the saddle in a tank of clear water, squashing the panels underwater for several minutes to get as much salt out of the stuffing as she could. Then she took it out and kept squashing water out of the panels (which mainly came out along the gullet) and finally hung it up to drip overnight. We both thought the saddle would rot away.

Next day she dressed it thoroughly with leather dressing, and continued to dress it every day. Once the stuffing had dried out (checked by inserting a flat hand into the stuffed panel from the gullet where it is always open), we started using it normally again.

It was intriguing to see how, over several weeks of using it and cleaning it with glycerine saddle soap, the saddle continued to ooze out salt, despite its treatment in the tank of clear water, not merely through the seams but through the leather itself. There was a regular white crust all over it, not just on the underside of the panels where one might have expected it to have oozed out from the stuffing, but from the seat and flaps, too – everywhere. The saddle was only in the sea for a few seconds, yet it must have absorbed lots of salt. The leather finally cleansed itself after a couple of months, and the saddle (a Stephen Robertson) was absolutely fine and did not even need restuffing for fit at that time.

Years later the same saddle was on the same horse when, crossing remote mossland, he shied and we fell into a very deep, overgrown drainage dyke at the side of the bridleway. As part of the fire brigade's (successful) efforts to get my precious horse out, they passed a rope under the saddle gullet (as well as hosepipes round his quarters) and hauled him up a ramp of straw bales, obviously putting great strain on the saddle tree. The saddle was submerged in slimy, liquid mud for about three hours, and I was sure that the tree must be broken and the saddle wrecked.

I washed it and sent it to Robertson's in Exeter, describing the whole

incident – and miraculously, they reported back that the tree (a conventional laminated beechwood spring tree) was not even sprained. All they had to do was replace the slimy, muddy stuffing. The leather this time strangely did not ooze mud or slime, but retained its perfect, supple condition despite stinking of rotten vegetation for a few weeks.

This tale just shows that well maintained leather has lifelong qualities, which surely means that in normal (and some abnormal) circumstances it does not need any help from numnahs. Moreover it is actually possible to buy leather-covered numnahs and saddle pads. However, as mentioned earlier, if a numnah is used ostensibly to help relieve the pressure caused by a saddle that is too tight or too narrow, it could well end up making matters worse as it takes up more space under the saddle and will actually increase the pressure on the horse's back. On the other hand, using carefully chosen pads and numnahs under a wide saddle, often now done as a temporary measure as a horse builds up muscle after experiencing wastage due to pressure from a too-narrow one, is a different matter. In these circumstances padding will stop the saddle rocking and moving too much on the back.

It may well be that a soft or resilient numnah or pad may make wearing a saddle more comfortable for the horse simply from the point of view of softness, and I do know a few horses who seem to prefer having their pad/s on. As with everything else to do with horses, what a pity we cannot ask them, but must rely on our own observation – which may or may not be accurate! My personal experience leads me to believe that any pads must be very carefully chosen and used.

The Proteq™ Saddle Pad was developed from human medical applications and contains polystyrene beads in an air-tight sac. The amount of air is adjusted so that the pad (which fits inside a lambswool cover) conforms to the horse's back on the underside and to the saddle on the top. Computerised pressure analysis has shown that the pad greatly alleviates saddle pressure

A good person to ask about an appropriate numnah or pad, if you really need one, should be a qualified saddle fitter. Many 'ordinary' pads simply do no good at all: for instance, ordinary plastic foam covered with cotton flattens to nothing, and the cotton often wrinkles and causes uneven pressure and rubbing. On the other hand, soft, acrylic fleece numnahs seem to be reasonably efficient at filling out wide saddles, provided they are not filled with foam but with fibre. The ubiquitous thin, quilted cotton numnahs do absorb sweat (if you feel this is necessary), but I know of at least two physiotherapists who maintain that the stitching on them can actually rub sores on fine-skinned horses. Natural sheepskin is rarely seen these days, but is not, I feel, a lot of use, largely because it can ball up and matt if not carefully combed out and kept clean; comfort can be provided more effectively with a modern, pressure-absorbing material.

A Prolite Relief Pad which, the makers claim, reduces the risk of sore backs. The material is a blend of viscose-elastic-gel polymer and latex rubber said to distribute pressure more evenly and eliminate rubbing by absorbing friction

SENSITIVE-SKINNED HORSES

Thin, quilted numnahs are very popular for use under saddles as a discreet, absorbent layer which also offers a slight padding effect. However, there is some evidence that they may not be the most comfortable thing for sensitive-skinned horses, particularly if clipped or in their summer coat. A physiotherapist pointed out to me that the stitching can easily rub such horses and cause significant back soreness.

Even in some of the more technologically-advanced-sounding products, the fillings may flatten and quickly become useless, or they may ruck up, matt and harden, or even actually rub the horse sore and encourage sweating. Some of the materials break down easily in use, too.

Gel pads sound like a good idea, but in those where the gel can move around, the pressure-relieving principles must be doubted. The claim made by some that they can 'even up' pressure by this means does not hold water, because if the filling will move away from a pressure point to the surrounding areas, it is too soft to support those areas to relieve the more prominent problem areas.

All in all, the best way to check the wearing and working qualities of any pad is to pick and choose a user: you need someone who does not take advertising hype for granted, who is concerned enough to really examine and understand the condition of a horse's back, and can recognise when a horse is, or is not comfortable, and who watches equipment in use very closely to see if it really does seem to be doing what it says it will do.

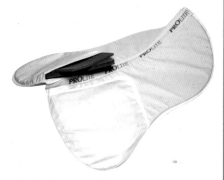

The Prolite Adjustable has pockets into which pads of the Prolite material can be inserted, as required

The Prolite Pressure Relief Numnah has four shaped inserts located at key pressure points which Prolite say are common to all saddles

GIRTHS

Girths have not escaped the technological revolution or the increasing interest in horse comfort and what girths really do to horses. Sadly, however, along with the current fashion of putting saddles on too far forward, another has developed for fastening girths much too tightly. I don't know where these fashions come from, but they are not at all appropriate for a supposedly enlightened revolution in horse welfare standards.

Girths still come in leather and these work fine provided, like all leather, they are kept clean and soft. The older type of natural fabrics are rarely seen, although they are still available, if only to order; these include: wool serge web – appalling, and likely to snap without notice; mohair – good, as long as it is well cared for; lampwick – the same, but a little inclined to 'pill' or 'bobble'; cotton web – better than wool, at least; and cotton string – easily surpassed. Probably the worst of the older girths were the nylon string ones which are quite primitive and must have been designed by the Devil himself – rough, harsh, totally non-absorbent and ungiving, with strands which gathered together into a hand rope as if they were magnetised.

Girths have been subjected to pressure-sensor tests in the same way as saddles and some pads, and more than one organisation world-wide has come to the conclusion that a good girth needs two vital features:

The Aerborn gel pad, probably the most used gel pad in the UK

1 It must spread the pressure evenly over the entire girth area, which must be neither too narrow nor too wide, about 3–4in (8–10cm) being a good, general width; and

2 It must have plenty of firm, even 'give' in it because the horse needs to

be able to breathe freely and also to move his forehand without restriction, and since the girth encircles his ribcage, he cannot do either if he is obliged to wear one that is made of an unforgiving material.

The conclusions of this research led to these practical recommendations:

1 Girths which have a narrow, reinforcing strip down them (usually down the middle) that is made of firmer material than the rest of the girth and is stitched on could not be recommended: this is because, in wear, the horse feels the pressure from just the strip, and not the whole girth – this concentrates the pressure in much too narrow an area, and is therefore very uncomfortable.

2 The most effective, practical way of providing 'give' for both breathing and moving is to have firm elastic inserts at *both* ends of the girth and/ or in the centre: like this it will provide a laterally even stretch, whereas an insert at one end only will give an unpleasant, twisting sensation.

Although some girth fabrics are claimed to have a small amount of give in them, in practice this seems to make no significant contribution to the horse's comfort or feeling of freedom of movement. The following anecdote should exemplify this:

I have recently lost an old Thoroughbred mare who was extremely sensitive and who made her feelings known about everything, including the effects that tack had on her person. I started off riding her in an ordinary, reinforced, permeable girth with a reinforcing strip down the middle, and one which I thought was a quite reasonable design; however, I soon noticed that she never let herself take a deep breath in, always stopping short, despite the fact that I ride with the girth only comfortably 'close' and

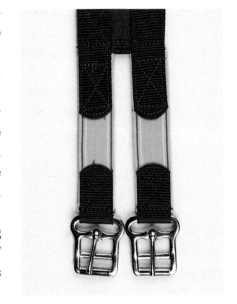

Elastic inserts on an Aerborn girth. Elastic inserts are much more comfortable for the horse if incorporated on both ends of the girth – if only one end 'gives', the girth will cause a twisting feeling

Below left: The Aerborn Humane girth allows more freedom of movement due to the buckles being fastened, at both ends of the girth, to one doubled length of fabric which slides on a strong dee

Centre: A standard Aerborn girth

Right: An Aerborn short dressage girth

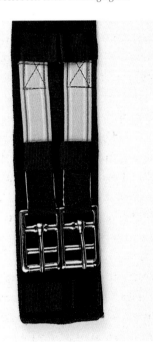

not at all tight. Then I bought an Aerborn Humane girth (see photograph) which slides and moves with the horse's movements on a strong central dee. I found this an improvement, but still the mare did not seem comfortable when taking a deep breath. Finally I considered the Aerborn elastic insert girth, but did not like the one-end-only design; so I asked the manufacturers, through Giddens of London, to make me a couple with elastic at both ends. They duly obliged, and the difference was obviously immediately tangible to the mare, and therefore most rewarding to me.

The first time she wore one, we warmed up on a hack, then went for a spin down our favourite bridleway specifically to test the girth. After her fun, she made to take a big, deep breath as usual, but stopped herself, also as usual, and presumably out of habit. But then she tried again and did a double-beat inspiration, stopping and then, realising that the girth was not going to restrict her, breathing in again without breathing out first. She then, quite comically, took a few deep breaths (even though I don't think she needed them), snorted hard, and pranced, high-blowing, all the way home. Enough said, I think.

Modern synthetic textiles for girths are very often the permeable ones which allow sweat to pass through them and evaporate, so keeping the very sweaty girth area drier. In practice, they do do this. As for fit, the tests mentioned found that, as expected, it is imperative that the girth does not dig in behind the horse's elbow: this is most likely to happen with a fat animal, one with no natural girth groove – a Balding or Atherstone girth would be helpful for a horse of this confirmation – and, of course, when it is used with a saddle which is positioned too far forwards (there is no excuse for this).

The tightness recommended for humane horse management was 'snug but not tight', so that 'the flat of the fingers can easily be slid down inside the girth from the front, to keep the hair smooth, but not then pulled more than half an inch away from the horse's side'. This is, in fact, the old fitting criterion which nowadays seems to have been forgotten. This degree of tightness, plus the two-ended elastic insert, makes an excellent girthing arrangement.

Good quality buckles on a girth are important, and are a giveaway as to its general quality. There is one point, though, on which I disagree with the tack experts, and that is about having a roller fitted to the top bar for ease of adjustment. Their argument is that, should the roller open up, it will cut the leather of the girth tab: however, if you keep an eye on it, you can press it back before it comes apart – and surely, ease of adjustment and avoidance of a wear line across the tab (because the roller evens out the pressure) are good enough reasons to use one.

The short belly girths used on some dressage and showing saddles do remove buckles effectively from under the rider's leg, but to my mind they can look clumsy, and they do create an unforgiving wodge which is often

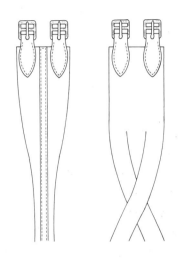

Girths which are shaped behind the elbow like this Atherstone (left) and Balding (right) give much more freedom of foreleg movement

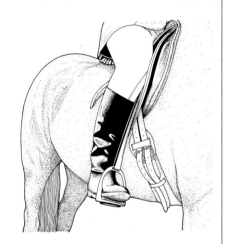

Short belly girths often used on dressage saddles can create an uncomfortable lump just behind the elbow; this girth is long enough to prevent that

too near the horse's elbow for his comfort. In fact it is quite easy to work out just how long a girth you need so you can avoid lumpy fastenings under your leg, yet have it long enough for the buckles to be hidden by the saddle flap and well out of the way of the horse's elbows. Ask a friend to measure carefully from just behind the angle of your knee, under your horse's belly and up to just behind the angle of your other knee – and that should be the length you need. Most saddles will have girth straps long enough to permit this, but if not, they can easily be replaced by a good saddler.

Measuring from side to side under the horse's belly to find out what length girth is needed, so that the buckles come behind the knee and not directly under the leg – provided the girth straps are positioned appropriately!

BREASTPLATES AND CRUPPERS

Breastplates are still seen quite frequently on hunters and riding horses, and often on competition ponies. Cruppers, on the other hand – formerly a standby of families who owned Thelwell-type teddy bears whose saddles you could not keep from slipping forwards for love nor money without a crupper – are now quite a rarity on riding animals, although they are a normal part of driving harness.

BREASTPLATES

Breastplates are most useful for keeping the saddle in place on certain horses: these might include one that is fit and fairly lean; one with slab-sided conformation; or one with an exceptionally big front and shoulder. They are also a great advantage when riding in hilly country.

The hunting breastplate that is used for general riding, and which can have a martingale attachment fitted to it, is the one most commonly seen

A racing breastplate in use. Fitting these can be a fine art as they must not interfere with breathing or the movement of the horse's shoulder. This one is about right

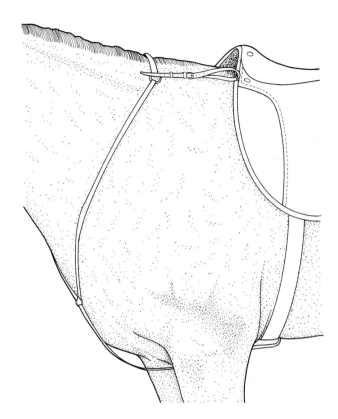

A breastplate correctly fitted, fastened to the saddle dees and the girth and adjusted just tightly enough to keep the saddle in the correct place. It is obviously useless if it is too loose. You should be able to pass the flat of your hand comfortably all round underneath it to allow for shoulder movement

outside racing. It fits closely round the base of the neck so that you can just fit the width of your hand between it and the horse, and fastens to the front dees of the saddle with leather loops; there is also a strap passing down between the forelegs with a loop through which the girth passes. The breastplate works well if it is fitted tightly enough, though most people fit them too loosely. On the other hand, if fitted too tightly, they are uncomfortable for the horse and can restrict his shoulder movement.

One type which is informally known as the halter-neck type has no strap passing between the forelegs and works well without it. It is more or less identical to an ordinary neckstrap which is invaluable for novice or unsteady riders: it is far better to hang on to one of these than to the horse's mouth, which is always a sin in riding! Some types of breastplate also have strong elastic inserts on the 'collar' part which enables them to be fitted tightly enough to work but still allow the horse to move comfortably.

The racing, or Aintree-type breastplate or breastgirth is basically a strap, sometimes padded, that passes horizontally across the base of the horse's neck and above the points of his shoulders; it is suspended from another strap that passes up over the horse's neck in front of the withers. The horizontal strap is attached by means of adjustable loops around the girth tabs of the saddle or the girth itself, depending on how high the buckles are. It must be fitted so that it does not press on the horse's windpipe or interfere with his shoulder movement.

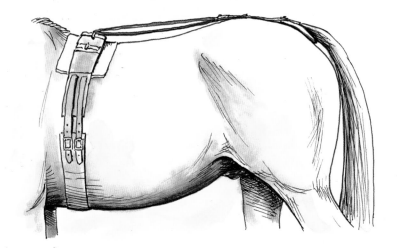

Many people do not use cruppers these days and most saddles no longer have a cantle dee to allow for crupper attachment; this would be a real boon for croup-high or tubby animals on whom the saddle invariably slips forwards causing considerable problems. Here a crupper is correctly fitted to a roller to keep it back from the elbows

CRUPPERS

Cruppers can cause the fat ponies who usually wear them a good deal of discomfort if they are not kept very soft and clean, or if they are not adjusted properly. A crupper consists of a well padded loop of soft leather, sometimes chamois, through which the pony's tail is passed. The loop must be positioned right up under the root of the tail, but without pulling on it or forcing it upwards; any tail hairs must be brought out of the loop as they can cause soreness. Once the correct position has been found, the adjustable strap passing from the loop and fastening to the dee at the cantle of the saddle must be carefully adjusted and buckled to keep that position. Most modern saddles, even children's, do not have cantle dees, in which case you will have to have one fitted (a simple job).

If the loop is too low the crupper will not work, and will irritate the pony; if it is too tight it will also be uncomfortable for him, and the tail may be pulled out of position and actually come out of the loop.

STIRRUP IRONS AND LEATHERS

STIRRUP IRONS

The stirrup, measured inside the branches along the tread, should be 2.5cm (1in) wider than the widest part of the sole of your boot

Possibly the two most important points regarding stirrup irons are firstly their size, and secondly the metal from which they are made (note, however, that there are now strong synthetic, usually plastic, stirrup irons available, too).

Size

The size should be measured along the tread or bottom of the stirrup on the inside of the branches: it must be 1in (2cm) wider than the widest

86

part of your riding boot or shoe. Even with modern riding trainers, an essential point about riding footwear is that there should be a noticeable heel which, combined with a stirrup of the correct size, will almost certainly prevent your foot slipping through the stirrup, and so also prevent you being dragged by the ankle in a fall. Conversely, if the stirrup is too narrow, your foot could become stuck in it with the same, if less likely, result.

Parting Company

Although synthetic stirrups are fairly common in the endurance riding field because of their lightness, for other forms of riding there is a definite advantage in having heavy stirrups as they are much easier to find should you lose them (ie your foot comes out of your stirrup); this is because they tend to follow gravity and try to hang straight downwards, despite the horse's movements. Losing a stirrup (of course you haven't actually lost them because they are always on the ends of your leathers!) can be a real nuisance and upset your balance, so it is an excellent plan to practise riding without stirrups at all gaits and over jumps – then losing one will not be such a disaster when it happens. However, I always have the greatest admiration for jockeys who lose their often lightweight racing stirrups, can't stop to get them back, and carry on and win races regardless – what strength and skill!

The Sprenger System 4 Safety Stirrup. Its forward-curved branches are a safety feature in themselves, but the stirrup also has four separate pivoting points allowing it to follow the movements of the foot for greater comfort and flexibility, and also allowing immediate release of the foot in emergency

You can 'train' your stirrups and leathers to hang so that you can find them again easily if they come adrift. Leave the irons down when you put your saddle away, twist the left leather twice round to the left and the right one twice round to the right, then tie them in that position from underneath the saddle with a piece of string. Eventually, you will find that when you are mounted but with your feet out of the stirrups, the latter are hanging at right angles to your horse's sides with the leathers turning naturally flat against your shins, as they should be in use. In this way, you can easily find a stirrup and slip your toe in without having to fumble inwards with your foot.

Metals

As regards metal, the strongest is some kind of stainless steel, with a guarantee ticket tied to your new pair when you buy them. Apart from in police and military circles, irons are no longer made of iron; however, quite a few are still made of a much weaker, easily bent and easily broken metal called 'solid nickel', and this material is positively dangerous: it is noted for cracking, bending and even breaking without warning, and should be avoided if you value your safety.

Talking of safety, although the standard English hunting iron has been used for generations quite satisfactorily, in these increasingly safety-conscious days various safety stirrups are to be found, and their

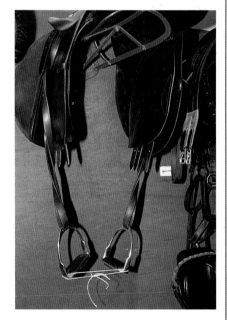

You can train your stirrups to hang slightly sideways to your horse's sides when your feet are out of the stirrups, making it easier for you to find them again. Tie them when your saddle is put up so that the left leather is twisted anti-clockwise and the right one clockwise

use for children is often highly recommended. The safety iron with its outer branch made of a rubber loop is probably the least satisfactory in use: because this loop releases under pressure, as in a fall, its all-round structure is not really strong enough, and in time the tread starts to slope outwards. There are other safety stirrups which are probably better, such as various snap-apart designs, those with shaped outer branches, higher eyes (the slot through which the leather passes) and so on, all aimed at allowing the escape of the foot in an emergency.

Comfort, and assistance in maintaining a good foot position, are both important factors now, and there are stirrups which help with this. Like horses, people come in different builds, and for some, stirrups which position the foot in a certain way do not suit their individual conformation. A generation ago, riders were taught to ride with the lower leg and knee turned inwards and with the outer sole of the foot slanted either up or down, according to which instructor you went to. There were, and are, stirrups which enabled – or forced – these positions (neither of which are good riding practice, incidentally), and if your natural lower leg/ankle/foot conformation did not adopt them easily you would experience a good deal of pain and discomfort; invariably your instructor would tell you that this would get better with practice!

If you are stiff, forced and in pain, you cannot ride well or in a relaxed way, no matter what position you assume. It is therefore important to choose a stirrup which enables your leg to be comfortable, and does not force it into any particular position. I like those with hinged treads or branches which make it easy for your heel to rest downwards without your having to think about it, simply because your weight is falling through your heel; these also make it easier for your heel to stay beneath your hip, I find, particularly if you are riding on a saddle (hopefully someone else's!) which does not facilitate this. Readers will have their own preferences.

One thing is certain: the choice in stirrups is now wide enough for everyone to be safe and comfortable.

STIRRUP LEATHERS

Your stirrup leathers are another vital safety factor as part of your saddle; moreover, not only must they be strong and reliable, they must also feel comfortable against your shins.

Widths start at around ⅝in (15mm) for children to around 1¼in (32mm) for heavyweight gentlemen riders. Generally if they are the right width for you, you are not conscious of them; but if they are too narrow or too wide they will be uncomfortable.

They are usually made out of some sort of leather, though synthetics such as plastic and nylon web are used, too; the synthetic leathers avail-

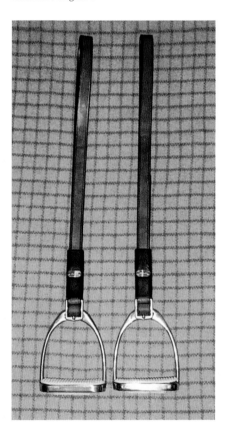

The Lauriche stirrup leather from Fosters, specially designed for dressage and adjusted near the stirrup, not at the stirrup bar, preventing bulk under the thigh. There is no loose end of stirrup leather and so one less thickness beneath the thigh. Although intended for an elegant appearance in the dressage arena or show ring, the leathers are claimed to be robust and practical for eventing or showjumping and, with a twelve-hole adjustment, come in sizes from children's to gent's

able today are much stronger than the early ones, and like all synthetics, they are cheaper and quick to clean. Leathers can be made of red buffalo hide, ox-hide or rawhide.

Red buffalo hide is so strong that leathers made of it are often sold as unbreakable – I for one have never known them break. Leather has a smooth (grain) side and a rougher (flesh) side which in good quality leather looks a bit like suede, though without the little fronds on it. Some leathers are made with the flesh side outwards so that the considerable wear they receive from the eye of the stirrup is borne on the stronger, grain side, but with buffalo hide leathers this point is insignificant because they are so strong anyway, so they are made with the better looking grain side outermost. They do stretch somewhat, but if you change them over very regularly at least they will do so evenly.

Ox-hide leathers are quite common and stretch less than any others.

Rawhide leathers come somewhere between the two as far as stretching is concerned, but they are rarely found and have no special advantages over the others.

Remember that all new leathers stretch somewhat when new.

Stainless-steel buckles of high quality should be fitted to all stirrups, and should have a firmly located tongue and a little groove on the top bar of the buckle for the tongue to lodge in to. Nickel buckles should only be used by those who like living dangerously.

Good quality leathers will have evenly spaced holes punched in them – and if they are not even, you will of course always be riding lopsided. The holes will be numbered, so if your leathers are on the same number and you have ensured even stretching by regular swapping over, you are likely to be riding 'level' even though it may not always feel like it. However, if you regularly feel that your stirrups/leathers are unlevel, you should check that the saddle is not unevenly stuffed or twisted, that your horse is symmetrically muscled, and that your riding is not at fault.

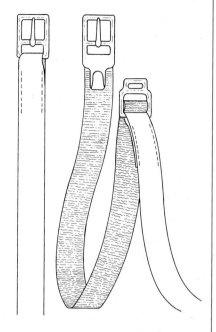

Extending stirrup leathers (normally fitted to the nearside) which unhook during mounting to make life easier for rider and horse. The leather hooks up again after mounting. A plain leather (left) is fitted to the offside

SEAT COVERS

A cover that fits over the top of the saddle can add considerably to your comfort when riding. Sheepskin ones of different colours can still be bought, as can synthetic fleece ones, but special 'technical' foam ones are also now available: these give support and can help the rider maintain a balanced, central seat on any saddle which seems to have an adverse effect on their position. For instance, they can be used to good effect on a saddle which tilts either backwards or forwards, helping the rider to avoid the effects of the tilt and sit centrally – but as ever, this should be only a temporary measure, and the real answer to such a problem is to change the saddle if it cannot be professionally adjusted.

3 BRIDLES and BITS

Why do we put bridles on our horses' heads, and why do we add bits to those bridles to go in our horses' mouths? This sounds like a really silly question, the sort no one ever asks because either everyone 'knows' the answer, or no one has ever thought about it. So let us do just that and think about it for a minute; then we will go into the more traditional and conventional aspects of choosing and fitting bridles and bits – and we will also overturn a few widely held beliefs about bits and bitting, and about nosebands.

Anyone who has had anything to do with horses and ponies – and this doesn't have to have been all their lives – knows that it is quite possible to control and ride a horse without a bit or even a bridle. Perhaps it is a counsel of perfection to say – rightly in my view – that it is the partnership and relationship between you and your horse that decides whether or not you ride well together, and not entirely what bit, if any, that you use. However, that relationship can easily be ruined if the horse is in pain or even discomfort because of what you have put in his mouth.

Bitless bridles, usually of the Blair pattern but often wrongly called a hackamore or even an English hackamore, were very popular among showjumpers in the 1980s and early 1990s, and a few still compete in them; however, they are not so much in favour now. Nevertheless they proved their point, that bits are not necessary even at a high level of performance; moreover some horses actually go better without a bit, usually because of previous abuse and the horse subsequently refusing to accept anything in his mouth, or because it just seems impossible to find a bit which really suits him. We are also now used to seeing displays by talented and empathetic trainers and riders, often of a Western persuasion, of bridleless riding in which the horse wears just a neckstrap or rope of some kind, and such trainers often teach students and clients the techniques of such riding to the extent that they can perform amazing feats on obviously willing horses who could easily bolt off if they wanted to. This certainly emphasises the partnership aspect.

Some decades ago a colleague and friend of mine, the late Dr Moyra Williams, habitually hunted and point-to-pointed without even putting a bridle on her horses, until the respective authorities asked her to put a bridle on because she was frightening the other participants! She obliged

by using a home-made bitless bridle of the Scawbrig (USA: sidepull) type, though never exerted any contact at all on the reins so the effect was the same. Her horses did not wear any kind of neckstrap, either. She trained them by means of weight, seat, legs and messages applied to the neck with her hands, plus of course that most valuable aid, the voice. Her book *Adventures Unbridled* is long out of print but is very well worth searching for; so too is a book by Shuna Mardon called *Riding Free*. However – and it is a big 'however' – I dare say we can all think of horses we would not care to sit on with no bridle, even in a safe, completely secure area such as an indoor school, a round pen or well fenced manège; and the older one gets, the more circumspect one becomes!

So, does putting a bridle on a horse's head and a bit in his mouth ensure that we have control? No, of course not! Again, it depends on our experiences, but most of us know that if a horse really wants to do something or go somewhere, he can and he will, under normal riding circumstances – that is, if he is not strapped up and down, lashed to a telegraph pole or has his head tied to his tail. The presence of a bit in his mouth and a rider's efforts to use it will, in themselves, not stop a determined horse.

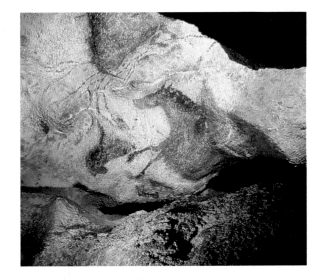

Like falling off, being 'carted' (run away with) is a valuable and sobering part of learning to ride; it really does put you in your place if you have been getting a little too big for your boots.

WE HAVEN'T COME VERY FAR

Ancient civilisations must have discovered quite early on that if you can control a horse's head you have more control over his body. Very old rock carvings exist – carvings much older than the 6,000 years or so ago which is generally taken to be the time that the horse was first domesticated – which show primitive halters on Przewalski-like horses. And whenever this happened, bits surely came second in the process. Probably at first these consisted of no more than a rawhide or horsehair or even textile rope that was passed through the horse's mouth or looped round his lower jaw, similar to the native American bridle. Later, wood, horn, bone and, later still, metal were used in the mouth for extra control. Although the use of horsehair for bridles no longer seems to be widespread, we still use animal skin, which, when well tanned and prepared is a source of pride to craftsman and owner alike, and results in a prestigious item one is proud to put on one's horse. Textiles, both natural and synthetic, are still used to some extent, and other synthetic materials, mainly plastics, too, continue to appear, each one claiming to be innovative. Bits now come in metals, rubber and various synthetic materials such as nylon, plastics and polymers.

Cave paintings from many thousands of years before the end of the last Ice Age – this one from Lascaux in France – occasionally show Przewalski-like horses wearing what look like primitive headcollars, even though the date for the domestication of the horse is usually taken to be about 3000BC

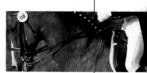

BASIC BIT FORMS AND THEIR EFFECTS

SNAFFLES

The simplest form of bit is the snaffle, and this exerts a direct, straight-line 'pull' on the mouth by means of the reins. The mouthpiece may be straight, curved, single- or double-jointed and occasionally ported. It attaches to the bridle by means of rings (usually) which may be fixed (eggbutt) or movable (loose- or wire-ring), and some snaffles have shanks or cheeks at the sides, a design which tends to put them in the fixed category. These are useful for horses that are not very responsive to directional aids, and for green horses, because the shanks effectively push on the side of the face, directing the head towards the side on which the rein aid has been applied; they also prevent the bit being pulled sideways through the mouth.

There is, in practice, a huge variety of weird and wonderful mouth-pieces for snaffles, all aimed at foiling a horse's little tricks to evade their action.

THE BRIDOON SNAFFLE

This is the thin snaffle used with a double bridle which, of course, has two bits – the bridoon itself, and the curb or Weymouth – the combination being called a double or full bridle. Like an ordinary snaffle, a bridoon can be eggbutt or loose-ring and may be mullen-mouthed or jointed.

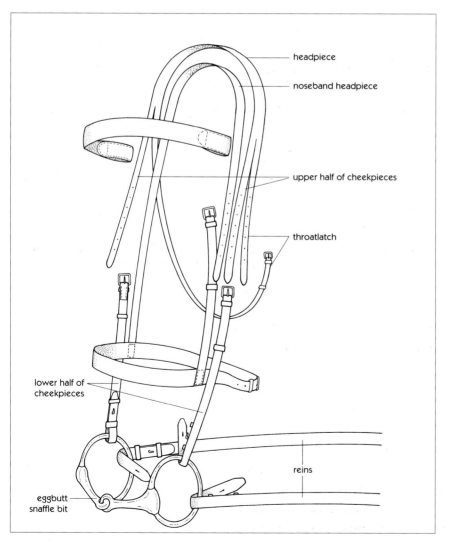

headpiece

noseband headpiece

upper half of cheekpieces

throatlatch

lower half of cheekpieces

reins

eggbutt snaffle bit

Harsh use of the reins, whatever bit is used, can cause overbending like this and the neck to be kinked downwards at the base, in front of the withers. The wrinkles there are an immediate pointer to a horse forced by discomfort to adopt a posture which is exactly opposite to the beneficial one of voluntarily stretching the neck up and forward from the base

Left: Parts of a snaffle bridle, showing an eggbutt snaffle

93

BRIDLES AND BITS

PELHAMS

An object of controversy since the day it was invented, the pelham is liked by many horses and riders simply because it is uncomplicated and it works. Its denigrators say that because it uses only one mouthpiece and tries to do the jobs of bridoon and curb in one, it inevitably fails – an opinion not borne out by practice, however.

The effect of the curb bit. The curb chain should normally be adjusted so that it comes into action when the curb's lower cheeks make an angle of about 45° with the lips. The idea is that the horse 'gives' his lower jaw (flexes the joint between lower jaw and skull just below the ear) and also flexes at the poll (the joint just between the skull and the atlas) with the poll being the highest point. If the use of the hands is not sufficiently tactful, or the horse has been previously worked incorrectly in draw-reins, the result may well be as shown – the horse's face is behind the vertical, the poll is too low, the highest point of the outline is behind it and the windpipe is compressed, hampering breathing

Mullen-mouth pelham

Jointed pelham

The pelham bit usually has a curved (half-moon or mullen) mouthpiece (although jointed and ported ones are also seen, and also straight-bar which are sometimes used for driving) with a ring at each end to take a snaffle or bridoon rein, and also a cheek or shank with a smaller ring at the bottom, to which the curb rein is attached. To produce the curb action, the bit is used with a curb chain. A pelham has a short upper cheek on each side with a ring on it, and to attach it to the bridle, the bridle cheekpieces are passed through their respective rings, and adjusted as necessary.

The rider should, therefore, have two pairs of reins; but pelhams are often used for children, who may not be able to handle four reins, so rolled leather loops called roundings (USA: converters) are attached to the bridoon and the curb rings on the bit (where the reins would go) and one pair of reins is attached to the loops, as shown. This does negate somewhat the double action of the bit, although the curb can still come into action; but this arrangement is preferable to a novice possibly using too much curb.

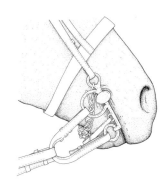

Pelham bit with roundings for the reins, curb chain and lipstrap. Some people like to pass the reins through the upper bit-ring which helps prevent possible chafing of the jawbones with a pelham, where the chain may operate higher than in a conventional curb which is fitted slightly lower

The Kimblewick

Kimblewicks (USA: Kimberwicke) are classed as a version of the pelham, having a single mouthpiece and a curb chain, in the same way as the pelham; however they have D-ring cheeks, sometimes with eyes in them, one positioned high up the ring, and the other lower down, to which the rein is attached. In the USA this type is called the Uxeter. The mouthpiece may be ported or curved, and occasionally it is straight.

In the type without ring eyes, the idea is that if the rider lightens his/her contact to the point where the reins can slide up the rings, then takes up a contact again when the rein is high up the ring, the Kimblewick acts rather like a snaffle with very little leverage/curb action; but if the rein is allowed to drop down the ring, and the rider then takes up the contact, the action will be more curb-like. This allows considerable variability in use. If the reins are attached to the upper or lower eyes, where these are present, the snaffle or the curb effect, respectively, is most prominent.

Kimblewick with ported mouth and curb chain

DOUBLE OR FULL BRIDLES

These must have two bits, the bridoon already mentioned, and a curb bit with a chain, its mouthpiece being usually ported but sometimes mullen-mouthed. Two sets of reins are always used, and the curb reins should be one size narrower than the bridoon reins for ease of identification in the rider's hands (the same applies to double reins used on a pelham). The curb is attached to the normal bridle cheekpieces, but the bridoon has a separate headstall of its own which fits under the headpiece and passes down through the browband loops with the ordinary cheekpieces. The browband loops on some modern double bridles are too narrow to allow this easily, with the result that the browband may feel uncomfortably fixed. Saddlers should not be allowed to get away with this; purchasers should insist on a correct double-bridle browband

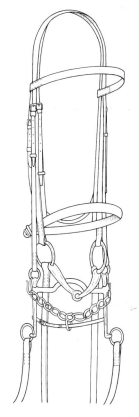

Double bridle, curb chain and lip-strap fitted

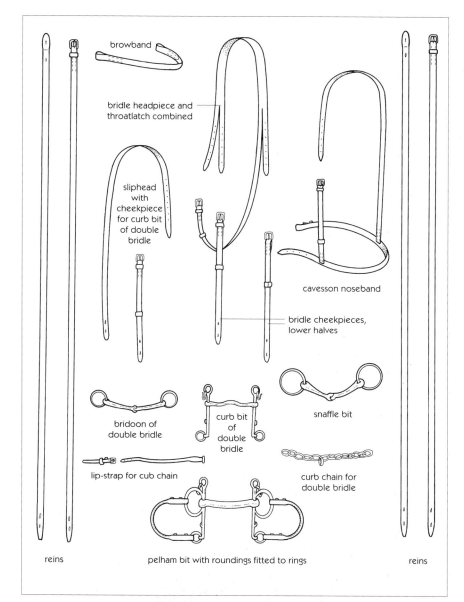

browband

bridle headpiece and throatlatch combined

sliphead with cheekpiece for curb bit of double bridle

cavesson noseband

bridle cheekpieces, lower halves

bridoon of double bridle

curb bit of double bridle

snaffle bit

lip-strap for cub chain

curb chain for double bridle

reins

pelham bit with roundings fitted to rings

reins

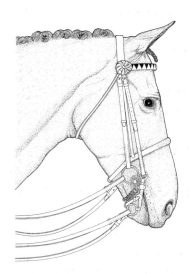

Above: A showing double bridle with velvet-covered, patterned browband and matching rosettes at the end, a raised stitched cavesson noseband, a loose-ring bridoon and a sliding-cheeked curb bit. The throatlatch should be a little looser and noseband lower, away from the facial bones

Right: Parts of the double bridle

with, incidentally, the split between the throatlatch and the cheekpiece coming below the browband on each side, again for comfort in use, but also looks. (This applies to any English-type bridle.)

The point of the double bridle is that it enables an educated, sensitive rider to achieve more finesse in the horse's responses to the aids and therefore in his elevation and collection. It is supposed to be the epitome of training and education in both horse and rider – although it must be said that at the time of writing, at least here in the UK, few instructors seem truly to understand this bridle, so that correct training in its use is hard to come by – yet children are allowed to use them in the show ring!

Dressage riders at the higher levels use them most, and they are also used by American Saddle Seat riders. Moreover up to about the middle of the twentieth century they were almost *de rigeur* with any reasonably fashionable pack of hounds, snaffles then being regarded as fit only for young horses, young children, novices, grooms and the mutton-fisted!

English-type riders often look askance at Western riders, considering their curb bits to be 'horrific' – but this, sadly, shows ignorance of the purpose and correct use of a curb bit. As with any bit, the hands on the other ends of the reins are far more important than the bit itself, and a curb bit, contrarily to the misinformed, often suits light-mouthed, sensitive horses much better than a snaffle. I have known several previous rearers who lost this highly dangerous inclination once they were ridden mainly on the curb of a double bridle or simply in a curb alone. It is much kinder to give a horse one firm (but not strong) tweak on the curb to remind him to 'give' to the bit, than to drive him repeatedly 'up to the contact' (being a snaffle) with a hard hand and unrelenting nagging, which could be regarded as harassment.

The longer the upper cheeks of a curb, the more poll pressure there will be, and the longer the lower cheeks the more leverage the rider will have. As pointed out earlier in this book, poll pressure alone will not cause a horse to lower his head, neither will a curb without a chain or strap. It is the combined action of a gentle request by the curb rein on a chain acting correctly in the chin groove (not higher up the jawbones), the subsequent slight raising of the mouthpiece in the horse's mouth and the pressure exerted on the poll via the curb which, in the educated, thinking horse, produces relaxation of the lower jaw (flexion of the joint between upper jaw and lower jaw) and tongue, and also the flexing of the joint between the upper jaw and the atlas which is the first (cervical) vertebra of the neck (known as C1). This principle also, of course, applies to a pelham, or to any other curb bit.

Compare the head carriages shown in these two photographs. The top one shows a classically trained competition dressage horse with correct carriage, the horse raising his own neck from

below, extending it up and forward in a smooth arc to the withers; his face is just on the vertical and there is an open curve at the throat.

The bottom picture shows a horse ridden in saddle seat in which the head and neck appear to be help up and back by the reins; the neck is compressed into a broken outline, kinked down in front of the withers and has a sharp angle at the throat which may be squashing and partly obstructing the windpipe, greatly increasing the effort needed for breathing

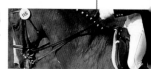

GAGS

Gag bits are ostensibly snaffles, but some have 'leverage cheeks', although there is no curb chain so there is no true leverage action.

Gag snaffles come with various mouthpieces and ring on each end, but there are eyes at the top and bottom of the rings, and the bridle cheek-pieces, which are made of rolled leather or cord, run right through these, the reins being attached to the ends of, effectively, the elongated cheek-pieces. The object is that pressure on the gag reins causes the bit to rise up the cheekpieces, so raising it in the mouth, whilst at the same time exert-ing pressure on the poll. This gives the horse a very firm message to get his head up and to stop. Such gags should always be used with an ordinary pair of snaffle reins attached to the rings in the usual way and used nor-mally, the gag reins only being used when needed.

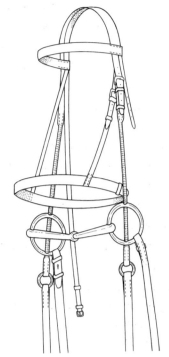

Gag snaffle bridle showing an extra pair of reins fitted directly, and correctly, to the bit-rings

Left: (top) A three-ring Dutch or continental gag; (bottom) An American gag

Leverage-cheek gags (known in the UK as American gags) have upper shanks to which the bridle's ordinary cheekpieces attach, and also lower shanks below the mouthpiece to which the gag reins attach. It is possible to attach a pair of snaffle reins to the metal loop (you cannot call it a ring) at the ends of the mouthpiece so that the gag reins are only used when really needed. The effect, again, is to raise the bit in the mouth and exert poll pressure at the same time.

Ring gags (called **Dutch** or **Continental gags**) have a number of rings one on top of the other (usually three) so the rein can be placed just where it is needed for the desired effect. The bridle cheekpieces attach to a ring above the mouthpiece, then there is a larger ring to which the rein can be attached for a simple snaffle effect, then below that there are two more smaller rings, each level down producing an increasingly severe gag-type leverage.

Strictly speaking, leverage-cheek and ring gags should, like gag snaf-fles, be used with a pair of reins on the snaffle ring and one on the shank ring of your choice, so that you are not 'riding on the gag' all the time; in practice, however, all three types of gag are often used with only one (the gag) rein. To my mind this does not help the horse – or, therefore, the rider – to produce a long-term improvement in his problem, be it boring, leaning, pulling or actually bolting, because if you are riding with the stronger effect all the time, it could well have a 'white noise' effect on the horse, ie it will make him pull against the stronger pressure all the time. If he only experiences the uncomfortable gag effect when he bores or pulls, but not when he goes more amenably, he will have more chance of learning what is wanted by his rider, and what is not.

An American gag in use on a showjumper

THE RIGHT BIT – THE RIGHT FIT

It is perfectly true that there is a key to every horse's mouth, and that key is usually his rider's hands. I have always maintained that there is no such thing as a magic spell in the form of a bit – that there is no perfect bit for every individual horse and all we have to do is find it. But in this, my most recent horse has proved me wrong (as horses often do). I had failed miserably to make her happy and give myself some control when riding her, until I tried an ordinary mullen-mouthed stainless-steel pelham. She had galloped through every snaffle and gag I tried – and that was a good selection – as well as other pelhams and also a double bridle, which she hated. In a mullen-mouthed pelham, though, she showed herself to be the lady she was bred to be.

So although one should really be able to ride any horse in any bit if one is a good enough rider, it does not always work that way, and it can certainly be worth a little experimenting.

THE HORSE'S MOUTH

We are all familiar with the layout of the horse's teeth, where the bars are, where his tongue goes and so on, but we may not all be aware of how diverse in make and shape the inside of a horse's mouth may be. Make no mistake about this: it is just as sensitive as ours: it is made of exactly the same skin, flesh, blood, nerves and bone, and immense problems may be caused if there is just one tiny sore spot, if the horse has dental problems, a mouth infection, or persistent discomfort or pain from a badly chosen or badly fitted bit, or one that is harshly or wrongly used.

I feel that all horse owners, trainers and riders should pay great attention to a horse's behaviour when he is eating and when he is wearing a bit, as any even slightly unusual behaviour can mean there is a problem, and this will almost certainly affect his performance in work, and maybe in his condition, too.

The lips are what we see most obviously of his mouth, and they can be long or short, fleshy or fine. The corners of the lips are where most of the abuse occurs when bits do not fit (particularly if they are too narrow) and when they are adjusted too high, a very common fault today. We often hear that bits should not touch the teeth, but if your horse has long lips (where the corners of the lips are close to the first, lowest cheek teeth or premolars) and his rider hoists the bit up high in his mouth, it will almost certainly be in regular contact with the teeth, it could chip them, and he/she could find him/herself out of control because the horse has found it easy to 'get the bit between his teeth' and negate its entire action.

Carefully slide your finger inside the corner of your horse's mouth until you can just feel his first premolar, or feel down the outside of his cheek to

Above and top: A too-narrow loose-ring snaffle, showing how easy it will be for the lips to become pinched

Above and left: A D-ring rubber-mouthed snaffle of a comfortable width

A loose-ring snaffle bit which is a little too wide; still a lesser sin than being too narrow

where the cheek teeth start, then you will have some idea of just how high or low you should fit his bit (see General Guidelines below).

The tongue plays a greater part than is realised in the type of mouthpiece we should use. Studies in Canada some years ago by Dr Hilary Clayton showed that there is almost never any excess space in a horse's mouth for a bit! As in humans, when the mouth is closed normally, the tongue takes up all the space between the soft tissue below the tongue and the hard palate above it. So what are we to do?

Some horses do have a very thick, fleshy tongue, and in some it is very wide, too. If you gently part the lips where the bars are (on which we imagine the bit lies – except that it does not), note whether the tongue bulges out at the sides or fits easily between the jawbones: then you will know whether your horse has a large, fleshy tongue or a thinner and maybe narrower one, although it will never be like that of a dog.

Dr Clayton's studies apparently showed that the tongue takes almost all the pressure from the mouthpiece of even a moderately ported bit. It is very mobile and quite strong, and horses are adept at using it to push the bit around even with the mouth closed. The 'fleshier' the tongue, the more it will protect the bars from bit contact.

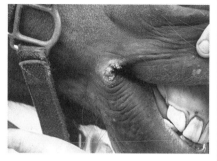

One example of the injuries which can be caused to a horse's mouth when the bit is fitted too high and/or is too narrow and becomes pinched

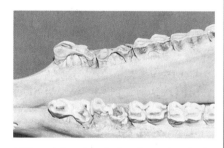

Milk teeth 'caps' pushed up by, and wedged on top of erupting second teeth. These can cause considerable problems in youngsters, both in eating and working and must be removed by a vet or equine dental technician

THE BARS OR DIASTEMA

It is on the bars of the mouth that we have always believed the mouthpiece rests in the mouth. In practice, only a bit with a very high port – one which can almost totally avoid the tongue – will permit this, but such bits unavoidably press so uncomfortably and even painfully on the roof of the mouth (the hard palate) that they have no place in modern, humane equestrianism. This action, of course, causes the horse to open his mouth wider than is reasonable for flexing and relaxation, and is not what we want at all. It takes a very hard pull on the reins to get any other kind of mouthpiece to press significantly on the bars.

The hard palate may be high or low, and this determines how thick a bit, or how many mouthpieces, or the type of mouthpiece, a horse can accept comfortably in his mouth; and as ever, if he is not comfortable his performance will always be adversely affected, as will his rider's expectations.

Carefully put your finger, knuckle upwards, into his mouth over the tongue and bend it to see if, or at what point your knuckle touches the hard palate. This will guide you as to whether the palate is high and arched or low and flatter. Even a moderately high port may press into it, as may a single-jointed mouthpiece, particularly if they have a supposedly 'kind', thick mouthpiece.

The teeth obviously need to be kept well smoothed and rasped (US: floated) if the horse is to eat well, but this should also be done to avoid the inside of the mouth being cut should the lips, cheeks or tongue be

The bit lies in the convenient space between the incisors/tushes and molars, but the size of the tongue is often overlooked when fitting the bit. It may take up much of the space available in the mouth and will not be comfortable with, for example, a straight-bar bit or maybe a half-moon/mullen-mouthed bit, any bit with a thick mouthpiece or the two bits of a double bridle

BRIDLES AND BITS

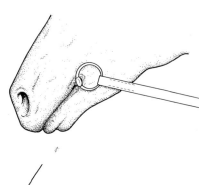

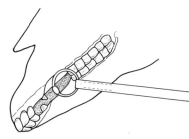

The snaffle bit should normally fit up into the corners of the mouth, making contact with the skin but causing only one wrinkle

compressed, for whatever reason, between the bit and the teeth. Snaffle bits used with harsh hands are the main culprits of this, and even if the teeth are in good order, bad bruising can still occur. When the rider pulls on the reins, the cannons of the bit (the parts between the joint and the rings or cheeks) are pulled out of the mouth, press onto the outsides of the cheeks, and therefore press the insides of the cheeks against the premolars, with very painful results. The pain is similar to you biting your tongue, but is much more prolonged. The edges of the tongue, too, can become trapped and compressed between bit and teeth, with similar pain.

The width of the lower jaw is also important if your horse has a thick, fleshy tongue. The old practice was to see if you could fit your fist between the rounded parts of a horse's jaw to check if it had good airway space, and it can be modified here: with the exception of a man with large hands, it should be possible to fit a fist between the straight, lower branches of the jaw, in which case the latter is wide enough to accommodate the tongue. If not, the tongue will bulge above the jaw, and this will create problems if we stick to the conventional wisdom of fitting a thick mouthpiece in the interests of mildness and comfort. In fact such horses are often much more comfortable, and so more amenable, with a thinner mouthpiece.

The bearing surface of a conventional rounded mouthpiece, which they nearly all are, is actually tiny, even in a thick one. Some jointed snaffles do have a mouthpiece which is slightly more oval – and here I am thinking mainly of those called German hollow-mouthed snaffles – but the majority are more or less round. If you draw a circle on a piece of paper and then draw a straight line at a tangent to its circumference, you will see that the tangent point represents a tiny 'bearing surface'.

We now know that it is the tongue which takes nearly all the pressure in normal, reasonable riding; we also know that the tongue allows very little space for the usual round bar of metal (or anything else) crossing over the top of it: so surely what we need are many more bits with an oval or even a flat mouthpiece, and rounded edges (like the idea of the Sam Marsh pelham – see illustration). These would take up comparatively little space between the tongue and the hard palate; they would increase the bearing surface on the tongue which would therefore not be so squashed, and by the same measure more comfortable; and they would be instrumental in teaching the horse that it is infinitely more comfortable to go with his tongue and bars parallel to such a mouthpiece in the flexed-poll-and-jaw posture which a good rider seeks.

This may be an inconvenient idea to adopt in view of the rounded shape of nearly all mouthpieces today, but I think Sam Marsh got it right, and I believe that, in view of our supposedly enlightened, more humane attitude towards horses today, it really must be implemented. Surely the loriners will want to keep up with their colleagues, the saddlers, in bringing out innovative designs and principles for the mutual benefit of horse and rider.

100

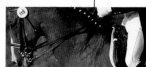

GENERAL GUIDELINES ON FITTING BITS

Snaffle bits in particular today are often fitted so high that they actually stretch the skin at the corners of the mouth. Incredibly, this is also done by some people with curbs and pelhams, displaying a total ignorance of the effects on the wretched horse (or a lack of caring) and of the purpose and function of such bits.

I understand that the people who do this believe that it makes the horse's mouth more sensitive. In actual fact it does just the opposite, ultimately 'deadening' the skin, and often causing it to split with subsequent callousing, nerve damage and, obviously, insensitivity. It certainly does not promote feel and lightness, nor does it permit a comfortable, co-operative horse.

By adjusting bits correctly and humanely, riders will find that because their horses are more comfortable and the bits are acting where and how they should (given reasonable competence on the part of the rider), the way is opened for the horse to offer co-operation and lightness with, ultimately, more enjoyment for both him and his rider.

Width

A jointed snaffle should fit so that about ½in (13mm) shows on either side of the mouth when the bit is held with the joint straight.

Pelhams, Weymouths or curbs and other straight-bar bits can be slightly narrower, but you should always be able to fit an index finger snugly between the bit's upper cheeks or rings and the corners of the mouth without having to push the horse's cheeks in.

Front and side views of correct-width bits in a double bridle

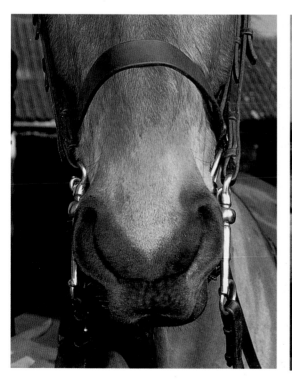

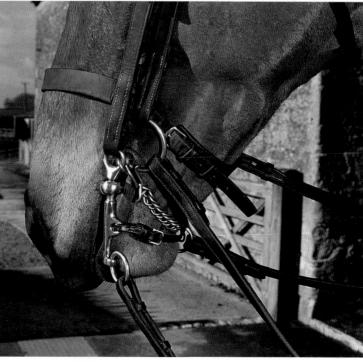

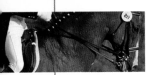

Height

A jointed bit should create one slight wrinkle at the corners of the mouth: and I repeat – one slight wrinkle – not the two, or even three commonly seen, unless your horse has genuinely short lips, when a jointed mouthpiece making just one wrinkle might bang on the incisor teeth.

A straight-bar snaffle, a pelham or a Kimblewick should just touch the corners of the mouth, creating no more than half a wrinkle.

In a double bridle, the bridoon fits like a snaffle, creating no more than one slight wrinkle. The curb bit rests just below the bridoon, about ½in (13mm) to ¾in (20mm) below, depending on the length of the mouth – and therefore not touching the corners of the mouth at all: this is most important. When checking this fit, make sure the bridoon is over, never under, the curb and that the bits are not interfering with the teeth.

Lip-straps are strictly correct and do help to steady the curb chain and keep it in position, whether used on a pelham or Weymouth. Kimblewicks unfortunately lack the small rings on the bit cheeks which are necessary to fit them. Perhaps some enterprising loriner could remedy this situation

Fitting a Curb Chain

The fitting of the curb chain or strap is also important in any bridle which uses one. It must always act in the chin or curb groove, and should never ride higher up onto the narrow jawbones, as this can result in severe bruising because they are protected by no more than a thin layer of skin. In English-type tack, curb chains, whether of metal, leather or elastic, are always fitted with a small ring called a fly link: a narrow strap, usually of rolled leather and called a lip strap, is passed through this and fastened to the small rings on the bit cheeks (with the exception of Kimblewicks), and this keeps the chain down in place; although it is better to ensure that it

falls in the groove naturally, rather than needing to be kept there. This is a more common fault in pelhams, because the longish upper cheeks may hold the chain too high in a long-jawed horse.

The curb chain should always be carefully fitted so that its links are quite flat; even one link twisted or out of place can dig in and cause pain and bruising. Check also that there is no hay, straw or anything else trapped in the links as these, too, can make a very sore place very quickly in this sensitive area.

BIT MATERIALS

Just as fashions in saddles, bridles, theories and bit shapes come and go, so do fashions in bit materials, and the current fashion is for materials which make a horse 'mouth' the bit and salivate, and so maintain a 'soft' mouth. Although some materials do produce this effect, I am not the only one who is quite sure that it is at the expense of the horse's contentment with his bit, because the materials concerned – mainly copper and sweet (pure) iron currently – have a definite and unpleasant taste.

Copper tastes really foul – try it and see, though beware, because in its pure form it is toxic: in humans it causes nausea, vomiting and lethargy, plus other gastrointestinal disorders, and in fish lethargy, suffocation and death. I looked into it with the help of my vet after I unwittingly poisoned two tanks of lovely tropical fish by doing their water change with water partly from the hot tap instead of warming water from the cold tap. The hot water had caused copper ions to pass into the water from the copper pipes (this only happens above a certain temperature), and this had killed our fish, even though cold water was added to make it the right temperature.

Although the temperature in a horse's mouth never reaches that required for such toxicity, copper and its alloys do taste appalling, as several horses have confirmed to me by their behaviour and demeanour – excessive salivation, going behind the bit, champing the bit, lolling the tongue out of the mouth, and tossing and shaking the head, and in one case, the horse stood with her head vertical to the ground and her mouth wide open so that the bit did not touch any more of her mouth than she could help! This mare did the same with all other metals except stainless steel, and she also did it with rubber; in fact she would only accept a bit made of stainless steel, or the plastic from which the soft German Nathe bits are made.

Sweet iron, too, tastes horrible and strong. It may be that it is called 'sweet' by its manufacturers because horses are known to have a sweet tooth, and they feel, perhaps rightly, that this will cause owners to buy it.

Synthetic materials – namely nylon and plastic – are strong and light, and are sometimes apparently said to be flavoured with apple, mint,

Copper

Sweet iron

Synthetic – in this case plastic with a steel cable

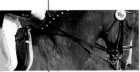
cinnamon or carrot with a view to pleasing the horse; although the intention here is laudatory, one wonders if he really likes it.

I think we should take great care to observe the horse very closely when he is wearing any bit, and decide from our own observation whether or not he looks content and happy. Any reasonably sensitive horseman or woman can surely tell when his or her horse is happy, unhappy, resigned, distressed or whatever, even if he is one which does not make his feelings too obvious. A discontented horse will lose that softness usually apparent in his eye: he will acquire a worried expression, or one expressing distaste, his mouth will not seem relaxed, and he will not seem to be enjoying the feel of the bit in his mouth even though he may be moving it around.

Excess salivation (including frothing) is a sign of distress in most animals, including horses: it is certainly not a sign of a so-called 'happy mouth', and neither is 'champing the bit'. What we need is a normally moist mouth with the horse merely gently mouthing it occasionally, and flexing in a willing, calm way at poll and jaw. Anything more than that should be cause for concern.

To be on the safe side, I feel we should choose the tasteless rather than the tasteful when it comes to bits, unlike other aspects of life. Again with the aim of making bits comfortable for the horse, we sometimes see them covered in leather (which tastes really terrible) or bound with adhesive plaster dressing or cohesive leg bandages, with no apparent regard for how these materials taste. We can only have a guess by sucking and chewing them ourselves, and by watching the horse's reaction to them closely. I feel such coverings are totally unnecessary if a comfortable bit is chosen and is used wisely and correctly.

Stainless steel is still used to make bits and stirrups, and is a material I feel we could go a long way to beat. It is very strong, hard to damage, wear-resistant, totally tasteless as anyone knows who uses cutlery made from it, and is easy to keep clean and hygienic.

Stainless steel

Nickel, the material that stainless steel has largely replaced – often called 'solid' nickel and correctly termed 'nickel silver' – is very weak and unreliable; moreover it has a slight but unpleasant taste to it, and needs cleaning with metal polish. Because it wears quickly, this creates a loose fit between the mouthpiece and the rings or cheeks in a bit so there is a gap between which the horse's lips can be pinched. This must be absolutely excruciating, like pinching your own skin hard with pliers. Furthermore some horses and ponies have a sensitivity or allergy to nickel, which produces sore mouths, inflamed skin, blisters and scabs – another excellent reason for avoiding it.

Nickel-plated iron

Rubber also tastes unpleasant (I know several horses and ponies who will not eat or drink out of rubber containers, presumably because the taste taints the feed and water) although some animals seem to mind it less than others. Watch carefully to check the horse's reaction. Even so,

Rubber

rubber-covered metal bits, usually jointed, are fairly common, and all-rubber bits in a mullen (half-moon) shape are popular as being very mild. These used to have a metal chain running through the middle of them, presumably with the intention of reinforcing them, but in fact this would often break without warning, perhaps because it had a weak link or suffered from metal fatigue and could not take the pressure, or because saliva had seeped through the rubber which had been chewed by the horse or which had cracked with age.

One of the world's best and most famous steeplechasers experienced such a breakage in 1962. The horse was Mandarin, a horse who has since become a legend, his trainer was the incomparable Fulke Walwyn and his jockey that superb horseman, Fred Winter. Mandarin was taken from his home in England over to Paris to contest the big French 'chase, the Prix d'Auteuil. Now Mandarin was an extremely hard puller, but rather than take the usual course of action and put a more severe bit on him, his trainer in fact always ran him in a rubber snaffle because a metal bit hurt his mouth.

The field set off and Fred Winter settled Mandarin, but fairly early in the race the rubber bit, for whatever reason, suddenly snapped in two, leaving only the cheekpieces attached to Mandarin's browband and headpiece as contact with his head. The field was approaching an enormous privet hedge, and Winter found himself with no means of control, no way of pulling up or pulling out or or doing anything else. So he gave Mandarin a kick, and he flew the hedge with the other horses. Miraculously the horse seemed happy to race on in the front of the field without ever attempting to take control or run away – and remember he was an inveterate hard puller – and tackled the formidable obstacles without thought of refusing, negotiating the turns guided only by Fred Winter's weight and the help of a French jockey, Jean Daumas, who had seen what had happened and who raced on Mandarin's outside, helping to steer him. Mandarin had the other horses round him and so was quite happy to take his lead from them – until the final stretch when Winter kicked him on and they won, to the utter amazement and admiration of the whole world.

Again this story just goes to show that the bit is far from everything, and that it is horsemanship which usually wins the day – but the other 'moral' to be gained from this story is, check your bit daily! Although rubber bits today normally have an extremely strong nylon thread running through them, imported ones from the Far East have been found still to contain metal chains – so check on the source of any rubber bit you buy.

Vulcanite is a hardened form of rubber usually used in mullen-mouthed snaffles and very often in pelhams. Presumably it does have a taste – you can always try it for yourself and watch your horse's reaction to it.

Bit dangling beneath his neck and browband behind his ears, Mandarin holds off Lumino in the 1962 Prix d'Auteuil

TONGUE PORT AND GRID

Tongue ports or grids are used to stop a horse getting his tongue over the bit. A rubber port is used on a mullen mouthpiece and is illustrated below. The tongue-shaped piece of rubber is passed round the mouthpiece and through the rubber loop at its other end and then all is pulled tight and straightened out so that the tongue-shaped piece lies flat on the tongue pointing towards the throat. It cannot feel very pleasant but it certainly does its job.

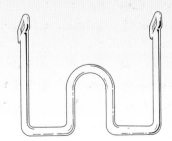

A metal tongue grid (above) is suspended by a separate sliphead above the bit, well into the corners of the mouth but not pulling on them uncomfortably; it is also very effective.

NOSEBANDS

The simplest noseband is a basic cavesson, from the French caveçon meaning to curb or restrict: it probably has this name because the lungeing cavesson (lungeing apparently having been invented by the French) was a means of restraining the young or green horse during initial schooling. (Lungeing cavessons are dealt with in Chapter 4.) As a noseband, the cavesson is fairly useless, but most people do feel that a stylish, well made one does add to the appearance of even the handsomest horse. If it is positioned on the high side – though it should never contact the horse's straight facial bones – it can make a long head look shorter; if positioned low – though without interfering with the bit – it can make a too-short head look more in proportion. If the horse has an unattractive dip in his nose, the cavesson can be positioned in this dip to disguise it, and so on.

A well fitted, workmanlike snaffle bridle, with a correctly adjusted cavesson noseband and a cheek snaffle. The throatlatch could be looser

If the cavesson noseband is positioned fairly low and fastened snugly (but never tightly – a subject to be dealt with shortly), it can be surprisingly effective in discouraging a horse from opening his mouth. It is also essential for fitting a standing martingale, of course, which is a useful item for young or green horses who may be going through a phase of throwing their heads about for apparently no good reason. (Note that a standing martingale is not the answer to a ewe-necked horse or one which has learned to evade the bit by raising his head above the point of control. This topic is dealt with in Chapter 4.)

Almost all other nosebands have the sole purpose of stopping the horse opening his mouth or of preventing him pulling, both of which 'sins' are the result of his trying to evade the action of the bit. Of course, this is a very sad reflection on our times, when no one, it seems, has the hands to make a horse not want to open his mouth, or the time to acquire the skill needed to train a horse properly! In an ideal world we should all be exquisite horsemen and women with hands like silk (firm when necessary, but soft and smooth most of the time) and with a harmonious, secure and independent seat, and all horses would be not only compliant but also beautifully trained to the highest standards – in such a world we should not need any nosebands at all – or any bits, come to that, and maybe not any bridles…. In particular it saddens me when I see people buying 'flavoured' bits which are said to 'soften' the mouth and cause the horse to salivate and mouth the bit, during which process he must unavoidably open it slightly – and then they clamp his jaws shut with a noseband which stops him doing exactly that. Crazy!

The drop noseband fits below the bit and well above the nostrils, as here. No noseband should interfere with the horse's breathing

However, in this world we live in, nosebands are a normal and accepted part of equestrianism, except in Western riding and in flat racing, particularly in the US and Australia. Some endurance riders, too, forego the noseband as being unnecessary extra weight and clutter encumbering the horse's head.

SHUT IT!

The photographs show different types of noseband, and I should like to investigate more closely here just why we think we should keep a horse's mouth closed in the first place. We have already seen, mainly in Chapter 1, how any muscular tension can affect the whole horse, stiffening muscles and reducing 'feel' and performance throughout his body. Tension in the jaw, mouth, head, throat and neck transfers down the spine and through other muscles of posture and locomotion, thwarting all our efforts at getting the horse to use his 'ring of muscles' properly, and to go from his back end in self-carriage and with swing – or *schwung*, as the Germans call it – that carefully generated and guided impulsion which results in

The Combination noseband is useful for strong horses with a sensitive mouth who would benefit from, or improve in, a stronger bit. There are two straps fastening at the back of the jaw above and below the bit, connected by metal arcs running down the sides of the face. The noseband discourages the horse from opening his mouth and crossing his jaw, so preventing him from setting himself against the bit

Top left: A Grakle noseband correctly fitted, not rubbing the facial bones with the cross-over high enough not to bring the lower straps too near the nostrils

Top right: A high-ring Grakle correctly fitted

Bottom left: A Kineton noseband correctly adjusted. Snaffle bits used with Kinetons should be a size wider than normal to allow for the metal loops on the noseband

Bottom right: The 'tieback' or 'turnback' effect on this flash noseband of passing through the dee on the left enables to handler to fasten the noseband very tightly indeed: this practice is inhumane and absolutely wrong. The device is useful in obtaining a precise, comfortable, fit in which a finger can be passed easily under the noseband and jawband all the way round. Padding under the jawbones does not make tightness acceptable

that elevated forward movement which makes riding so exhilarating.

Evasion of the bit causes tension, but so, most certainly, does a tight noseband of any kind because it simply causes more resistance, and resentment, in the horse. It therefore defeats the object. To my mind the situation nowadays has reached absurd proportions – how often do we see the following scenario: the horse tries to open his mouth, put his tongue out or slide his jaw from side to side, either because of the rider's or the trainer's failings, or because his bit is so uncomfortable, only to have this attempt at retrieving a modicum of comfort denied him because his noseband is then done up as tightly as possible. Today, we even have on the market little pads which you can put behind the noseband and elsewhere to protect the horse from the intense pressure of his bridle which some human has winched so tight, sometimes with patented devices or simply a pair of pliers, that this protection is necessary. These items are not illustrated in this book because they have no place in the armoury of a true horseman or woman.

A tight noseband will cause more tension and lead to other, different evasions, and so the situation described above escalates. Not least, the horse's mind becomes affected: his attitude to work and to his people deteriorates, the feeling becomes mutual, and eventually the entire relationship spirals downwards to the point where neither trusts the other.

I really do not know where this trend for tightness – and this is not only in nosebands, but in girths, bit fitting and in riding itself – has come from. I first noticed that it had become quite widespread by the mid-1980s, and now a whole new generation of riders has grown up thinking it is 'right' whereas, in fact, it is certainly 'wrong'. How can causing the horse such discomfort, and even pain, be beneficial? Surely anyone with the most moderate intelligence can see what is happening and what it does, and yet it continues.

The Worcester noseband from Shires Equestrian is a kinder, more effective alternative to the Kineton noseband. The straps to the bit-rings must be adjusted evenly, and add pressure to the nose should the rider need to take a pull, saving the horse's mouth. It also makes turning and lateral aids more effective and the turnback-style jawband offers fine adjustment, retaining the humane spirit of this noseband if it is adjusted, as any noseband should be, so that you can easily pass a finger all round the nose beneath it

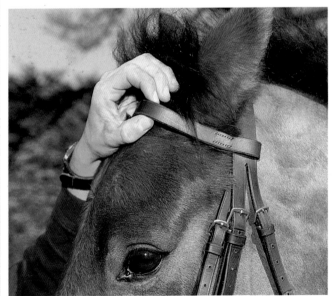

Tightness and restriction prevent the flexion of the jaw which is all-important in good equitation within any discipline, ie the flexion of the joint between the lower and upper jaws near the ear. Flexion means movement, and movement of this joint cannot occur if the horse does not open his mouth slightly. Tension in the muscles of this area (around the ear) also affects the flexion of the joint between the skull or upper jaw and the first vertebra of the neck, so a tight noseband will also stop the horse willingly flexing this joint ('flexing at the poll'). He can be forced to flex or bend here by the rider pulling hard on the reins or by having some device such as side-reins or draw-reins fitted to force him to 'bring his head in', but this will be at the expense of his raising his neck at its base and stretching along his topline, which is what we really want and need for hindquarter and hindleg engagement.

When we say we want the horse to keep his mouth closed, perhaps we mean we want him to open it only slightly, only so much as will enable him to flex the joint between his upper and lower jaws which is necessary for compliance to our bit aids and for willing acceptance of them. Everyone knows that opening the mouth wide is not what we want in equestrianism, but the horse mainly does it because we are making his life uncomfortable.

The only way we can suggest to him that we don't want this wide opening or twisting of the jaws, if we haven't the time or skill to retrain him, is to fit a noseband which is comfortable (so as not to cause any more tension) but which will suggest to him that he should open his mouth only slightly, which is all that is necessary. Force by means of tight restriction is plainly counterproductive in this process. Persuading him to open his mouth only slightly – the essential flexion of the jaw – can be achieved by making sure that any noseband we fit is just snug (as the Americans call it)

Below (opposite and this page): Checking the fit of the bridle

(opposite left) This browband is a comfortable length and will permit a finger easily underneath it, yet is not so loose that it will flop about, annoying the horse
(right) You should be able to fit the width of four fingers between the throatlatch and the horse's round jawbone

(below left and right) A comfortable fit for a cavesson noseband allows about two or three fingers width between it and the face bones and about the same between it and the corner of the mouth, Again, you should be able to easily slide a finger underneath it all the way round

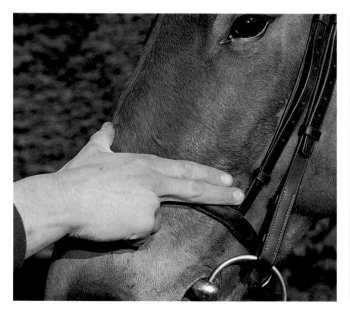

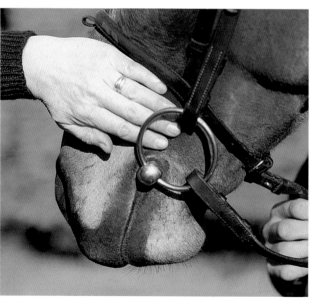

BRIDLES AND BITS

or close, but not so tight that we cannot run a finger easily underneath it all the way round the horse's jaws. This is how nosebands were meant to be used – and used in this way, they can be a big help.

REINS

On a double bridle and on a pelham used with two reins, it is expected that one should have plain leather reins. On a horse schooled to respond to light aids from such bitting arrangements and to obey his rider almost without question, there is no need for grip, and so no need for anything else.

I have to admit to using what is called a dressage rein (lined with rubber on the inside only so that it doesn't show) for my new mare's bridoon rein on her pelham, with a narrower, plain leather rein for the curb because when I bought her she had a reputation for charging off for fun whenever she felt like it and I thought it might help a bit. (It didn't.) Once I got round that trick with the help of a couple of friends, Roy King (psychology) and Heather Moffett (technique), I changed the bridoon rein to plain leather.

When pelhams are used with roundings/converters one frequently sees the same wide variety of grip-type reins as on snaffles – perhaps an indication as to the rider's competence! There is no 'law' about what to use on snaffle bridles, and people have many different preferences when it comes to reins.

SIZE AND COMFORT

It is important for the rider to have reins which are comfortable to handle, and to this end, I personally still feel that there is nothing quite like the feel of well cared-for leather – although it has to be admitted that they do become slippery when wet from rain, sweat or water should you fall in The Lake at Badminton. You can always wear gloves, of course (though avoid leather ones!).

Probably the material that is used the most to provide grip is rubber, although it does reduce the pliability of the rein. Otherwise you can have plaited reins (they stretch), laced reins (uncomfortable), webbing reins with handgrips (rarely seen nowadays), or you can buy one of the new synthetic reins with a suede, super-grip feel and pliability, too.

Some years ago it was easy to get plaited cotton reins, and these gave a lovely, soft and pliable feel in the hands with superb grip – and, of course, they absorbed moisture beautifully. They tended to stretch, but were cheap enough to replace frequently. Now, however, they can only be made to order by some of the more traditional, specialist saddlers – but it is an order well worth placing. Their nylon counterparts are abominable: harsh,

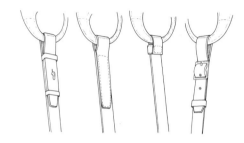

Rein fastenings (left to right): hook stud (which fastens on the inside), stitching (rare now and mainly seen on show bridles), loop and buckle (fastening on the outside)

The Balance Eeezy Reins make it easier for a rider who may be learning or who finds it difficult to keep the hands steady to maintain a comfortable, consistent contact

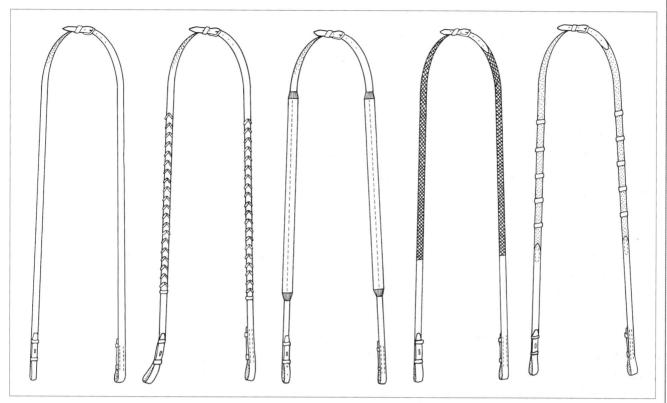

Various reins (left to right): plain leather, laced leather, rubber-covered, plaited and webbing with handgrips

slippery, totally non-absorbent and they look awful, too – well worth avoiding!

The width of the rein is very important. Even though the UK has 'gone metric', tack in Britain is still sold in imperial measurements – that's British logic for you! Curb reins and children's show pony bridle reins can be as narrow as ½in, otherwise reins can be as wide as 1in; the most common widths are probably ⅝in and ¾in. Obviously, the smaller your hands are, the narrower your reins will need to be, and vice versa.

If the reins are too wide for your hand they will be difficult to hold or handle comfortably, and this will affect your technique; if they are too narrow, your hands may tend to turn into fists and will lose sensitivity.

BITLESS BRIDLES

If bits are no real help in controlling horses, why don't we all use bitless bridles? This way, we'd have some directional control, and the horses would surely be more comfortable. Well, it has to be said that, because of equine and human weaknesses as described above, not all horses go well or amenably in bitless bridles – some will always try every little crime in the book if they can to avoid working. Even so, some horses do actually go better in a bitless bridle. There is more interest in them than ever nowadays, possibly thanks to such horsemen as Monty Roberts, Pat Parelli and many others, and some newer designs are illustrated and explained here.

E. Jeffries & Son Ltd, Walsall saddlers, have produced a new rubber coating for a range of reins called New Grip. The coating is bonded onto top-quality leather which makes the reins much easier to hold than the conventional stitched type as the reins stay soft and supple. They are so durable that they are guaranteed for two years

Competition in the horse world continues to increase in popularity, and of course, you cannot enter a conventional dressage test with your horse in a bitless bridle because he will not be 'on the bit'! Unfortunately, the more hidebound of us are still coming round to realisation of the fact that it is not the acceptance of the bit (the state of being 'on the bit') that is important, but the horse's whole physical and mental way of going – the correct use of his muscles and his attitude – which is important in equitation: the bit is therefore really only a means to an end, its acceptance not being the end product of schooling. Occasionally one sees informal competitions for bitless and bridleless riding where dressage is involved, but they seem to be very rare.

Bitless bridles are very useful for horses which cannot take a bit perhaps due to a mouth injury, a sore mouth due to teething in youngsters,

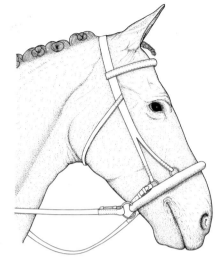

A jumping hackamore which is simple, kind and effective. It is open at the back of the padded nosepiece which is stabilised by the jawband (seen just above it) and the split cheekpiece

Left: A type of Blair-pattern bitless bridle popular in showjumping. This is a leverage bridle exerting pressure on nose, jaw and poll and is obviously much 'stronger' than the jumping hackamore shown above. It requires knowledgeable, sensitive use

An American bitless bridle very similar to the jumping hackamore above

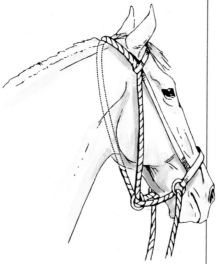

and for those in the process of being mentally rehabilitated having been abused by harsh use of the bit.

Riding without a bit

I feel that every rider should ride his horse in a bitless bridle for a while. Training a horse to go in a bitless bridle is surprisingly easy. It is usually the rider who needs to adapt most. If you have attended a riding school where emphasis is placed on bit contact and getting the horse on the bit, you may find the lack of a bit disconcerting. However, bit contact and being on the bit are means to ends, ie to get the horse to accept the rider's aids, to go with impulsion with the neck and head relaxed and the poll flexed. All this is possible in any bitless bridle. Your feelings still travel down the reins and if you pull or are tense and harsh, the horse will still resist or pull back.

A good start is to concentrate on your own seat. Relaxing down into the saddle, perhaps without stirrups, and with your toes hanging freely and being allowed to point wherever they wish (probably downwards). In this position, which some classical teachers use for lunge lessons, there is no tension in the leg muscles nor, provided the rider concentrates on relaxation, in the seat muscles. This enables the rider to really feel what the horse's legs, via the back are doing. A sensitive, balanced seat, which can be obtained through correct instruction on the lunge, helps give the rider the confidence to guide the horse more by means of seat, weight and legs – riding the horse from the back end forwards rather than concentrating too much on what the bit would be doing with a conventional bridle.

Of course, you do still keep contact with the horse's head, and the type of

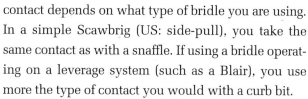

contact depends on what type of bridle you are using. In a simple Scawbrig (US: side-pull), you take the same contact as with a snaffle. If using a bridle operating on a leverage system (such as a Blair), you use more the type of contact you would with a curb bit.

You may prefer to start off in an enclosed school of some kind if you are uncertain of your horse's response, but few react adversely and many go better and more kindly depending on the kind of contact they have been used to via the reins. Use a few school exercises to start, keeping a light contact on the reins and trying to guide to the horse with your seat, and using it to feel where his feet are.

Progress from gait to gait and keep the horse alert and listening to you, Keep using your weight and body position. By the time you progress to canter the horse will be used to this new technique and you will feel sufficiently confident to jump from trot and canter, and hack out.

Above: The American Spirit bitless bridle. Allan Buck, a horse trainer from Ramona California, has developed the American Spirit bitless bridle which Professor Bob Cook of Tufts University veterinary school, Massachusetts, believes could be the biggest advance in equine technology since people started riding horses and will, he says, significantly improve the welfare of horses.

The reins pass through side rings to another ring below the jaw. A loop passes through this ring and over the horse's head. Rein aids thus gently cause pressure behind the ears and under the jaw rather than exerting the downwards and backwards pressure the horse would feel with a bit in his mouth or when wearing a leverage-type bitless bridle.

Professor Cook believes that wearing a bit confuses a horse, stimulating salivation and feeding reflexes: a horse cannot breathe and swallow at the same time so he has to stop breathing to swallow the saliva otherwise he may choke. If the natural angle of the head and neck is changed, bending the windpipe, this may cause air turbulence and increase the effort needed for breathing. This process is much less likely to happen with this bridle

Left: The Scawbrig bitless bridle has a front padded noseband and a padded piece in the chin groove, with the reins passing through rings on the ends of the nose band. The bridle is stabilised by the jowl strap and there is a normal throatlatch and browband. When the rider applies pressure to the reins, the padded parts tighten around the lower parts of the jaws. The noseband must be fitted high enough above the nostrils so as not to interfere with the horse's breathing

4 SCHOOLING AIDS

LUNGEING EQUIPMENT

THE LUNGEING CAVESSON

Anyone who has lunged a horse off a headcollar (US: halter) or even a bridle cannot fail to appreciate the extra control and stability afforded by a proper lungeing cavesson – so long as it is properly made and of good quality. Most English-trained (which means almost any non-Western school) horses and ponies will be lunged at the beginning of their working life, whether their intended career is for riding or driving, and they will probably be lunged at various times throughout their life, too, either as a means of getting back to basics or just as a form of exercise.

Control is essential to achieving obedience and safety for all concerned, including the horse, particularly when he is young and still forming his ideas about humans, and using proper equipment is vital to this objective. A good quality lungeing cavesson is, therefore, an invaluable piece of equipment in any stable yard.

There are several types of lungeing cavesson, particularly since the advent of synthetic materials, but amongst all these most experts still prefer either the strongly made traditional Orssich pattern, or the lighter-weight Wels pattern, both made of leather.

The Orssich has not only a throatlatch but also a jowl strap which passes under the jaw and helps to keep the cheekpieces in place: these can slip round and interfere with the horse's eye on the outside of the circle if the cavesson is too loose or of unstable design. Other refinements are a short strap under the jaw passing from the jowl strap down to the back of the nosepiece, which makes for extra stability; and also an adjustable face strap (sometimes this is even made of metal) running from the centre of the nosepiece and passing between the ears to the headpiece: this prevents the nosepiece of the cavesson from dropping too far down the nose, and again gives added security and stability. Any cavesson, or headcollar come to that, benefits from having a browband because it is then more efficient at keeping the headpiece, and therefore the whole arrangement, in place. Short diagonal straps that pass from the top of the nosepiece to the cheekpieces are another means of stabilising the cavesson.

The Wels cavesson consists simply of the padded nosepiece (about

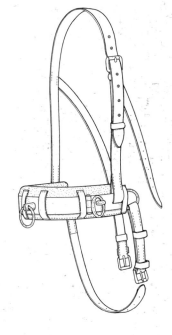

An Orssich-pattern lungeing cavesson

which more below), a simple strap passing over the poll and buckling to its shorter partner on the near side, and a throatlatch to help keep it steady and in place. The nosepiece is the most crucial part of any cavesson. In a well made item it consists of a metal bar padded with leather, with a metal ring on a swivel on the front of it; the lunge-rein is attached to this ring. There are almost always two other rings towards the sides which, in establishments where haute école training is carried out, are used for fastening the horse between pillars for work from the ground – and for any other purpose they are useless: for instance, you might want to attach riding reins so that you can ride a youngster from the cavesson before introducing a bridle, but the rings are usually too far forward and would interfere with the action of the rein. For attaching long-reins (US: long-lines), these two side rings need to be fixed further back behind the cheekpieces – and then you can certainly ride off them.

The nosepiece must be adjustable, and capable of being fitted firmly and snugly enough to keep the whole cavesson in place. Sometimes – for instance if the horse plays up or tries to bolt off – considerable force may be placed on the centre ring from the side, which unavoidably has the effect of pulling the cavesson to the side towards the trainer; however, if it is strong and closely fitted, this slippage is much less likely to occur.

If you want to introduce a bit simply to lie in the youngster's mouth whilst he is being lunged, you can buy little clips which will suspend the bit by its rings from the side dees of the cavesson. You can, as his training progresses, then attach reins to ride him, and carry on from there.

LUNGE-REINS

The old-fashioned tubular cotton webbing lunge-reins are still widely used – and I cannot understand why, because lighter-weight, easier-to-handle synthetic ones have long been available. All lunge-reins (usually also used for long-reining, although you can get specially rounded, braided reins for this) need a swivel-mounted fastening, either a strong clip or, more secure, a buckle on the end to fix to the cavesson's centre ring.

I should also like to see lunge-reins made without a hand loop on the trainer's end (which they always have) because inexperienced or blasé trainers can easily be tempted to slip their wrist through this loop to get a firmer hold should a horse play up, and they then risk being dragged.

Left: The lightweight Wels cavesson

PESSOA TRAINING AID

Invented by showjumper Nelson Pessoa, this finds favour with many people who may otherwise use side-reins: it is more effective than side-reins and is intended for lungeing. It encourages the horse to enhance his natural 'rear-wheel-drive' way of going as well as persuading him to lower his head and stretch his neck long and low.

It is a cord which can be used in three positions, although most people use the first and lowest position. It attaches to the bit-rings and passes through a choice of positions (as mentioned) on a normal lungeing or driving roller and then passes through rings on the end of a sheepskin-covered strap behind the horse's thighs, finally passing up in front of the hips to the roller, level with the horse's back

Lunge rein

ROLLERS

Although many people lunge their horses without a roller (not requiring to fit side-reins), I find that to dress him up in one has an advantageous psychological effect from the point of view of accustoming him to 'clutter', pressure and some discipline. For long-reining of much finesse, the fitting of a roller is essential.

The roller should be fastened snugly but not tightly, sufficient to stay in place but without causing discomfort. Some rollers that are specially designed for lungeing and long-reining have rings fitted to the saddle part, the padded section on the back of the horse: long-reins can then be passed through them, or side-reins fitted. There are usually three sets of rings or, if a driving pad is used, terrets, where each ring is fixed to the end of a short metal rod so that it stands up and away from the roller, rather than flopping down. The highest set permits the reins to be carried at about the level they would be held by a rider, and is used for fairly advanced-level training when the horse will have attained the higher head carriage which goes with better balance and steady self-carriage. The lower fittings are used for younger, greener horses, to allow for the lower head carriage, and for the fitting of side-reins.

This little drawing is taken from a photograph of Miss Sylvia Stanier, LVO, using the Danish method of long-reining

A dee may be fitted in the centre of the roller's back edge so that a

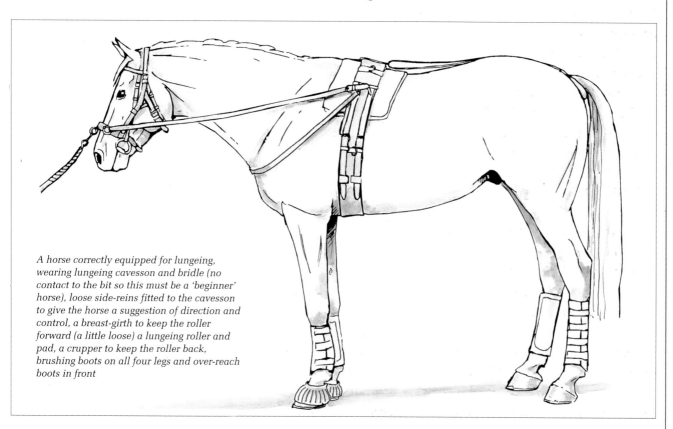

A horse correctly equipped for lungeing, wearing lungeing cavesson and bridle (no contact to the bit so this must be a 'beginner' horse), loose side-reins fitted to the cavesson to give the horse a suggestion of direction and control, a breast-girth to keep the roller forward (a little loose) a lungeing roller and pad, a crupper to keep the roller back, brushing boots on all four legs and over-reach boots in front

crupper can be fitted to prevent the roller from slipping too far forwards; and a breastgirth, a simple strap which clips to dees on the front edge of the roller, does the opposite job, of preventing the roller from slipping too far back. If this happens it could induce bucking and kicking, and if it slips too far forward, digging in behind the elbows, it will cause discomfort, and in the longer term could possibly diminish the free action of the forelegs and shoulders.

TRAINING AIDS

THE PHILOSOPHY OF THEIR USE

The above paragraphs cover the basic equipment needed for lungeing or long-reining; protective boots are covered in Chapter 7. Some other individual training or schooling aids are considered below, and are also shown and described in the accompanying illustrations. However, with a view to removing some of the mystique which has come to surround their use, I think it is appropriate to consider the whole concept of the use of such aids before we continue.

If we accept that the main objective of good riding is to have the horse going as described in Chapter 1 – and this applies to any discipline of riding except possibly racing, and including the American Saddle Seat – what we are aiming for ultimately, if we wish to progress that far, is a horse that holds up his own head and neck in self-carriage from its base, with well developed muscles in front of the withers so that, from the saddle, this area seems 'meaty', and from the side, the sunken triangle which is often apparent at the base of the neck in front of the withers, is filled out with muscle, creating a smoothly arched crest to the neck, joining with the withers and flowing on down the back, loins and (engaged/'tucked under') hindquarters.

We can perform exercises which will develop all the latter areas, but only the horse's own efforts can develop the neck muscles and carriage. As far as schooling aids are concerned, this means that using 'gadgets', as they are often called, in such a way as to force the horse ultimately to go with his head and neck up, usually results in him arching his neck in a forced posture, with the angle of arch not at the poll, but at the base of the neck in front of the withers; and like this, he can never produce the shape described in the preceding paragraph.

The object of training aids must always and only be to suggest to the horse that carrying himself in a particular manner makes for easier movement, praise from the rider and a relatively comfortable way to carry his or her weight. Training aids, therefore, are to be used for as short a period as

Below: One possible effect of tight side-reins, here fixed at 'hand' level for a more advanced outline. The horse has come slightly behind the vertical and, in trying to make himself comfortable, has kinked his neck downwards just in front of the withers, the complete opposite of the effect desired

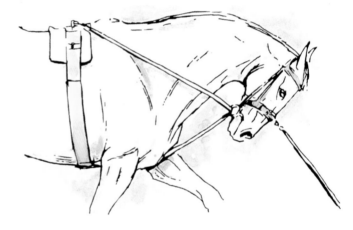

What an appalling picture! Not on the part of the artist, we hasten to add, but in regard to what it depicts. Sadly, this is an all-too-common sight: a version of draw-reins for lungeing which have been fitted much too tightly so that the horse is grossly overbent, creating considerable stretching tension on the nuchal ligament in the poll area. This does not teach the horse any useful physical movements or willing acceptance of the bit, nor does it enhance advantageous muscle development because he will be adopting compensatory movements to counteract his discomfort. In addition, the horse must be harbouring resentment, confusion, puzzlement and anger at such gross abuse – unless he is far too good for this world, as so many are

it takes for the horse to get the idea of what we want and what is best for him. Their use is then discontinued. Their continued use, and certainly their incorrect use – usually by inducing forced posture due to over-tight adjustment and harsh or strong use – is counterproductive and cannot produce the results that knowledgeable trainers and riders seek because they do not permit – indeed, they often prevent – the use of the very muscles needed to develop and maintain correct posture and action.

With that in mind, let us look at some schooling aids.

SIDE-REINS

These seem to be almost standard equipment for lungeing these days, but opinions vary, as ever, regarding their use.

They can clip to the side rings of your cavesson or the bit-rings of the bridle, if required, and pass back to the dees of the roller, or if a saddle is used instead, to its girth straps under the flaps. Side-reins are not meant to set or hold the horse's head in a certain position, although they do discourage him from throwing it around because he soon learns that he can cause himself a certain degree of discomfort should he position it outside the area permitted by the side-reins. Their initial purpose with a green horse is to give him a preliminary suggestion of the contact he must come to expect from a rider's hand via the bridle reins.

Side-reins fitted loosely to bit and girth tabs, appropriate for a young horse

It is essential to remember, when using side-reins, that the horse must learn to position and carry his own head and neck by means of correct muscular action: forcing or strongly suggesting a head position can only result in incorrect muscular use and development, in a false carriage and in possibly encouraging the horse to lean on the cavesson. All this, as described earlier, results in him using his body wrongly, and if this way of going is allowed to become established early in training, it can be very difficult to correct.

The matter of their adjustment is one of observation and fine-tuning: if they are too long the horse will barely feel them at all, and if too short they will actually prevent him from stretching down and out with his nose, as we want him to do, particularly a young horse – instead they will force him, if he does offer to stretch down, to go overbent, with the highest part of his neck part way down the crest, his nose tucked in towards the chest and the front of his face behind the vertical, a posture which is wrong and not to be encouraged.

Another point to consider is, should the side-reins be rigid or slightly elastic? Elastic inserts are probably not helpful, because even when the horse does learn to 'give' and flex his jaw and poll in response to a contact, the elastic keeps 'taking' and does not reward him with lessened contact, so he never knows where he is. Rubber rings in the reins will have a similar, if lesser, effect. Ordinary side-reins, carefully adjusted to create exactly the right amount of contact for a horse's stage of training, are probably best – but remember his need to stretch down and out.

THE CHAMBON

This is a very useful and helpful item of equipment originally designed for lungeing and loose schooling only, but which some people now also use for riding. Its main benefit is in the early stages of a horse's education or re-training, because it encourages the 'long and low' posture generally required in novice horses. It consists of a padded poll strap with rings or a little pulley on each end. A cord is clipped to the bit-ring on each side, each is then passed up the side of the head and through the ring on the poll strap, then down to the breast where they both buckle to two short pieces on a single strap that passes between the forelegs and fastens round the girth or roller.

The horse 'works' the Chambon himself, as it only comes into effect when he raises his head above a level that is acceptable to his trainer. The poll strap exerts downward pressure on the poll and the bit is drawn rather uncomfortably upwards in the mouth (although there is no backward pressure as can be exerted from the saddle with draw-reins); the theory is that, in order to avoid this uncomfortable feel, the horse lowers his head again. It works very well in practice, too, many horses going with a lowered head and neck and rounded topline just from the feel of the Chambon in position.

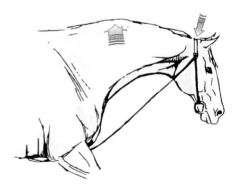

The Chambon is regarded as standard lungeing equipment on the continent of Europe because it encourages and suggests to the horse, rather than forcing him, to go with his head low and his neck stretched up from the base and forwards. It has no direct influence on the hindquarters

THE GOGUE

Is this to be called the 'de Gogue' or just the 'Gogue'? I have heard many explanations from various knowledgeable horsemen and women, all of them equally convincing. I call it the Gogue because that is the essential part of the surname of its inventor – René de (meaning 'of' or 'from') Gogue, as in François Robichon de la Guérinière who is called la Guérinière. So much for the French lesson: I shall be pleased to be corrected if I am wrong.

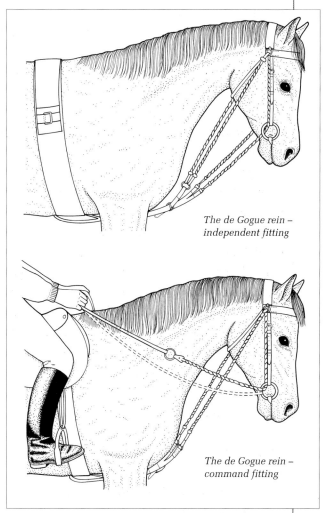

The de Gogue rein – independent fitting

The de Gogue rein – command fitting

The Gogue was designed with two ways of adjustment: the independent fitting, for dismounted work; and the command fitting, for ridden work. In the independent fitting, cords run from a strap at the breast (fastening round the girth and passing between the forelegs), up through a ring or pulley wheel on each end of a padded poll strap, down the sides of the head and through the bit-rings, and back down to the breaststrap again. As with the Chambon, the horse operates this fitting himself and, depending on expert adjustment, it only comes into effect, with its bit-raising and poll-pressure technique, when the head is too high. It is used during lungeing and loose schooling in this position, although some trainers also use it during initial ridden schooling.

In the command fitting, the cords pass up through the rings or over the pulleys, down the face and through the bit-rings again, but thence back to the rider's hand, clipping to special short reins with rings to take the Gogue clips. A pair of ordinary reins is also used on the bridle, and the rider can use the ordinary reins and/or the Gogue, as considered appropriate. Some experts, particularly on the continent of Europe and especially in France, use the command Gogue without a direct rein; but this does take great finesse, knowledge and ability on the part of the trainer. Incidentally, the Gogue can also be used when jumping and has been used in actual competition. Many European trainers consider it standard schooling equipment and not an accessory at all.

RUNNING REINS AND DRAW-REINS

Running reins and draw-reins are often confused, but they both have the object of 'drawing' the horse's nose in if his trainer thinks he is poking it out, and this usually also results in his lowering his head, though often with the highest part of the neck some way down from the poll. Because the reins 'run' through the bit-rings, they are called running reins by some people.

What is important is their effect on the horse in their various fittings,

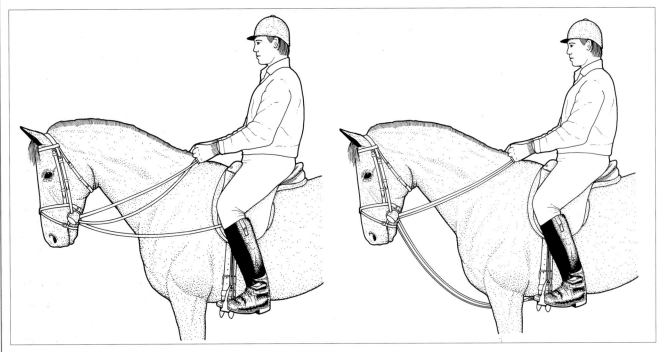

and they are currently used in three main ways. The least severe way is to have the reins running from the rider's hands, through the bit-rings usually from inside to outside, and back to the girth under the saddle flaps. The more severe fitting is for the reins to pass down from the bit-rings between the horse's forelegs, fastening round the girth at the breast-bone. Both these fittings have the effect of encouraging the horse to lower his head and neck and to bring his nose in a little, so suggesting an easier way of going. Of course, we are all familiar with the depressing scenario of riders hauling in their horses' heads in a strong, forcible manner which does far more than 'suggest' and which has the ruinous effect described above.

A pair of ordinary reins must always be used on the bridle too, and the rider should differentiate between the two reins, and hold them as he/she would double bridle reins, with the snaffle rein between the third and little finger and the running rein outside the little finger (one method, at least), only using the running rein when the horse is going with his head up, his nose poked out and with a hollow back and trailing hind legs. The rider should certainly ride mainly on the snaffle rein, and not constantly on the running rein, if this rein is to be used as intended and without harming the horse.

Running reins are sometimes mistakenly put on a horse which 'takes off', in the belief that they will provide additional control. In fact they will have the opposite effect because such horses usually take off with their heads down, and the lowering effect of the running reins simply makes their task easier. Running reins should also not be put on horses prone to bucking, as the head-down posture is exactly what a horse needs to be able to buck effectively.

Above: (left) Running reins fitted in their least severe way, passing from the rider's hands, through the bit-rings, to the girth tabs under the saddle flap
(right) The more severe fitting for running reins, in which they pass between the horse's forelegs to the girth at the breastbone

Right: Draw reins, which pass over the horse's poll, down the sides of his head, through the bit rings to the rider's head

Below: When a horse is forced into such an extreme outline by the use of draw-reins, here in their most severe setting, there is tremendous stetching tension on the nuchal ligament at the poll and horse often kink down the neck at the base, to try and raise their heads and relieve the tension

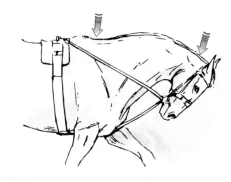

Draw-/running reins can also be used as one continuous rein, passing from the poll, down the sides of the face, through each bit-ring from outside to inside and then straight to the rider's hands, and like this they have quite the opposite effect to the previously described fittings as they raise the bit in the mouth and encourage the horse to raise the head, although there is a lesser downward pressure on the poll, rather like the feel of a gag. In this fitting they are useful for buckers and horses which plunge and get their heads between their forelegs, or for those which bore and lean on the bit. They can also correct horses who have found that a good way of unshipping some riders is to suddenly throw the head down and stop, especially when performed at speed. (Such horses should, in any case, be ridden

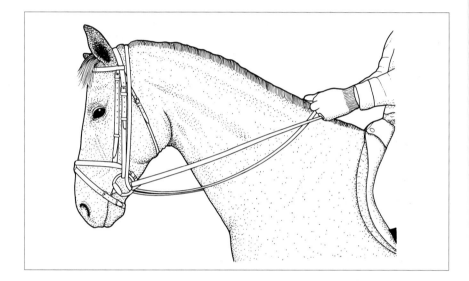

with bridged reins, jockey-style, so that the rider has some frontal support over the base of the neck to keep him or her from being lurched forwards.)

Lungeing draw-reins are a better alternative, in my view, to side-reins for lungeing. They fasten to the front dees of the roller or saddle, pass from outside to inside through the bit-rings, down between the forelegs and fasten round the saddle girth or roller. They are adjusted comfortably when the horse has his head in a normal position, only coming into effect if he raises it too far and pokes his nose. They allow the horse more freedom of movement than do side-reins, and do not promote over-bending in the same way. They are not seen much in the UK and Ireland, but are very common on the continent of Europe.

MARTINGALES

Usually used as a fairly permanent fixture on mature horses under saddle, martingales do have their place on horses with ingrained habits, although the only ones which might have an actual training effect are the Market Harborough and the Harbridge (see page 126).

MISUSE OF TRAINING AIDS

There is a good deal of ill-feeling developing in some quarters at the time of writing against the use of 'outline-fixing devices' such as side-reins, draw-reins, running-reins and certain patented/branded schooling devices – indeed, anything which can be used to forcibly bring a horse's head up, down and in, because they obtain their results incorrectly, that is by more or less forcing the horse from the front to assume what we feel is an appropriate posture. This, of course, is not the way to go.

Sadly, many such devices are wrongly used by people of little knowledge and judgement and can certainly do much harm in such hands. When used by knowledgeable riders with a great deal of tact as a temporary measure, and correctly adjusted, just to help a horse get the idea of giving to the bit and flexing at poll and jaw, they may be an acceptable aid to schooling, being removed once the penny drops.

They should certainly never be used all or most of the time, adjusted too tightly or used too strongly as they can simply result in a hard-mouthed horse, heavy in hand, on the forehand and with an untrue way of going. Also, horses so abused will never learn to go properly from the hindquarters and learn to lift their necks up and forward themselves, developing true self-carriage.

The Standing Martingale

The standing martingale is a traditional standby for horses which habitually throw their heads up higher than their trainer/rider wishes. They are almost standard equipment in the polo field where horses constantly throw their heads up in evasion of, and response to – dare I say it – pain in the mouth inflicted during the heat of play. This action must be encouraged,

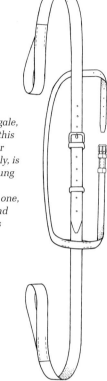

*Left and right:
A standing martingale, fitted as shown in this picture, correctly or slightly more loosely, is useful to stop a young horse, or an older, poorly-disciplined one, tossing his head and breaking his rider's nose*

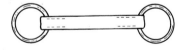

contrarily, by the fact that most polo ponies are played in head-raising gag snaffles these days as a devastating stopping aid considered essential for today's very fast play.

A standing martingale is useful if it is adjusted correctly (see picture) as a safety measure on a horse whose head position is not established, to prevent the rider being bashed in the face.

The standing martingale must only be fitted to the back of the nosepiece of an ordinary cavesson noseband, and to the same place on a Flash. It should only be used with a snaffle bridle. It is far too severe if fixed to the bottom strap of a Grakle or drop noseband, and is not at all appropriate for use with a pelham or a double bridle – if the horse is sufficiently educated to wear those bridles he does not need a standing martingale.

If adjusted at all tightly a standing martingale will encourage the horse

Above: The Irish martingale is often used on racehorses who may be prone to throwing their heads about, to stop the reins being tossed over to the wrong side of the neck

Right: Bib martingales are used a lot in racing because it is not possible for the horse to get hold of the straps with his teeth. Stops should still be used on the reins, though. These two horses are both wearing wire-ring snaffles favoured in racing because they are most unlikely to be pulled through the mouth. The horse on the left also wears an Australian cheeker noseband believed to have a psychological anti-pulling effect

to lean on it, and in doing so he will develop all the wrong 'riding' muscles; it should therefore be adjusted very carefully so that it only comes into effect when the horse's head is raised too high. When the martingale is fitted correctly, the strap running from the back of the noseband, down between the forelegs to the girth should reach almost up to the horse's throat if pressed into that position by your hand.

The Running Martingale

The running martingale's objective is to achieve a steadier feel on the bit in the horse's mouth – even if he raises or throws his head around, the rings keep the reins down and maintain the action of the bit across the tongue instead of into the corners of the lips, preventing evasion. For

green horses, it produces a steadier feel on the bit and helps prevent the reins being thrown around and possibly over the neck if the horse indulges in high jinks.

It is also a useful item of equipment for novice riders who have not yet attained full control of their hand position; such riders tend to keep their balance by hanging on tight to the reins and, by using the martingale, the

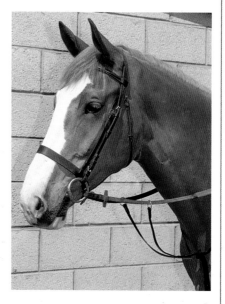

Above: The running martingale has a steadying effect on reins and bit when fitted correctly, as here. If the horse raises his head, the martingale will keep the action of the bit down on the tongue (and maybe on the bars, although this is debatable) rather than up on the corners of the mouth where it is far less effective. A too-short martingale (shown left) has the same effect as the rider holding the hands low and stiff: the horse tries to raise his head in resistance and goes in an 'upside-down' way

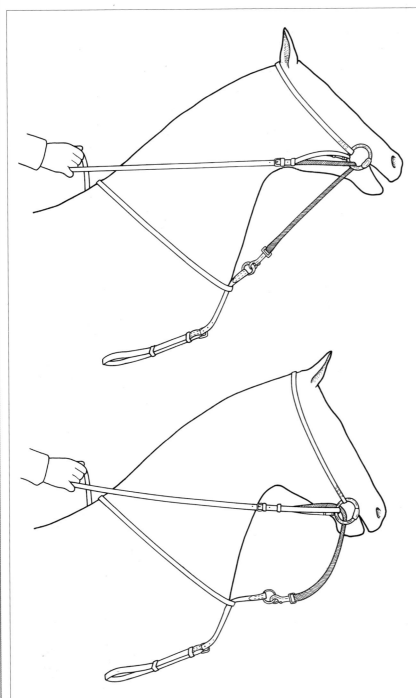

Sometimes called a martingale and sometimes a rein, the Market Harborough takes its name from the place where it is thought to have made its début. It consists of a neckstrap and a strap passing under the breast to the girth at one end, and towards the other, dividing like a running martingale into two thinner straps. However, these are longer than those on a running martingale and each ends in a snap hook not a ring – these pass through each bit-ring, then are brought back to snap on to one of normally four pairs of metal dees sewn to each rein.

The influence of the Market Harborough directs the horse's head downwards should he raise it above the height at which control can reasonably be exerted. It has the feel of a running martingale to the horse and can be fairly severe or quite ineffective according to which pair of dees it is attached to and how loosely it is adjusted

THE HARBRIDGE

The Harbridge Training Aid was launched in 1995 and is now well established and highly regarded as a training aid able to produce horses kindly, simply and correctly along classical lines.

It is comprised of three leather straps joined by a central ring. Two of these straps are elasticated to provide a sympathetic feel since they join directly to the bit and are designed to imitate perfect hands as they always give the moment the horse assumes the required outline. However, they offer no opportunity to lean on the hand, a common drawback of some other devices.

The Harbridge, correctly adjusted, encourages the horse to find his own balance and cannot be operated by the rider, only coming into effect with an elastic give-and-take (pressure-and-release) feel when the horse raises his head too high. It works with any length of rein, allowing the horse to step under and elevate his forehand, stretching and rounding his topline and lifting his belly, so enabling development of the correct muscles for a strong, safe way of going. Because it is not a 'fixed' device and is operated by the horse himself, given correct adjustment, in my experience and opinion it comes into the same category as the Chambon and the Gogue as a safe and beneficial temporary aid for certain horses.

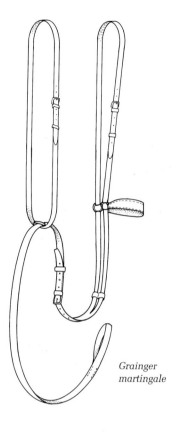

full impact of this is not transmitted directly to the horse's mouth as much as it would be without the steadying effect of the rings on the reins.

The running martingale should be fitted so that the two straps which separate at the breast, when not on the reins, can be passed up the shoulder almost to the withers: when the reins are through the rings they should not come into play when the horse's head carriage is correct. However, when the head is raised too high, the rings should exert pressure on the reins. Again, if the straps are too long, the martingale is useless; and if too short, so that they exert constant pressure on the reins, they hamper communication between mouth and hand and are too restrictive. When correctly adjusted, the running martingale is quite safe to use when jumping.

It is vital to use a 'stop' on each rein – a small piece of leather or rubber which slides onto each rein and is positioned between the bit end of the rein and the martingale rings; these prevent the rings running too far down the reins and getting caught on the rein fastenings, or even on the bit cheeks.

Other Combinations

The **Pulley** martingale is a variation of the running martingale, but instead of a simple device of the strap at the breast there is a little pulley and a cord with a ring at each end runs through it; the reins then pass through the rings in the normal way. It allows greater lateral movement of head and neck than a conventional running martingale and us useful in, for example, polo and gymkhana games.

The **Combined** martingale, as its name suggests, is a combination of the running and standing martingales for horses who seem to need both effects. A somewhat 'belt and braces' piece of equipment, it is not seen very often.

A **Grainger** martingale, rather than being fitted directly to the back of a cavesson noseband, or sliding along the bridle reins, is attached to the ends of a noseband. As the latter is adjustable, it can be positioned like a cavesson, like a drop, or in between (although the difference should not be that great), the lower position giving more control but having the possibility of interfering with the horse's breathing if fitted too low. The breast buckle allows two straps to be adjusted as desired, generally the same fitting as for a standing martingale, being both effective and safe.

*Grainger
martingale*

*Combination
martingale*

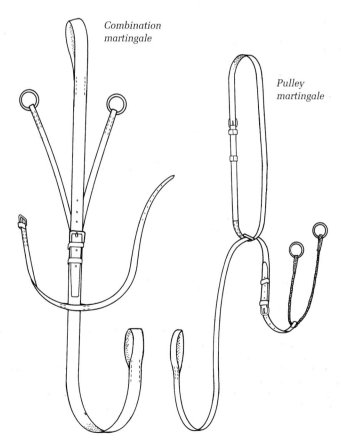

*Pulley
martingale*

127

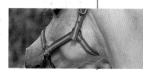

5 HEADCOLLARS and HALTERS

Headcollars and halters are two more items of tack which have changed little from the very earliest examples used by ancient peoples. The idea of a rope or a piece of rawhide around the neck, particularly around the top of the neck just behind the ears which gave reasonable control, was soon extended to passing the loose end around the two jaws and securing it with a twist or knot. A piece of rawhide or rope left dangling was found useful for catching the horse, and if it were long enough, for tying him up; other variations of early halters also incorporated a strip of hide or rope that passed through the mouth or just looped round the lower jaw for more control. However, I have not come across any ancient version of today's so-called restrainer halter, the best known one in the UK probably being the 'Be Nice' halter, although there are several others both here and in the USA and Australia.

I must explain here that in the UK and Ireland, a headcollar and a halter are two different items. In using the word 'headcollar' I am referring to the everyday item we are all familiar with, and which looks like a heavier version of a bridle but with no bit, and often no browband. To the British and Irish, a 'halter' is usually made of rope or cotton webbing with an integral leadrope; it will be described under that heading below. To the Americans, a 'halter' describes all of these. (Wasn't it that famous English-born American comedian, Bob Hope, who said that England and America are two countries separated by the same language?)

Let us look at traditional headcollars and halters first before considering what are currently called 'pressure' or 'restrainer' halters and which do give much more control, when used correctly, than the traditional items.

Native American horsemen often used the Indian war bridle which has a horsehair rope or rawhide strip or plait through the horse's mouth, but just as many seem to have been ridden in halter-type bitless bridles. Although they captured Spanish horses, they do not seem to have adopted wholescale their riders' use of saddles and metal bits

129

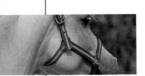

HEADCOLLARS

This little matter of control over a half ton of what is, underneath the veneer of domesticity, a wild animal, is rather important! The horse is the only domesticated animal which descends from wild forebears which used flight rather than fight as their first line of defence. All others fight readily in defence, but not horses – almost always their first instinct is to run, and only to fight if prevented from running, unless they are protecting young. As well as being easily startled, horses – and indeed even small ponies – are very fast and very strong.

The traditional headcollar offers little control over a horse who has even the least intention of not going where he does not want to. It was not designed for real control, but for securing horses in stalls (US: standing or tie stalls) and for leading quiet, obedient animals around. It was therefore a very stout leather affair with iron or steel fittings; brass, the metal of choice on high quality headcollars today, is relatively soft and easy to bend or break, so it is only intended for 'Sunday best' headcollars.

The horse would be tied in his stall by means of a strong rope: this would be passed through a ring on the manger in front of him, and a heavy wooden ball threaded through the end of it; the ball kept the rope down and away from the horse's forelegs, whilst giving him room to look around and to lie down and get up. Sometimes a chain would be used instead, with a T-fitting on the end to stop it coming through the ring.

Most readers will have had the experience of a horse being difficult or suddenly frightened by something when they have been leading him around in a headcollar, and will undoubtedly remember how little use the ordinary headcollar was for control, and how their own strength could do nothing whatever to stop him. Nevertheless, headcollars are in wide use all around the world because they are convenient and easy to slip on and off, and we are all accustomed to them. Most these days have regressed to the point of not having a browband, always fitted at one time: a browband prevents the headpiece slipping uncomfortably down the neck, where it will scrub the mane and create an indirect pull on the nose which can mark the hair, chafe the skin and cause considerable irritation. It would be very well worth while going back to using a browband on a headcollar.

LEATHER HEADCOLLARS

The very best quality headcollars are in the style known as Albert (after Queen Victoria's consort, Prince Albert, I understand); they have three rows of stitching down the cheekpieces which are of double leather, the throatlatch will be of rolled leather, and the headcollar will have brass buckles and fittings. There is often an engraved brass nameplate down the near-

This little renegade is wearing a catching strap dangling from his foal slip (which is a little tight) to make it easier to catch him. Catching straps must not be long enough for the animal to tread on them

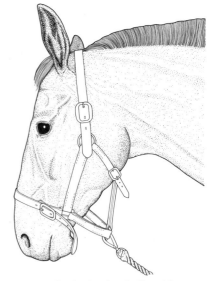

A good quality leather headcollar with adjustment buckles not only on the headpiece, as usual, but also on the throatlatch and noseband. A beneficial addition would be a browband. The noseband on this headcollar is a good height (midway between the corners of the lips and the sharp face bones) but could be a little higher

side cheekpiece with the horse's name on it, a sensitive touch which can be applied to any headcollar. Other best quality headcollars are even better than the Albert because they may have adjustment buckles not only on the headpiece but on the noseband (most non-adjustable headcollars being too big here) and often on the throatlatch as well.

Everyday leather headcollars are available with galvanised metal fittings, and they are often rivetted rather than stitched together; much cheaper than best quality items, they last just as long if properly cared for, and longer than modern nylon web headcollars which are prone to fraying and sometimes shrinking after being wet.

Most leather is vegetable tanned, but chrome-tanned leather – usually pale green, softer and rougher – stretches more before breaking and so is stronger, although certainly not as strong as buffalo hide. Even the best kept vegetable-tanned leather will break under the sort of pressure exerted by a determined horse pulling back on a tie-ring (horses can exert a pull of two-and-a-half times their own weight in this situation) and so are safer than chrome leather or nylon as probably the horse will ultimately break free, rather than risk seriously injuring himself.

NYLON WEB HEADCOLLARS

As already mentioned, these are extremely strong and too dangerous to be left on a horse at any time. I am not in favour of leaving headcollars on horses, anyway: I think it must be somewhat uncomfortable for the horse, and it is potentially dangerous as a horse can easily catch a foot in even a well fitting headcollar when, for instance, scratching his head with a hindfoot, as they do. In the field, they can catch on hedges and trees and anything else available. Nylon is also harsh on the coat and skin and can easily rub a horse if left on.

TIPS ON TYING UP

By way of an aside on this subject I would like to comment on tying a horse up: in the UK the conventional teaching is that horses should be tied up to a loop of string (never binder twine which is too strong) on the metal tie-ring so that it will break should the horse pull back: apparently the authorities consider that it is safer for the horse to break free than to risk injuring himself struggling. However, many people know from personal experience that once a horse has broken free when tied up he will make a point of doing so at every opportunity, and soon becomes a menace. You can never leave such horses for a minute, and the only place it seems safe to tie them and leave them is when they are travelling in a close compartment in transport. This is possibly not the place to discuss this matter in detail, but in a nutshell, such horses need retraining by a competent horseman or woman with something like a Galvayne's harness to break them of this dangerous habit. If all breeders taught all their foals to tie up properly, we should never have this problem.

Far left: A basic design of headcollar, which, however, is too tight. The throatlatch should come halfway down the rounded jawbones, and the noseband should be at least two fingers' width below the face bones and permit three fingers' width between it and the head

Left: This headcollar is much too tight in the throat region and should be let down a couple of holes. The lead rope is attached to a chain coupling passing through the side dees which will tighten when pressure is placed on the rope, giving more control provided the handler does not keep up a sustained pressure (which may cause the horse to panic)

SAFE HEADCOLLARS

Headcollars are now available for paddock and field use which will come undone or break if they get caught up on anything, and so fall harmlessly off the horse's head: some have breakable (easily replaceable) rubber rings, others have snap-open devices, and some have velcro inserts. Moreover you can often fit a fly-fringe browband to them for field use, so they are ideal for this purpose. Mares on large studs are often turned out in named headcollars for identification purposes, so wider use of safety headcollars would remove the slight but undeniable risk this involves.

FLY FRINGES AND BONNETS

The best fly-fringes are those made of heavy cotton with knotted ends as they have a good swing to them and are very effective because they swing and flick about with every move of the horse's head. The stiffer and more lightweight ones of plastic and various synthetic materials are pretty useless, in my experience, as are those which simply fit on the ears and round the throat without the need for a headcollar, as they soon come off.

Bonnets (see-through to the horse) seem like a good idea, but in practice it is almost impossible to get a totally fly-proof fit, so that flies can crawl inside but cannot get out again, driving the horse absolutely mad.

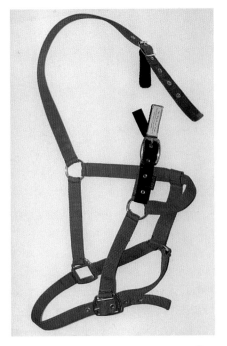

The Fly Free Link fits an ordinary headcollar: when set in the 'Secure' position, it allows the full strength of the headcollar to be maintained, as when leading. The 'Safe' position is for field use, when the link allows the headcollar to come off the horse's head should it become caught up

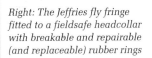

Right: The Jeffries fly fringe fitted to a fieldsafe headcollar with breakable and repairable (and replaceable) rubber rings

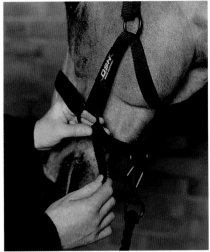

The Day Son & Hewitt Quick Release Safety Headcollar

132

FITTING A HEADCOLLAR

* You should be able to slide a finger quite easily under all the straps.
* Always use a browband: long enough that it does not pull the headpiece into the back of the base of the ears, nor rub itself around the ears; but not so long that it gapes or flops around.
* You should be able to fit the width of your hand between the throatlatch and the round jawbones, but no more.
* The height of the noseband should be adjusted by means of the cheekpiece buckle and headstrap so that it is 2in (5cm) below the straight facial bones, perhaps a little more if the horse has a large head. A very common fault is for the noseband to be too high and to rub the horse raw on these bones. If much lower, though, the horse may rub the noseband down over the muzzle so that the headcollar becomes completely displaced or comes off and is left dangling dangerously round the neck.
* Adjust the noseband so that there is ample room for the horse to move his jaws when eating: the width of four fingers should fit between the noseband and the front of the face – if it is looser than this it will catch on things and swing round annoyingly as the horse moves his head.

Below: Checking the fit of a headcollar

(top left) You should be able to slide a finger, very easily, beneath the straps all the way round
(top right) You should be able to fit the width of you hand between the throatlatch and the jawbones
(bottom left) The noseband must come a couple of fingers' width below the facial bones ... and (bottom right) you should be able to fit four fingers' width between the noseband and the head

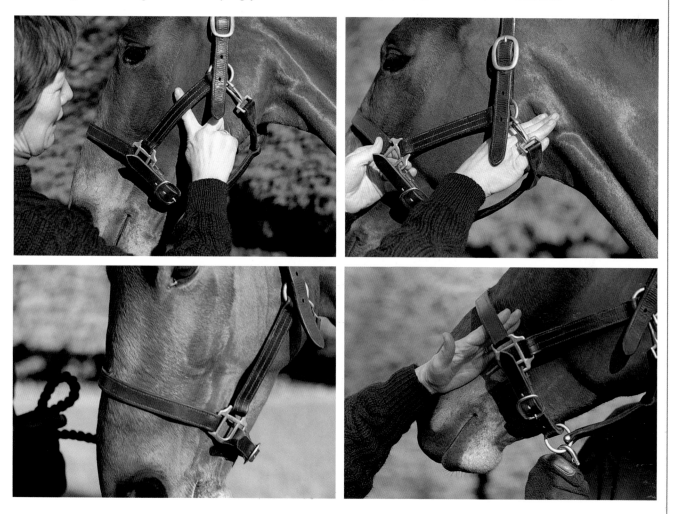

RESTRAINER/CONTROLLER PRESSURE HEADCOLLARS AND HALTERS

Surely none of us can have escaped the information now readily put about that the horse is an 'into pressure' animal – that is, he leans into pressure. At least, he leans into sustained pressure. He does not lean into intermittent pressure. In fact, he backs off from intermittent pressure which is the sort used by horses on their herd mates, usually with the teeth to make an unwelcome colleague keep his or her distance or to reprimand an underling, or with the feet when delivering a rather stronger message.

Intermittent pressure to exert dominance is the principle upon which all restrainer or controller headcollars and halters work. There are several different sorts of these now, and they are finding a ready market because they do work, even on big, really stroppy horses – if you know how to use them.

A sustained pull on the leadrope of even an ordinary halter or headcollar will not produce any desired results; it will simply result in the horse pulling back against you (this instinct is strong even in young foals) and maybe twisting his head and neck rapidly from side to side whilst still pulling and also half rearing up and back. No human can withstand this if a horse means it. However, if the handler, even with an ordinary headcollar, jabs strongly, quickly and repeatedly on the leadrope, this has a chance of having more effect, particularly if used with simple, clear voice aids given in a commanding tone.

HOW NOT TO USE THEM

Many people buy them and use them quite wrongly, hanging on to the leadrope with a long, strong pull which tightens the halter round the horse's head, simply terrifies most animals, turns a fraught situation into a dangerous one and so makes matters much worse instead of better. A very few animals do not seem to respond to them even when they are used correctly. These halters must never be used to tie up a horse.

Short, sharp pressure is used, in horse society, to indicate rejection and to say 'go away'

134

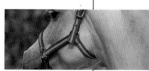

With restrainer headcollars, however, the situation is unlikely to escalate into a dangerous one because they transmit pressure to the horse's head so much more effectively and do bring horses to hand better, with apparently lasting effects. Pressure on the leadrope tightens up the headcollar/halter and is transferred to the nose and lower jaw (in a tightening ring of pressure round the lower part of the head) and to the poll. The pressure is momentary, and is then released, only to be repeated quickly if the horse does not respond. Consistent voice aids should also be used and the horse praised profusely the instant he responds well. He learns that when he behaves well, the pressure is released.

This sort of quick correction is one the horse can understand, and is therefore much kinder to him than allowing him to walk all over humans and perhaps, in some hands at some time, receiving regular thrashings or ending up in a pet food tin because he is unmanageable. Horses do not need to be young to learn manners from such a halter, either: very mature, nasty characters have been reformed with their correct use. Often a few lessons are needed and the principles maintained over a few hours, days or weeks, depending on horse and handler, but there seem to be very few failures.

The whole idea is to use intermittent pressure (which the horse already understands as a part of his own social mores) in the form of short, sharp jerks on the attached leadrope. 'Check and release' is the key to success, and if you do this in time with the horse's stride it is much more effective, checking as a hind foot is coming forward to start the next stride and releasing as it lands, then checking again, if necessary, as the next hind foot comes forward and releasing as that lands, and so on. Some trainers use a short series of checks and releases to give the horse the idea of the principle, and some do it whilst circling him, first in one direction, then the other.

As with any item of specialised equipment (although the principle of restrainer halters is elegant in its simplicity and equine logic), it is as well to read thoroughly any instruction leaflet which comes with it, and even better, to have a lesson from a trainer who is expert in its use.

The results obtainable by the correct use of these headcollars are remarkable, and they have been used for ground training to high-level dressage movements, as well as simply to induce a horse to follow his leader (trainer) anywhere willingly even when not actually being led. They act as attitude adjusters, and seem to improve the entire disposition of a previously recalcitrant horse or pony towards his handler(s). This is because the horse recognises the type of discipline he is getting as naturally dominant and so submits to his herd leader.

These halters and headcollars could surely form a standard part of the equipment of any yard, to be used with more than a few horses and certainly with known difficult ones, and are a beneficial, modern addition to our range of tack if used properly.

The Dually headcollar devised by Monty Roberts. It is important to read the instructions which come with the Dually headcollar. Basically, there are two side rings which are used for schooling from either side, and one normal ring for tying, beneath the jaw (Credit: Horse Magazine)

USE AS A BITLESS BRIDLE

I know of one person who uses her restrainer as a bitless bridle by simply attaching a pair of reins to the ring under the jaw which her model has, and then bringing one rein up each side of the neck, although I am sure the halter was not meant for this. She rides on a loose rein all the time, however (not conventional English-style with a steady contact, but more Western in ethos), using mainly her seat, legs and voice, and she only puts pressure on the halter on a check-and-release basis when necessary.

BE NICE HALTER OR HEADCOLLAR

The Be Nice halter or headcollar is a training item working on the pressure-and-release theory, like similar designs. It is made of rounded rope rather than flat, smooth straps, which concentrates its feel on the head. There are two throat pieces which cross through a ring below the jaw then thread through rings on each end of the noseband and finally join together behind the lower jaw to form a single lead rope. The noseband must be 2cm (1in) below the cheek bones and the plastic tab behind the jaw must be pushed up snugly, but not tightly, into place.

It is used with a lunge-rein or long lead at least 4.5m (15ft) long to teach the horse to respond to tension on the lead by giving to the pressure and so being rewarded. Responsible sellers of such halters will enclose a leaflet or booklet on their use or sell them as a package with an instructional video. These types of headgear can do a great deal of harm if used wrongly.

COME ALONG HALTER

Before ready-made controller/restrainer halters were easily available, we heard much talk of magical items called 'come-along' halters which 'horse whisperers' deftly put together themselves out of a long piece of rope whilst nonchalantly explaining their benefits to a rapt audience. 'Ordinary' horseowners found it impossible to really discover how to make them but Dr Tristan Roberts, former Chairman and Scientific Editor of The Equine Behaviour Forum, worked it all out for members thus:

Fasten one end of a reasonably long lead rope safely round the horse's neck using a non-slip know such as a bowline, leaving about a hand's breadth of slack. Have the knot on the far side of the horse and pass the standing part towards you under the horse's chin, up over the poll, down on the far side, and back towards you under the chin, where it will come to lie alongside that part of the rope coming towards you from the knot. Take a loose bight of the standing part of the rope and tuck it round its neighbour, up from behind, forward, over, and down, as in the drawing. Pull through enough slack and pass this bight down, forwards and up onto the bridge of the horse's nose. Tighten up gently until all is snug, up on the near side towards the poll, down on the far side, and across the nose from far to near. Any tension on the leadrope now presses on the horse's face.

A brief, gentle pull on the rope can be used to nudge the horse forward. Alternatively, if the horse tries to break away he comes up against the pressure of the rope on his face and quickly realises that this pressure is the result of his own action, since the pressure is instantly

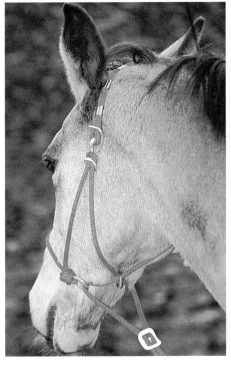

The Be Nice Halter was probably the first restrainer or controller halter to come on to the UK market. Although it may look flimsy, the rounded rope from which it is made (in contrast to the flat straps of ordinary headcollars) concentrate pressure and, when used correctly, it is highly effective in training even the biggest, stroppiest horses

Pressure on the leadrope creates pressure on the poll and around the head. When the horse takes a pull the handler keeps up a slight tension. The handler must not speak or look the horse in the eye so as to avoid his connecting the handler with the discomfort. The instant the horse himself comes forward to relieve himself of the pressure, he is praised profusely. Full instructions should come with your Be Nice Halter and, ideally, new users should have a lesson from a teacher experience in its use

relieved as soon as he, even accidentally, allows the tension to relax. He is, effectively, schooling himself, and violent struggles against a headcollar or neck noose can thus be avoided. The handler should on no account allow himself to get into a tug-of-war with the horse. It is important, also, to be vigilant and to watch the rope to ensure that, when the tension is slackened off, the rope does not slide down off the bony part of the horse's face. Used gently, this device can be even more effective than the Jeffrey loop, especially if the rope is kept reasonably slack, with only occasional gentle nudges. It is very effective in prompting the horse to approach you from the far end of a longish rope. Remember that the device is a schooling aid, not a tether.

THE STABLEIZER™

A unique piece of equipment invented by American R. C. 'Buck' Wheeler aims to restrain fractious horses whilst maintaining the ability to lead, ride, hold, load or otherwise treat or deal with them. It acts not only as a humane restraint but as a training aid for difficult horses, particularly those which are wild or very frightened and defensive. Called The Stableizer, it works on the dual principles of ancient Chinese acupuncture/ acupressure and Native American horse-handling techniques and is proving its worth in veterinary practices, competition and racing yards, mustang rehabilitation centres, farriers, educational establishments and in professional and amateur yards in over seventy-five countries.

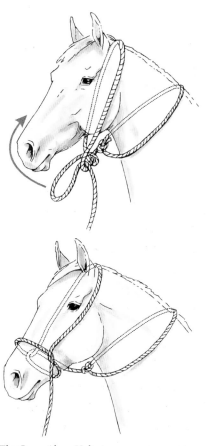

The Come Along Halter

Fitted as shown in the accompanying photographs, The Stableizer consists of strong cord very carefully and individually adjusted by means of a pulley system, with plastic tubing covering the parts which pass under the top lip and behind the ears. A highly detailed instruction leaflet comes with it and there is also a training and instructional video which is strongly recommended.

The part of the cord which passes under the top lip is believed to activate acupuncture point GV26 and the two knobs at either end of the covered head part activate two other points, one below each ear, numbered TH17. The net result is that endorphins are released into the body which have a marked sedative effect on the horse within about two minutes. The horse experiences pleasure and euphoria rather than fear and pain and, unlike some other forms of handling and sedation, these effects seem to remain after the device is removed. It seems that the horse associates being ridden, handled or whatever with pleasure so that the continued use of The Stableizer on that particular horse is unnecessary. Horses do not appear to resent its use or become head shy: it is particularly useful for those who work alone with difficult horses.

Full details of The Stableizer are available from the address in the Suppliers List at the end of this book.

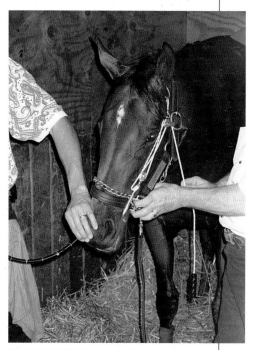

The Stableizer™ in use as during a veterinary procedure

Foal slip

FOAL SLIPS

A foal slip is a lightweight headcollar for a foal (see picture) with a leadstrap hanging from the back ring. Most big studs fit a headcollar from the foal's second day onwards, although he is first taught to lead with a stable rubber or towel around his neck and various hands and arms from two or three helpers around his breast and buttocks, before any pressure is put on his head. Also, never get between a mare and her foal when doing this, at your peril!

A foal slip should be made of leather or soft cotton webbing, as nylon is much too strong and harsh. Keep a very close eye on its fit, as a foal's head grows amazingly quickly. Sadly, most horse charities have frequent experience of being called out to youngsters whose slips or headcollars have been left on permanently, with no regard on the part of their appalling owners for their rate of growth, with the result that the straps have actually become embedded in the bones of the skull, permanently deforming them or even setting up an infection which, due to neglect, killed the animal.

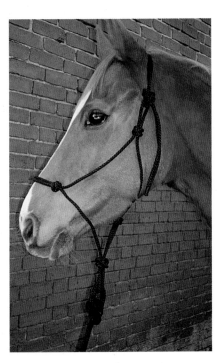

The Traditional Spanish Rope Halter. When a horse takes a pull, the stategically positioned knots exert pressure on the nose without tightening the halter on the head. A sharp tug teaches horses to respect the handler as this slight discomfort only comes into play when the animal misbehaves; at other times, it is loose and comfortable

HALTERS (ENGLISH AND IRISH!)

In the UK, a halter is an all-in-one design of headgear and leadrope made of cotton or jute webbing or of rope. It consists of one section of rope or webbing that passes over the poll, and one that passes round the nose and jaw, with a bound loop where they join on the nearside. Some people simply thread the integral leadrope through this loop so that it pulls the halter tight if the horse takes a hold and so acts as a sort of mild restrainer halter. Unfortunately this does not really work in practice, except with a rough jute rope halter which must be used with an intermittent, jabbing pressure from the leader, and this is nothing like as effective as a modern restrainer halter.

A webbing halter with a detail of the all-important knot

To fit this sort of halter, be sure that it is a comfortable size, then tie a knot at the loop by passing the lead-rope round the noseband behind the loop and back through it; this will secure it without allowing it to be pulled tighter and tighter.

Whitened halters are used to show the foals of heavy breeds and cobs and some native ponies.

Because the leadrope is 'built in', this design of halter cannot be left on when the horse is at grass or untied in the stable.

LEADROPES

Anyone who has spent any amount of time walking a horse about on the end of a normal-length leadrope, letting him graze, cooling him down, giving him in-hand rehabilitation exercise, or just leading him around for the pleasure of it, will know that the usual length rope today of 6ft (1.8m) is not a lot of use. It is fair enough for tying a horse up, but for most other purposes you need a good bit more. A lungeing rein (25ft or about 7.6m) is better, but rather too long.

What you need is a short rein or a little lunge: this invaluable item is used with a long schooling whip (instead of a lungeing whip) to introduce a youngster to lungeing without having to handle excess coils of rein and the long lungeing whip, and to school a horse from the ground in anything from basic movements to High School. It is simply a rope or short lunge-rein roughly 12ft (3.6m) in length. It is also excellent for leading horses out and about, allowing you and the horse some freedom, and it also means you have enough leeway to 'play' the horse should he spook or jink about, without having to cope with extra loops of rope in your other hand.

These double-length leadropes or short lunge-reins are not readily available from most saddlers, but they should certainly be able to make up such a simple item for you. You could ask them to make up two out of one lunge rein – and you will wonder how you ever managed without them.

Years ago plain-end, double-length leadropes with no clips, buckles or loops on either end were readily available. One end would be threaded through the back (jaw) dee of the headcollar and brought back to the leader, who would then be holding both ends in his or her hands. If the horse managed to break free whilst being led and trod on the rope, he was more than likely to tread on just one of the two ends, and the rope would thus be pulled through the dee without any risk of injury to him. If he were to tread on the end of a clipped-on rope, this would exert considerable force on his head and could very well bring him down. Obviously a knot should not be tied in either of the ends of a double-length rope, as this could easily prevent its being pulled through the dee, which is the whole point of having the longer rope. A good tack shop or saddler should be able to get one of these for you today. If not, try a ship's chandlery or an outdoor or climbing shop, or look in *Yellow Pages* for rope makers and have one made.

Some authorities advise that a rope should not be long enough for the horse to tread on anyway, but this is quite ridiculous and impractical because if the rope is that short it will be of no effective use for leading and tying up.

Kelly Marks teaching a young horse to back away from the slightly unpleasant feeling of Kelly shaking the leadrope. Note the safe length of this long leadrope, which is far more useful than the normal shorter type (Credit: Horse & Rider *Magazine)*

CLIPS AND FASTENINGS

There is a variety of ways of attaching your rope to your horse's headcollar, but the main two devices are the ordinary spring clip and the trigger clip usually found on dogs' leads. Both are good, and the only comment to make, for what it is worth, is that it is generally considered safer to attach the clip with its fastening facing away from the horse's jaw to safeguard against the remote event of the horse getting his lips caught in it – rather obscure, maybe, but it has happened.

There are also, now, several safety-type clips which will release if the horse pulls back determinedly enough when tied up. Their idea is that the rope will snap free and hang down the wall, rather than be left dangling in front of his forelegs when he could bring himself down on it prancing around the stable yard, showground or wherever.

HEADGEAR FOR SHOWING IN-HAND

Because the range of bridles, headcollars and halters for in-hand showing is now so extensive – and to many people, confusing – my advice to those wishing to know more is to study an authoritative book on showing which will surely cover this topic. It might also be helpful to go to a good show and study what the winning entrants wear.

In the UK and Ireland, hacks, riding horses and children's riding ponies often wear coloured, patterned browbands, but hunters (both horses and ponies) have plain leather. Stallions are led in bridles that no one would ever use to ride in, and broodmares, who are probably never ridden in their lives, are shown in hand in full 'riding' double bridles! More British (and Irish) logic! Conventions in America are slightly different from those in the UK and Ireland, but if in doubt it is always safer, certainly in English-style classes, to err on the side of discretion and to go for a look of underplayed elegance in both human and horse. Discreet, tasteful turnout has often won the day for a lesser horse competing against a better but flashily turned out competitor. Of course, much depends on the taste of the judge!

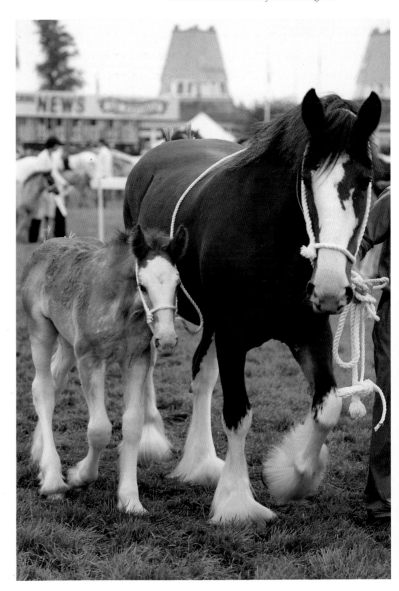

Below: Mother and baby in clean, white rope halters. Note how the foal is being led

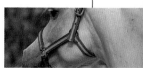

Foals should be shown in a smart leather or white cotton webbing slip with a leather or webbing leadrein. Older but unbroken youngstock wear smart leather headcollars of narrow, stitched leather with brass fittings and maybe a white browband, and with a leather or webbing lead, possibly with a short chain section at the clip end.

Pure-bred Arabs and Arab crosses in particular, but also youngstock of other breeds as long as they have a 'refined head', generally wear a showing headstall made of fine, maybe rolled leather, often decorated with metal or coloured inserts, and with no backstrap under the jaw. At the junction of the noseband and cheekpiece on each side is a ring through which a fairly insubstantial chain is passed: this chain also has small rings on each end and these are caught together under the chin by a clip on the end of the leadrein. When pressure is put on the leadrein, the chain tightens under the jaw and the noseband across the nose, giving a certain amount of control. Unfortunately, many such showing headstalls are not strong and can be easily broken by a robust, unschooled youngster excited by the sights and sounds of the show – how often have you seen some young Arab careering around a showground, having broken loose from one of these?

A finely-rolled Arab showing headstall with coupling for the leadrope attached to the bit

Although it is not essential to show **youngstock** in a bit, it is considered more impressive for three-year-olds. A simple mullen-mouthed snaffle can be used, perhaps of vulcanite or rubber, attached to a showing headcollar (though not the very fine sort) by means of a little bit-strap on the bottom of each cheekpiece. However, most sensible handlers will not wish to risk ruining the mouth of a virtually unbroken youngster by leading directly from a coupling attached to the bit-rings and thence to the leadrein; they will, therefore, buy special couplings which attach to the bit-rings as before but they also attach to the headcollar dee and are adjusted so that the dee and, therefore, the headcollar noseband take most of the pressure before the bit comes into action. Young horses which are broken in or at least mouthed can wear a showing snaffle bridle with the coupling attached to the bit-rings – but this arrangement should only be considered if the handler can be relied on to use it sensitively, and if the animal has been well handled at home, and thoroughly taught to lead in hand, and to behave.

In-hand hunter youngstock – or indeed, any in-hand riding youngstock – can wear this arrangement, or a smart show bridle with coupling and leadrein. Where a double bridle is the norm for in-hand showing, the reins are brought over the head and used as a leadrein; in which case it is advisable to buy long-length reins for this purpose to make leading easier.

Pony youngstock is usually shown in a snaffle bridle with a coloured browband, but a headcollar with or without a bit could also be used. Native pony and cob breeds are often shown in whitened cotton-web halters, as is heavy horse youngstock.

A **stallion** is normally defined as an entire from three years old and will wear a special stallion bridle with a bit. The bridle is strong but not

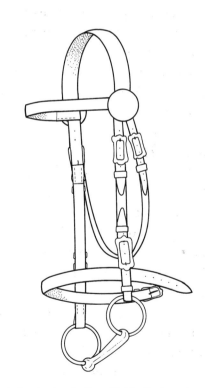

A showing headcollar with bit attachment and straight-bar snaffle bit

A smart, ornate and substantial stallion bridle with characteristic bit

over-heavy, often of stitched, padded leather and usually with a brass browband with a brass disk or boss at each end, depending on breed, fashion and preference. He will usually wear a straight-bar bit, maybe with a port, or perhaps a mullen mouth, and there may be brass horseshoe cheeks, although these are not so common as they used to be. A brass chain coupling is used with a leather or webbing leadrein; this is often longer for stallions in case they rear.

Rollers and side-reins are often used on stallions, particularly of heavy, cob and pony types, partly for appearance but also because they do facilitate control: the side-reins should be attached to the bit-rings and there should be a crupper attached to the roller. A roller on its own without side-reins or crupper looks ridiculous. The subtle positioning and width of a roller can create a significant optical illusion concerning the length of an animal's front or back and his depth of girth. If the roller is wide it 'shortens' the back, as it does if placed a little further back than normal; and vice versa. If you can find a roller with discreet stripes or stitching going the length of it, when on the horse this will create the illusion of a deeper girth. Different breed societies and discipline organisations have different turn-out rules for animals being shown under their auspices, and it is obviously best to check on these. For instance Thoroughbred, Arab and many sport horse stallions and youngstock are not shown in rollers and side-reins and may wear simple jointed snaffle bits. You have to err on the side of safety and control when deciding how to turn out your horses – besides being very careful not to over-feed them, and making sure that you school them well at home to instil discipline.

LEADING 'LAWS'

The following observations regarding safety have little to do with horse equipment, but are rather to do with protection for the handler. First of all, it is always a good plan to wear strong boots, a hard hat and gloves when leading a horse or pony; this may be considered unnecessary and a nuisance, and most people don't do it when just leading around their yard, but it has to be mentioned. To elaborate on the same theme:

LEADING DIFFICULT HORSES

Horses who are difficult to lead in hand can also be improved. Extra control can be obtained by using a bridle but the bit should be used carefully and never roughly. It has a psychological effect on the horse as much as anything else but can come into play when the need arises.

In cases where a difficult or green horse has to be led on a road or somewhere he may play up, such as passing his friends or through a crowd of people, a well-fitting lungeing cavesson should be used, maybe on top of a bridle, with a lead rope attached to the front ring. The bridle reins, if present, should be passed over the head as usual and used for leading, maybe in addition to the rope on the front ring and don't hesitate to use two people in such a case.

The handlers can use schooling whips in their outside hands (one on each side of the horse) to control the quarters when needed.

Another method is to take a long, soft rope or lunge rein, place the middle under the tail, knot the two pieces over the quarters to stop the loop you have formed falling down and again over the withers for the same reason, then pass both free ends through the back dee of the headcollar. At the instant you give the command 'walk on' pull firmly on the rope which will jerk the horse under the tail without hurting him and usually result in his springing forward in surprise and distaste!

A few horses will baulk and may even try to sit down, run backwards or half-rear, but they are in the minority. In any case, to be ready for this, start the horse off in a corner such as that made by two meeting lines of fencing, a corner of a building or, ideally, a holly or hawthorn bush. When the horse tries his usual backward rush he will be met by either solid resistance or very uncomfortable prickles. Interestingly, a horse will always learn best a lesson he seems to have taught himself rather than had inflicted on him by humans.

Keep repeating the procedure and the command at exactly the same time so the horse is sure to associate the two and a vast improvement will become apparent in no time.

* The boots should have protective toe-caps but not of metal, as half a ton of horse standing on a metal toe-cap can easily press it into your foot, and being metal, it will not spring back but will stay there, maybe causing severe and dangerous pressure to your toes. Toe-caps can be of reinforced leather, or one of the protective synthetics now available. Rubber riding boots, wellingtons and so on are useless for protection.

* A hard hat up to your national standard could save your life, either from your head hitting the road, or from the horse kicking you should you trip, fall or be brought down.

* A sudden pull or head movement from the led horse, or a meaningful effort to get away, can tear the leadrope through your hands and badly burn them; gloves not only give a firmer grip but will also help prevent friction burn.

* It is a good idea to tie a knot in the end of an ordinary leadrope so it will be less easily pulled right out of the hand.

* Always make sure your yard gates are kept firmly closed, and are never left hooked or wedged open, so that any horses which get free cannot get on to a public highway or anywhere they should not be.

* When leading a horse in a public place or any unenclosed area, he should always be led in a bridle and bit, a lungeing cavesson with the leadrope clipped to the front ring, or a restrainer halter. An ordinary headcollar is not safe enough as it offers hardly any control, as explained above. Difficult or very strong horses should be led in such areas by two handlers, one on each side, obviously with a rope or rein each and maybe a long schooling whip in their outside hands.

Top right: Correct leading practice. The horse is being led in a well fitting headcollar with the handler wearing a hard hat, gloves and sensible boots, holding the horse near the headcollar and carrying the spare end safely in the other hand

Right: When teaching foals to lead, use your arms around breast and buttocks to control and guide

6 RUGS and SHEETS

Every horse is equipped with a perfectly good coat to keep him warm enough, and cool enough, in the climates in which he and/or his ancestors evolved. We may not like the almost furry look of some equine winter coats, or we may despair at having to buy expensive rugs for a Thoroughbred whose winter coat is useless against our regional climate – but the animal's genes simply produce what his evolution developed. When removed from that climate, or asked to do physical work such as he would never do in the wild, his coat – or the insufficiency of it – can cause problems. In the UK and Ireland the climate is termed 'temperate' (although it seems to be gradually changing, as are many other regions of the world); North America has a very wide climate range, Australia somewhat less so, and New Zealand is rather like the UK but milder and windier, especially in the North Island.

THE SKIN AND COAT

The horse's coat grows from the lower layer of skin, the dermis, and protects the skin from outside influences including the weather. Nerve endings in the dermis detect temperature, pressure, friction, pleasure, irritation, vibration and pain. The dermis also contains blood vessels and

TERMINOLOGY

In the USA, horse garments are called blankets. In the UK, horses' top garments are called rugs, and blankets have the same definition as the household article – they are placed underneath the rug for extra warmth, and can only be kept on by means of fastening the whole lot with a separate roller or surcingle. Because of this necessity, and the final acceptance throughout most of the UK and Ireland of the type of horse clothing which does not need separate rollers, blankets are used less and less now. In the same way, the word 'sheet' does not mean the household article: it refers, first, to a lighterweight top garment of linen or cotton used – though less nowadays – in summer (in the UK it is called a summer sheet); and also to a short one without a front used under the saddle for exercising fine-coated or clipped horses in winter – in the UK it is called an exercise or quarter sheet, because it is used during exercise to cover the (hind)quarters.

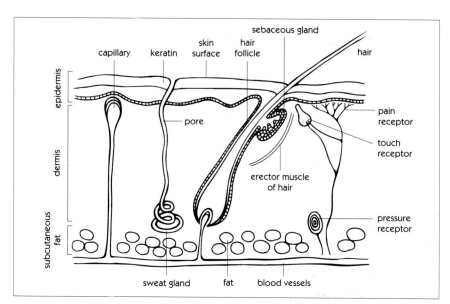

Cross-section of the skin and hair

capillaries for supplying oxygen and nutrients and removing waste products; it contains sweat glands to help remove waste products, excess moisture and body heat; and oil glands which produce sebum to lubricate the skin and coat and make them water- and friction-resistant. Each hair has a tiny erector muscle at its base to raise or flatten it, in response to nervous messages. This action increases or decreases insulation: when the hairs (which are themselves hollow) are raised, the warm-air layer next to the skin is increased and the animal is warmer; but when they are flattened, the warm-air layer is much thinner so the animal is cooler.

The equine's summer coat is short and fine and his winter one longer and thicker, both for obvious reasons, although there are considerable differences in these qualities depending on the type of horse or pony he is, where his ancestors evolved, where he now lives and how he is kept.

The hair also grows in directional patterns and whorls which help with water run-off. (The whorls such as are often found on the head, at the roots of the mane hair and the flanks, as well as some other areas, are believed by some people, not without foundation, to reveal a horse's character and temperament, if you know how to read them.)

THE POINT OF CLOTHING

Horses, depending on their type, can survive in world-wide extremes of climate, and the clothing made for them ranges from that with waterproofing and/or polar-type insulation, to fine sheets aimed at protecting them from the sun and insects. As with many animals and humans, humidity is one of the horse's worst enemies: it seems that they do not

These native ponies's natural coats are better than any rugs. The top photograph shows a Shetland in summer coat and the bottom one shows an Exmoor in furry winter coat

Left: Removing all or part of a horse's natural winter coat, as in this trace clip, deprives him of warmth and protection which rugs cannot entirely make up for

Below: This Shetland pony in traditional show condition has a shorter, shinier summer coat than he would ever have normally

thrive as well in humid regions as in drier ones, regardless of the ambient temperature.

Most horse people in westernised societies like their horses to look sleek, smooth and shiny, although feral horses are rarely in this condition; they are usually dirty by our standards, like a horse at grass, with plenty of mud, grease and dandruff in their coats, and they look rough – except perhaps at the height of summer (as long as the sun is not excessive, when it can bleach and burn the hair and also the skin if the coat is fine). Only at that time do they approach our artificial standards of what a horse's coat should look like.

More important from the point of view of the horse's well-being, is the thickness and length of the coat. If we are going to work a horse at a time of year when his natural coat would be long and thick, we usually clip some or all of it off, believing that he will otherwise sweat off condition and will become chilled or even hypothermic because his long coat will hold heat-conducting moisture which causes body heat to pass out too quickly. There is no scientific evidence for either of these points however, and in practice, I have not found that a horse 'sweats off condition' or that one sensibly managed becomes chilled (only a callous idiot would leave a wet horse standing around in a cold wind, but it does happen). These two points would make an interesting research project for someone....

Working on the above theory, the point of using clothing on horses is mainly to keep them warm and dry in winter, particularly if they are clipped and working, or if horses with fine or clipped coats are turned out in inclement winter weather. Summer clothing was originally designed to protect the coats of stabled horses from dust, and to help keep off flies.

Today there are other purposes for clothing. The development of

innovations in horse-clothing textiles has probably moved faster than any other field of equestrian equipment. Winter clothing has moved on from traditional fabrics such as wool, jute and canvas, although these are still available, so that we have all sorts of synthetics with various qualities (not all of which are present in all fabrics); these include the following:

* **Moisture removal** (strangely called 'wicking', at least in the UK). This implies that the fabric actually draws moisture away from the horse, although in fact only fabrics which are actually hydrophilic can do that. The term 'hydrophilic' means having an attraction to water: thus rugs with what the manufacturers call a 'hydrophilic layer' or 'coating' are said to work by means of the horse's body heat activating the proofing, which then attracts moisture molecules into the fabric and through to the outside air, so drying off the horse whether he is wet from water or sweat.

* **Permeability**. Permeable or 'breatheable' fabrics are passive, allowing

Below: The Day Son & Hewitt heat-retaining Solarium Rug contains a panel of Mirotec, a material which reflects heat back into the body to boost circulation whilst also allowing moisture to pass through to the outside. It is claimed to help horses recover after hard work and to help them warm up beforehand and is said to help back and muscle injury, hypothermia and osteoarthritis

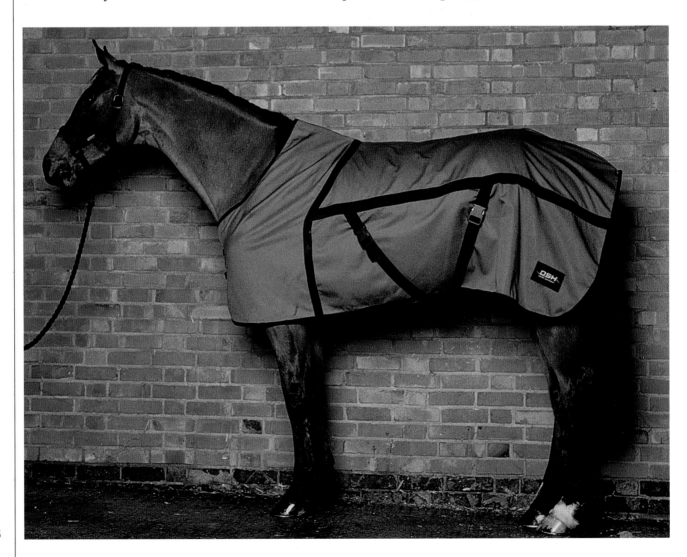

the horse's body moisture and heat to pass through to the outside air, but they do not actively draw moisture away unless they are also hydrophilic. They do help to maintain a more pleasant atmosphere next to the horse, and because of this quality, are probably healthier for him to wear than a non-permeable fabric would be (such as a rubber, plastic or solid polyurethane coating) which will not allow moisture or excess heat to escape, or sweat to evaporate (like wrapping him in a polythene bag), so you end up with a hot, wet horse, depending on his activity.

* **Heat retention.** Some fabrics are claimed to be capable of reflecting body heat back on to the horse, and not letting it out to the outside. Some are very effective: an acquaintance of mine once sent a horse to a rehabilitation centre where he was put in a loose-box (US: box stall) with a heat lamp whilst wearing such a rug and he ended up with hyperthermia.

* **Temperature regulation.** At the time of writing, one firm has developed a 'highly advanced double-weave fabric which has reflective qualities, allowing your horse to maintain an even body temperature' so that he remains cool in summer. This should be a boon to performance horses and ponies working in hot weather.

* **Protection from excessive sunlight.** Several rugs are now available which are made from fabrics with stated SPF ratings (sun protection factor ratings148) to help protect horses' coats and skins from bleaching and burning.

* **Protection from insects.** Although almost any fabric normally used for rugs would stop insects making direct contact, most would make their wearers far too hot for comfort, besides which some flies can bite through thick fabric. However, some fabrics are now available which are very fine but apparently do stop insects biting through them. One is being developed at present which is very lightweight, permeable and which has a built-in smell said to repel insects – an interesting item to watch out for.

SYNTHETIC VERSUS NATURAL FABRICS

NATURAL FABRICS

These are, of course, completely permeable or 'breatheable' by nature. Good quality cotton, linen and woollen fabrics can last a long time if well cared for and kept repaired, and they are said to be easier for a saddler to repair than synthetic fabrics. They usually drape well around the body, and if the general fit is correct, may well be more comfortable for the horse, particularly woollen winter stable rugs. Woollen rugs and sheets are certainly warmer than most quilted synthetics.

On the down side, natural fabrics hold moisture and are generally heavier than synthetics. Wet, natural-fabric turn-out and New Zealand rugs are very heavy to handle and presumably for the horse to wear, and most natural fabrics are not as easy to launder as synthetics.

SYNTHETIC FABRICS

These have a wider range of qualities than natural ones, although not all are permeable. They are usually non-absorbent, and lighter both to handle and to wear. Many can be washed and dried at home, although some of the bulkier ones will certainly not fit in a domestic washing machine. However, we tend to feel that they are warmer than some of them actually are, and it is not always true that the thicker the quilting or filling, the warmer the rug. On the other hand some, particularly the heat-retaining ones, make a horse much too hot. Also the non-permeable fabrics are not 'healthy' for the horse to wear: they can cause sweating, and moisture retention inside the rug, and so produce an ideal breeding environment for skin disease micro-organisms.

In general, it seems that synthetics are excellent for turn-out and New Zealand rugs and where real waterproofing is required – for instance, if you have to hack out on a rainy day (provided your exercise sheet has a permeable lining to take up sweat from the horse). On other wintry days, even in showers, I have never found anything to equal a woollen exercise sheet: they are warm and breatheable so the horse stays at an equable temperature, and dry even when the rug is damp on the outer surface due to a shower, since water will not soak through wool; also they stay in place much better than anything else, are comfortable for the horse if put on properly (pulled well up into the saddle gullet all the way along), and easily dried on a central heating radiator. Modern wool can often be washed on the wool cycle in a domestic washer, though it should not be tumble-dried.

For stable use, my favourite rug in all but very cold weather is the Goldson acrylic fleece stable rug. Made on a cottage-industry basis in England, it has an elasticated neckline which

Top right: The Goldson stable fleece rug in use on the author's old Thoroughbred mare. Made of knitted acrylic fleece, it is lightweight, warm and comfortable like a cosy jumper, with its stretchy, knitted texture, elasticated neckline, back edge darts and leg straps. It is not bulky, and machine washes and dries very quickly with no shrinking. The one shown here, bought 'off the peg', could be deeper

Bottom right: A lightweight rug from Bucas which is both waterproof and breathable. Bucas say that its Active Stay-Dry lining makes it a 'high performance turnout rug'

Below: The Goldson turnout rug has an elasticated neckline to help keep it forward

Bottom: The Shires Tempest Rug is technologically advanced, resulting in warmth, durability and permeability

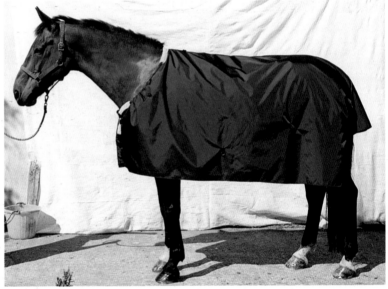

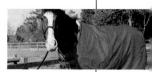

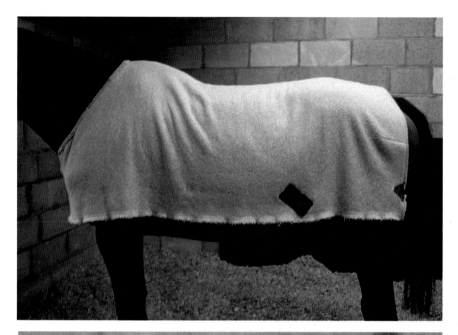

Apart from general suitability, we all want our rugs to be comfortable for our horse and to be long-wearing. Running repairs and regular laundering or dry cleaning are essential for this. I emphasise the 'clean' bit because so very many people think nothing of standing their horses in filthy rugs for a whole winter, only having them cleaned or washed once a year in the spring! This does the fabric no good at all, because grit and decaying organic debris rot it, which encourages skin disease and infestation with insects. All rugs should be given plenty of chance to air daily, and not just be folded up or dumped in a corner when removed — and in the case of turn-out rugs, these should be allowed to dry properly before the next day's use — and surely normal standards of cleanliness and hygiene should tell owners when a rug is dirty!

One quality of synthetic fabrics that promotes a long life is that they are often what is called 'rip-stop'. Of a special reinforcing weave, this means that a rug's outer fabric is extremely tear-resistant, so is a godsend for turn-out rugs and horses which tear their rugs.

Some rugs suffer constantly from seams that come undone, or tear along their length. Reinforcing strips or pads are often placed, particularly at the withers, on stable rugs and turn-out rugs, and the latter may have protective flaps which run their length; these protect them from wear, but are mainly intended to make them leak-proof, or at least leak-resistant. Seams on outdoor rugs should be stitched with thread which will swell at the same rate as the fabric to help ensure that rainwater does not get in through the needle-holes. There is no way to decide this in the shop: I find the best plan is to contact the manufacturers and really quiz them for an answer.

helps to keep it forward (an idea which has been copied by others now) and is ruched round the neckline so there is plenty of room for the horse's shoulders — it will not rub him in this area, nor will his movement be restricted. (New Zealand rugs are available in a waterproof synthetic fabric and are the firm's main line.)

The stable rug comes in a jersey fabric with fleece next to the horse, and is as cosy as a soft, fleecy jumper. Several features make for a super-light, cheap, comfortable and warm stable rug: the elasticated gathered neckline, the darted back end (for shaping), the fabric which moulds to the horse's body, and the hindleg straps. My late-lamented old Thoroughbred mare had high withers which were entirely white-haired along the top from possibly a lifetime of badly fitting rugs (and probably saddles) before I bought her at 23 years old, but never had any more

problems once I discovered Goldson rugs. One rug on top of the other copes with all but the coldest UK winters; however, I found that the bottom one tended to slip back underneath the top one (they never slipped when worn alone), and they also did this when used as an extra under the New Zealand rug. I never solved that problem, but stopped it in the stable by putting on the top rug slightly behind the bottom one; I would also put the top rug's straps through the bottom rug's grippers and clips, which helped keep them together.

FITTING AND FASTENING

Decades ago, when the British were still clothing their horses with rugs and separate rollers (a few still are), a friend brought me back from America a weird-looking garment called a Baker blanket. This was very horse-shaped, with an appropriately undulating back seam and darted shaping. It was cut right back at the withers (like a Lane Fox/cow-mouthed saddle) to avoid pressure, which I thought was a brilliant idea – but it also had no attached, conventional surcingle or roller to go with it, but the bewildering and totally useless feature (so I thought) of dangerous-looking straps which, horror

An uncomfortable, old-fashioned rugging arrangement thankfully not often seen today. Anti-cast rollers were/are meant to prevent a horse rolling right over against a wall and becoming cast, but they can cause significant and often unrecognised bruising to the back, because when the horse rolls in them they jab him in the back exactly where the saddle goes. Rollers round the ribcage like this are also most uncomfortable compared with belly surcingles and leg straps

of horrors, went somehow or other fairly loosely underneath the horse; there was no fillet string, and I could not see how it could possibly stay on or be safe. I had never seen anything like it, and simply did not believe my benefactor when he said that the Baker was the most-used and best 'blanket' in the States – even the word 'blanket' was strange, too, since I understood this to mean something that went underneath the rug.

'Just try it', said my friend. 'I'll help you!' (He could see I wasn't capable of sorting it out myself.) We fiddled around putting it on, and once I had got my head round the new design – the self-righting shaping, the lack of a tight 'belt' round my horse's middle, and the warmth of it (not needing a separate blanket) – I began to think that perhaps we British did not have all the answers after all!

Well, I used and loved the Baker blanket for many winters, and gladly put up with the derisory comments of stablemates who would rush to my horse's box every morning hoping to see it trampled on the floor, hanging round his neck, in shreds and whatever else. But it never was: it stayed beautifully in place, kept him warm and cosy, and as you might imagine, he lay down much more in the Baker than he had in his old-fashioned contraption with a roller round his ribcage.

Soon after I got the Baker I became aware of the Emston New Zealand rug which was becoming available in Britain; this works on much the same principles as the Baker: self-righting due to the shaping, hindleg straps in this case, and darts and a drawstring round the back edge to create individual fit. I bought one of these, too, and it worked beautifully, and I could not understand why other owners thought I was mad and stuck rigidly to their separate, unshaped rugs and awful rollers. Then a few years later, horse-shaped, self-righting stable rugs started to creep onto the British market – not imported Bakers, but other firms' designs, and now it is fairly unusual to see a horse kitted out in an antiquated and uncomfortable rug and roller.

CORRECT SIZE AND FIT

We tend to forget that horses often wear their rugs for many hours a day, sometimes all the time, and immense discomfort and injury can be caused by badly fitting rugs, certainly equal to that of a badly fitting saddle. Also, any rug should be removed, the horse checked and the rug carefully replaced and readjusted, or changed if necessary, at least twice a day.

Rugs are made in 3in (7.6cm) size increments, although a few are now sold in metric sizes in the UK.

MAGNETIC RUGS

In line with the current vast interest in complementary therapies, there is now available on the market a wide range of therapeutic magnetic aids for horses. Boots, wraps and rugs of various sorts contain magnetic inserts in pockets or sewn into the garments. Some work by means of electrically pulsed 'doses' of magnetism which require an inbuilt battery or which work off the mains. Others have 'free' magnets inserted at strategic points depending on the area to be treated.

Many people feel that magnetic therapy has helped both themselves and their animals but just how does it work? There are various theories, none of which are yet proven. A GP who often wears a magnetic wrist strap on the advice of his practice's physiotherapist told the author 'I'm quite willing to believe that it may improve the oxygen-carrying capacity of the haemoglobin in the blood. This may, in turn, help a variety of other systems of the body to function better, not least those biochemical systems which remove toxins from the soft tissues such as muscles and ligaments, also the joints'. This may well be the case because haemoglobin carries iron in the blood, and iron is a metal to which magnets are attracted, so it is not surprising that the blood may be affected by magnetism.

Another theory is that a magnetic field is generated which may increase molecular agitation within the blood and so improve its efficiency to carry oxygen and dispose of waste products.

Electrically pulsed magnetism is claimed to work much better than other sorts, but there is no doubting that very many people and animals seem to have benefited from the therapy in general.

Photograph courtesy of MagnetoPulse

To measure a horse for the right size:

Measure from the centre of his breast, along his side to the back edge of his thigh; this will give you the length (and so the size) of rug he needs. The following pointers are all important in getting the right fit – size is only one element.

* The rug should extend right back to the root of the tail, and slightly beyond it in a turn-out rug, for extra protection. Rugs, and particularly exercise sheets and coolers put on performance horses when they are hot, are often much too short and finish on the croup, leaving a crucial muscle mass unprotected.

* In depth, the rug should come just below the horse's elbow and stifle; extra-deep rugs, particularly in turn-out styles, are available, designed to minimise the circulation of draughts under the belly.

* Unless it is cut back at the withers (which very few rugs are in the UK), the rug must come in front of the withers, and the neckline must come up around the base of the neck; it should not lie down around or even behind the withers and shoulders as is so often seen, where it can dig in and rub, causing discomfort, restricted action and injury. Its front

BESPOKE RUGS

With a horse which is very difficult to fit, and/or very sensitive to wearing clothing, it is a good plan to get his rugs made to measure. This also allows you to incorporate your own features – and you never know, you could find yourself with a new business!

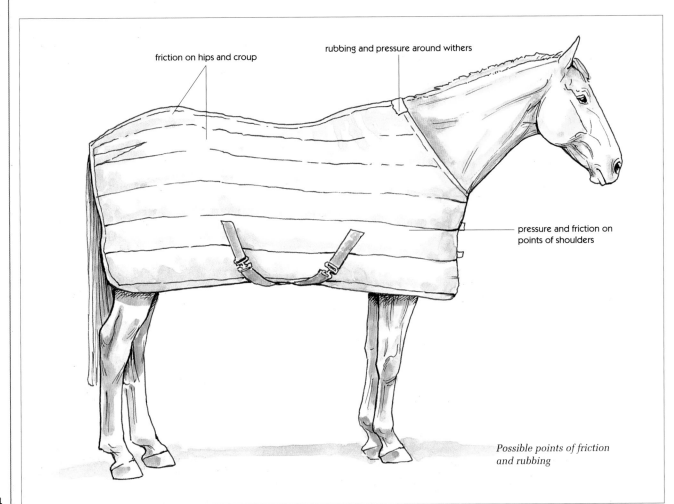

friction on hips and croup

rubbing and pressure around withers

pressure and friction on points of shoulders

Possible points of friction and rubbing

must be sufficiently roomy so there are no creases radiating out from the point of the shoulder, because this would indicate pulling and pressure at these points. With good shaping this is less likely, but it is still important to have the size and roominess.

* The rug must be strongly horse-shaped with a good rise for the withers, dropping down for the back, rising again for the croup, and dropping down towards the root of the tail; only with this shaping do you have any chance of approaching even, light weight-bearing down the horse's spine. Note particularly that there are no creases radiating down from the withers, because these indicate pulling and damaging pressure. This point is most important, and the most difficult one to get right: my experience is that in the UK it is almost impossible to get rugs that fit Thoroughbred horses at the withers, or any horse with reasonably prominent withers, a feature often found in a good riding horse since it is this which aids saddle stability. Stitching padding under the withers does not alleviate the problem because it does not stop the pressure.

* The breaststrap/s must fasten so that the horse can get his head down to eat and root in his bedding, turn his head and neck right round, or to graze if it is a turn-out rug, without discomfort and without creating an unreasonable pull on the withers; yet the breast fastening must also effectively prevent the rug slipping back, which it will do readily if too big. You should be able to slide your hand easily all round the neckline and over the withers.

* If the rug fastens with cross-over surcingles, you should be able to get the width of your hand sideways between them and the horse, and the same goes for leg straps, fore or hind. This fitting also applies to a fillet string if there is one; this lies behind the thighs under the tail to stop a rug, particularly an exercise sheet, from blowing up over the horse's back in a wind and frightening him.

* Turn-out and New Zealand rugs should be a slightly roomier fit than stable rugs, and the back edge should extend a few inches past the root of the tail for extra protection. On a normal-depth rug, you should only just be able to see the hindleg straps below the rug's bottom edge.

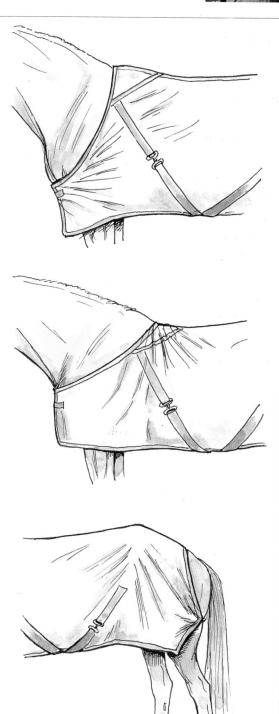

Top: A neckline which is far too loose and is pressing hard on the shoulders. It should be up round the base of the neck

Centre: Another effect of a loose neckline, here having slipped behind the withers and exerting a bruising pull on them

Bottom: A rug which is not shaped at the back end and is probably too short, being pulled forward from the front, pressing on the hip bones and via the fillet string behind the thighs

TO RUG OR NOT TO RUG?

Another awful trend which is now very prevalent is the practice of rugging up horses and ponies when they do not need it – and when they do, of using far too many rugs and under-rugs, and even old bed duvets. Basically, horses should only be rugged up for warmth when the horse himself feels chilly or cold, not when we think he might be.

Horses, like people, vary in their sensitivity to cold, but in general, horses withstand cold much better than we do. They are also unlikely to be bothered by cold, still and dry weather. What they hate are cold and wet conditions, especially when combined with wind. (I feel strongly that horses turned out at any time of year should always have access to effective shelter, except in really mild, fly-free weather; but few do.)

Obvious signs of cold are a staring coat or a miserable-looking horse wanting to come in, and of course actual shivering; otherwise the best way to tell if a horse is cold is to feel the base of his ears and to place the flat of your hand on his belly, flanks, loins and quarters. Allow a few seconds for any heat to come through to your hand, especially if the horse is not clipped, and only then decide whether or not he really needs a rug.

Reflective strips like the ones shown here on the Shires Tempest rug are an excellent aid to visibility when leading in the dark. Ideally, on a public highway in the UK, this handler should be on the horse's off (right) side between the horse and the traffic, and should himself be wearing reflective clothing; most importantly of all, he should also be carrying a light on his right showing red to the rear and white to the front. The rug also includes a tail flap (shown right) to shield this vulnerable area from bad weather

It is also important to remember that the natural insulating qualities of a dry coat are excellent, and that putting a rug on top of a full coat in winter will flatten it and partly remove the warm-air layer, thus certainly defeating your object in still, dry weather. Unclipped horses should not need rugs when stabled in a decent box with good ventilation but no draughts. Outdoor horses may well benefit from a rug to protect them from wind, rain, sleet, hail and snow. In summer, a light sheet to protect susceptible ones from sun and flies may be a help.

The practice of turning out horses and ponies in heavy rugs in warm weather to keep them clean is, to my mind, really unkind: if you must put on a rug in these circumstances, do make it a very lightweight one. Another practice which I think is actually cruel is to load animals with rugs in the belief that this will encourage the summer coat to come through early in the year. However, the main factor in coat change is actually exposure to light, not excessive rugging: horses exposed to light (natural or full-spectrum artificial light) for sixteen hours a day from Christmas onwards will cast their winter coats well in time for the earliest shows without suffer-

156

ing the extreme discomfort, itchy skin and overheating – and, incidentally, often spoiled coats – caused by too many rugs.

People who clip their horses in winter when they really do not need it and then pile on rugs to keep them warm are also, in my view, being unkind to their horses and not employing effective or humane horse management. Many working owners do not have time to give their horses enough exercise even to take the itch out of their heels, let alone work up a sweat, and to give such a horse any more than a bib clip (breast and gullet) or low trace or Irish clip is not being fair to the horse. Lightly clipped horses need fewer rugs (possibly none on good days) so will be more comfortable, and they can also be turned out for longer which is better for them than being stabled most of the time.

Conversely, few things are more cruel than leaving a sensitive horse out in bad weather with no protection. Many finely bred horses and ponies die of this each winter, or end up like skeletons in the care of horse rescue charities. A properly fitting, well designed rug is a real boon to such a horse, but still does not take the place of a good field shed or run-in barn, and possibly being stabled at night with a good bed, and plenty of roughage to keep him warm with its slow-release energy – and, of course, ample clean water.

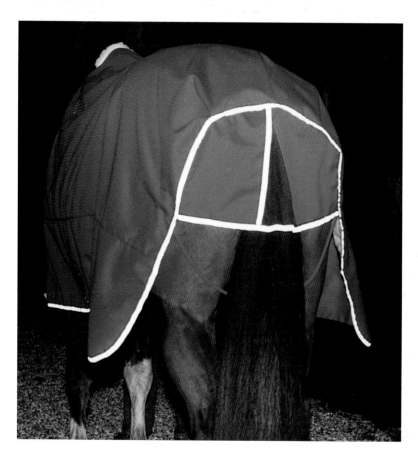

TAKE CARE

Because many people seem to think that clothing is not as important as tack itself, I should like to end on two warning notes.

A dressage horse, noted for his extravagant foreleg and shoulder action, was given a winter off work due to a back injury; he was sent by his owner to a trusted friend who would care for him. He had company, shelter, a good stable and correct feeding and was checked, fed and groomed daily – everything he needed to recuperate. He was also equipped for his days in the field with a very expensive turn-out rug. An observer mentioned that the rug was not big enough in front and was pulling on the horse's shoulders and withers, and round the tops of his front legs. The carer, however, could not see this, despite having the problem areas pointed out to her.

The horse returned home in the spring, back injury healed, and went back into work – but his action had changed, his extensions were a shadow of what they had been, and in passage and piaffe he did not 'lift' as he had before. Several months of steady, knowledgeable work produced little improvement, and it was not until the previously mentioned observer met the owner and her horse (they knew each other slightly) at a competition that the problem was traced back to months of wearing a restrictive, badly fitting rug.

The horse had apparently developed the habit of shortening his action and changing his muscle use to avoid the discomfort of the rug, and hours a day of this had ruined his action. His previous flamboyance never returned, despite physiotherapy and careful remedial exercises – all because of a rug that was top of its range, but did not fit the horse for whom it was bought.

The final story is really tragic, but not unusual. An international three-day event horse, a handsome and kind-natured chap who lived at a big teaching centre, was turned out by a student into his paddock for his daily run. The student adjusted the legstraps on his turn-out rug so they were a little too long, to give him plenty of room to stride and move about. But when getting up from rolling, he managed to end up with both hind legs inside one strap and broke a leg in his struggles to free himself. He had to be put down.

Failure to realise the potentially disastrous consequences of badly fitting clothing had therefore ruined the career of one horse and killed another.

7 PROTECTIVE EQUIPMENT

One of the most vulnerable parts of our athletic horses is undoubtedly their legs, and this chapter is mainly about the boots and bandages available to protect them. Lameness is most likely to occur in the feet and lower legs as a result of stress and strain, concussion, torsion (twist) injuries and wounds such as kicks, over-reaches, brushing or interfering generally; it might also be caused by cuts from wire, glass (unusually) or litter and equipment that has been left lying around. The source of lameness is less likely the further up the leg you go.

Many people go much too far in protecting their horses from the hazards of life, some to the extent that they don't allow them any time at liberty at all, not even in a small, enclosed space, for fear of them hurting themselves: truly this is being downright unkind to the horse. Horses do not go wild and turn themselves inside out at liberty when they are used to their daily turnout, and they certainly stay stronger, fitter, healthier and happier when they can remain gently – or sometimes not so gently – on the move most of the time, as they were designed to be.

Many owners and carers fit protective boots to their horses during turnout, and this is fine because these may well help to prevent knocks, cuts and bruises, and may also lessen concussion and strain, depending on the type of boots.

The tendons at the backs of the horse's legs – known as the superficial digital flexor tendons – have hardly any skin and connective tissue to protect them from external or self-inflicted injury, the front tendons probably being most at risk from impact by the hind toes. Thus combined tendon/heel/brushing boots (which are available, though you might have to search around the suppliers to find them) are undoubtedly a good idea.

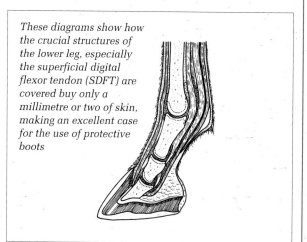

These diagrams show how the crucial structures of the lower leg, especially the superficial digital flexor tendon (SDFT) are covered buy only a millimetre or two of skin, making an excellent case for the use of protective boots

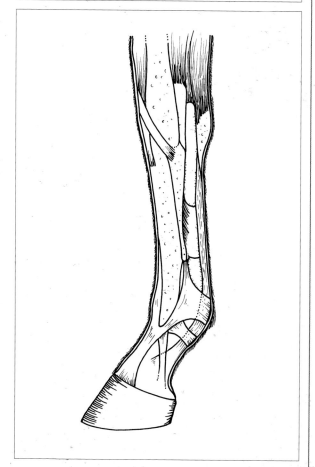

159

BOOTS

The range of boots on the market now is vast in every country where horses are popular, and it is not easy for novice owners to choose the right sort.

BRUSHING AND SPEEDICUT BOOTS

These are probably the most common boots in use, to the extent that they may be used when not needed, or when another type of boot would be more appropriate. Brushing boots protect a horse who brushes or hits the inside of one leg (called brushing or interfering) low down with the opposite hoof, and speedicut boots reach higher up the leg to just below the knee or hock, to protect against similar injury in those parts; the hind boots are always longer than the fore boots. They have a protective hard shield which fits around the inside of the fetlock and up the inside of the leg.

They must be fastened (usually with velcro or patented fastenings, but sometimes still with straps and buckles) so that the fastenings are on the outside of the leg, pointing backwards (this is normal for most similar boots). This is so the horse cannot kick the fastenings open, and if they are pointing backwards, they are less likely to be pulled open or caught up when the horse goes through scrub or undergrowth. The lowest strap should always be fastened first so that the boot cannot slip down over the hoof as you put it on and trip the horse should he move; for the same reason they should always be undone from the top strap down. They must fit snugly enough so they will stay firmly in place, but not so tightly that they will be uncomfortable and possibly hamper the action of the tendons or even restrict circulation.

FETLOCK OR ANKLE BOOTS

These are a shorter version of brushing boots and used for the same purpose. Some pass underneath the fetlock to protect the ergot (that little piece of horn growing down out of the point of the fetlock).

HEEL BOOTS

Like fetlock boots with ergot protection, these pass under the ergot and are normally used during fast work or jumping when the ergot may be pressed to the ground during galloping or landing from a jump. Combined heel/fetlock and brushing or speedicut boots are available.

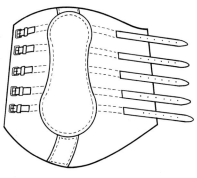

A brushing boot with hardened shield to cover the inside of the fetlock and lower cannon arca

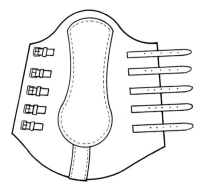

Speedicut boots reach higher up the leg than brushing boots

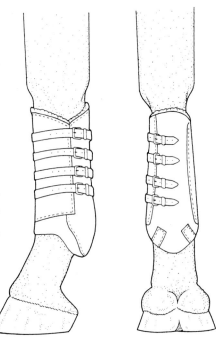

Heel boots do not actually protect the heels but the ergots on the points of the fetlocks

YORKSHIRE BOOTS

These are simple soft pads of thick synthetic fabric or felt with a tape round the middle. Cheap and effective, they are useful for horses whose interference at the fetlock is only slight and who just go a little close behind. The tape is fastened round just above the fetlock, tied on the outside of the leg in a firm but not tight bow, and the top part of the fabric turned down to cover it, as shown in the picture.

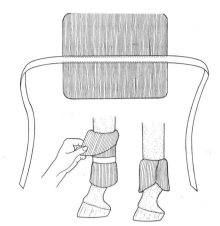

Yorkshire boots simple but effective

FETLOCK RING BOOT OR ANTI-BRUSHING RING

These are not so successful at preventing interference as the Yorkshire boots described above. A ring boot is simply a rubber ring fitted only to the leg which needs protecting, just above the fetlock. It acts to keep the opposite leg and foot away from the leg wearing it, but horses often become upset by the way the ring interferes with their natural action, and some horses trip because of this.

Anti-brushing ring

SAUSAGE BOOTS

These are much thicker than fetlock ring boots, and are fitted round the pasterns to prevent the horse bruising his own elbows on the heels of his shoes when he lies down; they are not for use during exercise.

POLO BOOTS

Polo boots are like heavy-duty brushing boots; they usually come right down over the pastern and coronet, fastening around the pastern to stop them flapping around, as well as with the usual straps further up the leg. They can have conventional fastenings, or they can be fastened with cohesive bandages (which adhere to themselves only and can be reused) which can also be sewn on – this makes a very secure fastening. Velcro is not secure enough for polo boots or, in my view, any active pursuit.

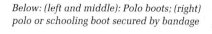

Below: (left and middle): Polo boots; (right) polo or schooling boot secured by bandage

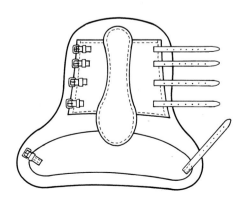
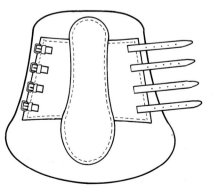
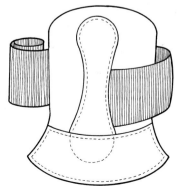

OVER-REACH OR BELL BOOTS

Although pull-on boots are still available – the bane of countless grooms' and owners' lives – there is now no need to struggle with them, as many kinds can be bought today that are split, and fasten with easy-to-manage fastenings. These boots are excellent for stopping a horse treading on his own front heels and coronets, and are used during work, particularly for horses prone to over-reaching, during travelling (maybe on all four feet to prevent sideways treads), and usually when a horse is lunged.

Note, however, that these boots can rub sensitive horses around the pastern and must be fitted with care. They must not touch the ground at the back, as this sets up a constant chafe; some of the more advanced designs have fabric protection inside the tops. Also available are patented designs made in petal or leaf sections which stop the boot turning upside-down when on, a very common occurrence with the old type.

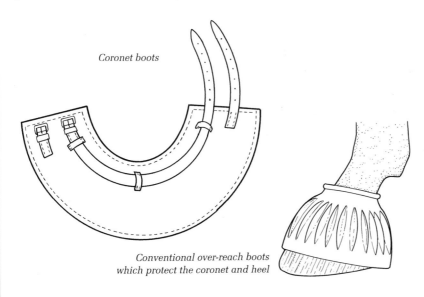

Coronet boots

Conventional over-reach boots which protect the coronet and heel

TENDON BOOTS

Tendon boots are intended to protect the front tendons against the horse's own hind feet: they cannot, and do not, protect the tendons from stress and strain. They are therefore good for horses likely to hit into themselves and for use in the field, particularly if you can find the combined tendon/brushing boots for the forelegs. They have a thick pad which fits down the back of the lower leg, and are often fitted with a leather-covered bar-shaped pad on the inside to provide side protection too. These features also help to keep the boots in place.

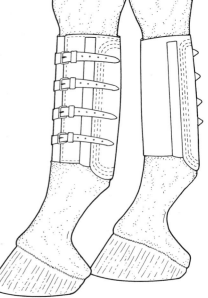

Tendon boots. The reinforcing protective 'bars' can be seen down the sides, plus the padding down the back. It is a common mistake to use these boots back to front as shin boots

SHIN BOOTS

These have pads down the front rather than down the back, to protect the front of the cannon bone against knocks when jumping; they can therefore usefully be put on all four legs.

TRAVELLING BOOTS

Many styles of these boots are now available, usually with integral knee and hock protection. They are simply padded 'leggings' that reach from a point above the knee and the hock, down to the hoof, covering the coronet and often the heel, too. They are much easier and quicker to apply than bandages over padding combined with knee pads and hock boots, and probably do a better job.

KNEE PADS

These come in two types: full knee pads with a woollen or synthetic surround, for travelling; and skeleton knee pads for exercise. They consist of a padded upper band with fastenings that lie on the outside of the leg and just above the knee, below this a hardened shield which covers the front of the knee, and a strap to keep it loosely in place. The top band needs to be fastened very snugly to prevent the knee pad slipping down when the horse is moving, but the lower strap must be fastened more or less as loosely as possible to prevent any interference with the horse's knee action, and so there is no pull on the shield which would encourage the top band to slip down.

HOCK BOOTS

These come in various designs, but generally consist of a padded, sometimes hardened, section which fits over the point of the hock to protect the horse when travelling, or in the stable if he is the type who injures himself on the walls. Again, the top strap fastens snugly around the top of the hock but not too tightly, bearing in mind that it encircles a main tendon here, and the bottom strap fastens more loosely.

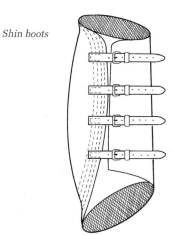

Shin boots

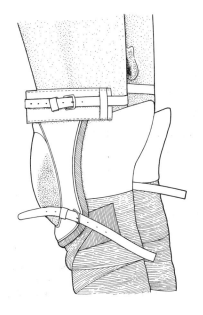

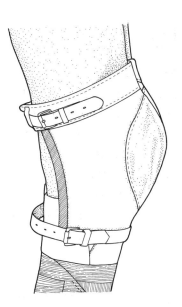

Right: Knee pads used here for travelling in conjunction with stable or travelling bandages and padding. Skeleton pads are used for exercising by some people

Far right: Hock boots, used mainly for travelling

SPORTS BOOTS

The range of sports boots which claim actually to absorb concussion and/or force passing up the leg, so protecting the tendons and other parts of the leg, is now quite wide. The problem, however, from the buyer's point of view, is that unless you can obtain some sort of proof of the manufacturer's claims, you can never be certain that the boots actually do what they claim to do. However, any reputable firm will have comprehensible literature written for non-scientifically minded readers which details how the boots work, and gives references and traceable details of tests that have been carried out to prove their claims.

Professional's Choice Sports Medecine Boots are scientifically proven to help absorb concussion in the leg and to help support tendons and ligaments

Most boots today are made of synthetic fabrics or specially treated leathers. With 'ordinary' boots such as brushing boots there are countless makes of cheaply priced, cheaply made boots on the market which wear badly, tear easily and do not usually offer much protection. Sports boots are normally better made – if quite expensive in some cases – and they do last well; so provided they can prove that they do what they claim to do, they must be a worthy addition to any tackroom. They often come in synthetics such as neoprene, polycarbonates for shields, and various polymerised materials, protective fleeces and patented composition materials normally aimed at shock absorbency such as orthopaedic foams, gels and other materials derived from the medical and aerospace industries.

For many years it was mistakenly believed that exercise bandages, conventionally applied from just below the knee or hock to just above the fetlock joint, actually supported the tendons and ligaments. Normally, the only way actual support could be given would be to hamper the action of the associated joint (in the case of equine athletes it is normally the fetlock joint which comes in for injury). Sports boots seem to lessen stress and offer a significant degree of support to the lowers legs without interfering with fetlock action.

THERAPEUTIC AND REMEDIAL BOOTS

Wearing boots whilst working may have definite advantages, but it is worth considering the fact that they may insulate the legs and thereby cause them to heat up; and it is known that when the core fibres in a tendon heat up, the structure is more susceptible to injury – which is exactly what we do not want. If more work can be done to produce work boots, like some of the remedial and therapeutic boots which are available, but stronger and which will keep legs cool during work, this would be another breakthrough in equine protection.

Therapeutic boots are now readily available, and may have built-in magnetic inserts for the general benefits of applying an external magnetic field, or with batteries for pulsed magnetic therapy; boots incorporating

cold gels are also available, or with pockets for either cooled or heated gel pads, according to the treatment required, and there are also boots with attachments for cold hosing.

The fit of all boots is most important, not only for the horse's comfort but also so as not actually to cause friction or pressure injuries, or to restrict the horse's action during work. Some of the newer sports boots are quite tricky to fit, and cannot be just slapped on and velcro-ed up like some everyday brushing boots. Bearing in mind that some therapeutic boots are kept on for several or many hours, attention to comfort and fit is most important, and allowance must also be made for any swelling of an injured area. Veterinary advice should be taken in such cases as to whether the boots would do more harm than good.

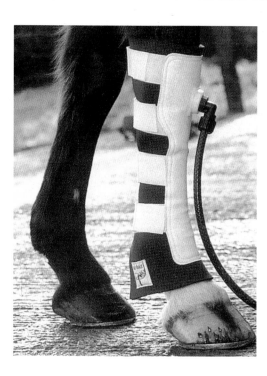

Cold-Hoze boots are designed to take the time-consuming waiting out of hosing legs, as the attachment fits to the yard water supply, the supervisor can therefore be doing some other task whilst supervising the horse

BANDAGES

COHESIVE BANDAGES

There do not seem to have been many advances in work bandages for horses apart from the appearance of cohesive bandages for work, stable or first aid. Cohesive bandages adhere firmly but not permanently to themselves, making them secure and reusable a few times, although not once they have become wet. They have a certain amount of stretch, and are excellent for keeping padding in place for work, or for holding on dressings. They also work well as a tail bandage for a brood mare when she is either foaling or receiving some kind of veterinary treatment or examination. They form a valuable part of any yard's general equipment.

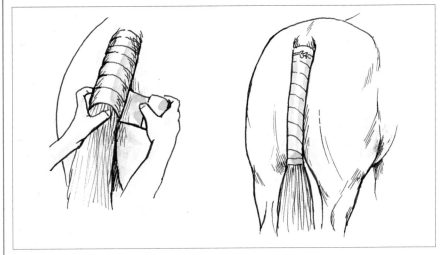

Left: Applying a tail bandage needs practice, so that the tension is comfortably loose and even but sufficient for the bandage to stay on; so practice on days at home in the year when you are not going anywhere. They are not put on over padding so if they are too tight, or if the material is bunched up under a fold, they can cause pressure injuries, particularly on the underside of the dock, wavy hairs on the dock, injured hair follicles and subsequent white hairs, and they can impair the blood supply

TAIL BANDAGES

Crêpe bandages are still popular for bandaging tails to keep them looking trim and groomed, or to protect them (albeit usually without padding underneath) for travelling. Again, there is a skill to applying tail bandages, and wavy hair down the dock is a sure giveaway that the 'bandager' is incompetent! Because no Gamgee is used underneath a tail bandage when it is put on in the conventional manner, when badly applied it can easily bruise and cut the skin underneath the dock.

EXERCISE BANDAGES

Bandaging a horse's legs correctly, effectively and safely is certainly an acquired skill. It is extremely easy to put on bandages too loosely, when they might come off and trip the horse; too tightly, when they will cause sometimes severe pressure injuries; or unevenly, again causing pressure and friction. It is amazing the number of horses from so-called 'top' yards which are seen with wavy lines round their legs (and tails), indicating very inexpert and potentially dangerous bandaging.

Although bandaging a horse's legs is a job for the experienced and competent, you can only become so qualified through practice under expert supervision – first on table legs, then on your friends' arms, and then on a quiet horse or pony – all the time absorbing a feel for tension, until such time as you are considered fit to be let loose on a horse on your own. Everyone has to learn, and competent bandaging, whether for working, travelling or veterinary procedures, is an essential skill for all horse owners and grooms.

Bandages should always be put on over protective padding, either Gamgee Tissue, that good old standby, or synthetic felts and other paddings.

So-called 'work' or 'exercise' bandages are best made of some slightly stretchy fabric, but they must not be pulled tight during application, for

Exercise or work bandages are applied over padding (two thicknesses over the tendons): they are stretchy and have a self-tightening effect so must not be overstretched during application. They are applied to finish with the pointed end bearing the tapes pointing backwards on the outside of the leg so that brush and scrub do not become easily caught in the bandages

the reasons given above. Most have a self-tightening effect during application, and the nearer you get to finishing the job, the tighter they get. They may also shrink when wet, which should help you decide whether or not to use them under such conditions.

The old theory was, that exercise bandages actually supported tendons during work, but this is extremely unlikely, even when they are taken under the ergot; however, they may well reduce concussive vibrations up the leg and help it resist torsion injuries. They and their padding will help reduce the bruising effect of knocks.

STABLE BANDAGES

Bandages for use in the stable are wider and longer than exercise bandages – although it must be said that they are shorter than they used to be, and it is often necessary to sew two together to make one long enough, certainly for a hind leg. They are made of non-stretch, softer material; the best are knitted wool or cotton. The synthetic ones I have tried, also felted wool velour, do not mould well to the leg and tend to slip.

They are used for warmth, when travelling, or to provide slight pressure to keep down filled legs.

They may be put on top of other bandages to keep dressings in place.

THE SANDOWN BANDAGE

These are not often seen now, though are still available at a few select traditional-type saddlers. The Sandown bandage has its own built-in, fleecy padding; when always used on the same leg of the same horse, it moulds itself to a perfect fit. It is normally made of wool, and can be used as a stable or a travelling bandage, with no need for separate padding. The bandage is put on from the fleecy end, and as you roll it on, you will eventually come to a non-padded part which continues over the fleecy part to hold it and keep it firm. There used to be a cotton stockinette type, though I have not seen it for years; it is/was used for exercising.

Stable bandages are longer and wider than exercise bandages, and the easiest to use are of knitted fabric which mould to the leg. They are put on over two thicknesses of padding (typically Gamgee Tissue) and go right down to the coronet and back again

PADDING MATERIALS

There are various synthetic materials available now for use as padding under bandages, usually in a felt form which can be reused.

Plastic foam is useless as it instantly compresses to nothing.

Gamgee Tissue™ is still used in most yards: it is cotton wool with a gauze covering, and can be reused a few times. Usually, two layers are needed for reasonable protection. It is important not to let it wrinkle and crease during application otherwise you will get uneven pressure.

Cotton wool alone is not much use as it tears apart too easily.

OTHER EQUIPMENT

POLL GUARD

No horse should be travelled without a hardened poll guard: simply wrapping the headpiece of the headcollar round with gamgee is certainly not enough. A poll guard is a hardened cap with ear holes: it has eyes through which the headcollar strap passes, and is usually padded on the inside to protect the head. It may be made of leather or a synthetic substance, and it should be regarded as an essential piece of travelling equipment.

A hard poll guard which slots on to the headpiece of the headcollar should be regarded as essential travelling equipment

TAIL GUARD

This is a simple fabric or leather cover put on over the tail bandage when the horse is travelling or in the stable to prevent him dislodging the said bandage. It has a strap or tape that is passed through a loop on the back edge of the rug at the top, and the guard itself usually fastens with tape bows or velcro.

Below: A horse correctly dressed for travelling, wearing a poll guard on the headcollar, well fitting rug, a tail bandage under a tail guard, the latter being tied to a loop on the rug's back seam to keep it on and travelling boots which protect the leg from above the knee/hock to below the coronet

NECK CRADLE

Rarely seen now, most horses dislike a neck cradle intensely; however, it may be invaluable to prevent a horse turning round and biting at a wound or dressing. It consists of wooden or synthetic rods fastened together and fitted round the neck. If your vet considers it essential to use such a cradle, then the horse will need to be carefully supervised and watched for some hours, as many react in panic to the restriction the cradle imposes.

A neck cradle to stop the horse turning round to bite at a wound or dressing

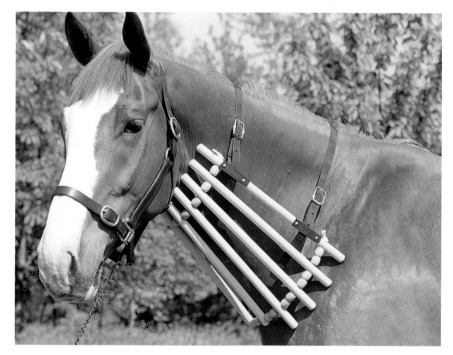

MUZZLES

A much less restrictive piece of equipment, a muzzle allows the horse to turn round with complete freedom, although he will not be able actually to bite the area he is trying to reach with his teeth.

A muzzle is sometimes recommended to be put on a fat animal at grass to severely restrict its grazing, and if you buy the coarse mesh type which allows blades of grass to penetrate the mesh, this will work – although it must be most frustrating for the pony. Of course, any muzzle must allow its wearer to drink freely.

Stallions, and any animals which are considered potentially (or actually) vicious are often muzzled for general handling.

The best type consists of a mesh cage which fits over the entire muzzle. It is usually padded around the inside top edge to prevent rubbing, and is kept up by a simple strap which passes up the side of the head, over the poll and buckles to a shorter strap on the other side. Some muzzles have a more closed-in bottom part with holes for breathing, but these must be much less pleasant to wear and I imagine they do not let in enough air for comfort.

A horse wearing a muzzle to stop him interfering with a wound or dressing. Some muzzles are specially designed to enable a horse to graze in a restricted way, and to drink, so are used to help prevent a high intake of nutritious grass

169

8 CARE and MAINTENANCE

Good tack is very expensive, and as second-hand tack in excellent condition has a good resale value, or will last its original buyer a lifetime, it is well worth looking after.

LEATHER TOPICS

Leather needs more care than other materials, although modern leather products, some saddles at least, are often treated with special waxes, coatings and resins which cut cleaning to an absolute minimum: in fact the makers may advise you not to clean and oil them conventionally but just to wipe off any surface dirt with a damp sponge or chamois leather. For conventional leather you can still use good old saddle soap, glycerine saddle soap in bars or in spray form giving excellent results – and with the spray type you don't have to use water as you do when using a bar, and so you avoid getting everything too wet and lathery. Various new leather dressings are available now, which make the whole tack-cleaning process much quicker and easier than the routine we are used to, and several

The way we were. A 'yesteryear' photograph of the Malta Branch of the Pony Club cleaning tack under the watchful eye of Brigadier R.C.Symonds, District Commissioner of the branch

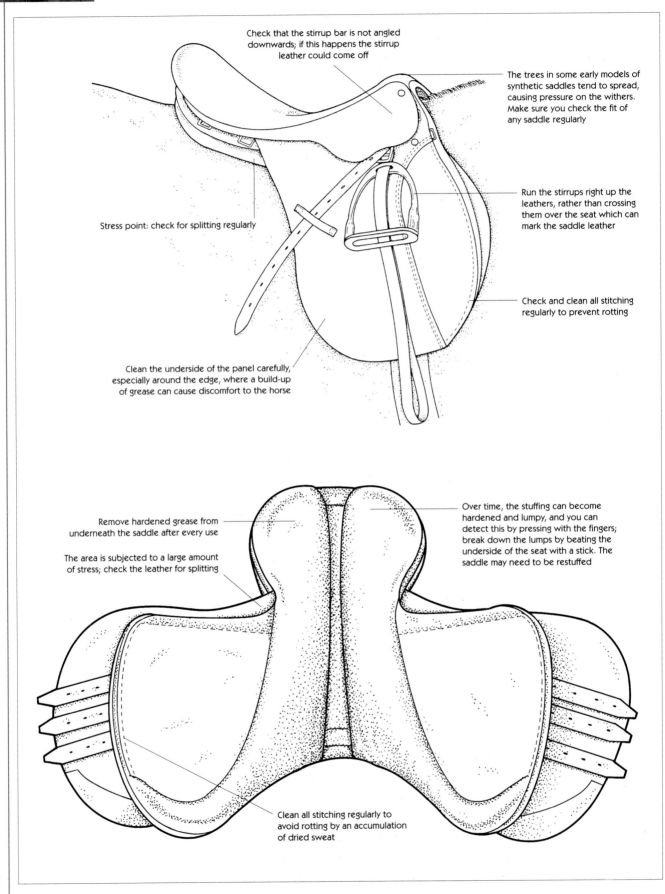

Check that the stirrup bar is not angled downwards; if this happens the stirrup leather could come off

The trees in some early models of synthetic saddles tend to spread, causing pressure on the withers. Make sure you check the fit of any saddle regularly

Stress point: check for splitting regularly

Run the stirrups right up the leathers, rather than crossing them over the seat which can mark the saddle leather

Check and clean all stitching regularly to prevent rotting

Clean the underside of the panel carefully, especially around the edge, where a build-up of grease can cause discomfort to the horse

Remove hardened grease from underneath the saddle after every use

The area is subjected to a large amount of stress; check the leather for splitting

Over time, the stuffing can become hardened and lumpy, and you can detect this by pressing with the fingers; break down the lumps by beating the underside of the seat with a stick. The saddle may need to be restuffed

Clean all stitching regularly to avoid rotting by an accumulation of dried sweat

'dressing' products which are infinitely better than neatsfoot oil. There are also all-in-one cleaning and preserving creams and lotions, although I have found that these do not actually clean all that well, particularly if your tack is quite dirty.

The important point is to check how your leather has been treated, if new, and make sure you follow the cleaning instructions so as not to destroy any in-built protection.

Muddy leather must be washed carefully, without exerting any pressure, otherwise the grit will scratch the leather. In fact it is quite all right just to dump bridles, driving harness and any non-padded items in a tub of clear water and swish it around to get the mud off.

Grease and sweat from the horse (which damages leather if left on) will need firmly sponging off, most effectively with tepid water (not even hand-hot) and a dash of washing-up liquid to dissolve the grease. You can wipe it over afterwards with a sponge dipped in clear water, if this makes you feel better, then wipe it with a damp chamois leather to partly dry it, and finally soap it in the normal way.

Proprietary dressings must be used according to the manufacturer's instructions for best results.

NEW TACK

Some new tack may not be treated with protective substances and may feel hard and stiff. To soften it, wipe over the underside with a damp sponge – damp leather is more absorbent than dry – then give it one coat of your favourite leather dressing, conditioning cream or oil, then one coat on the top surface, and finish with a second coat on the underside again. After it has soaked in for several hours, you can use and clean it normally. Always put plenty of oil in bends where the bit rings and buckle bars go, around fastenings, and behind and around where buckles fasten – anywhere which is hidden or gets a lot of wear.

OLD, NEGLECTED TACK

The first thing is to find out from a good saddler whether or not it is worth repairing should the leather be actually cracked, badly worn or the stitching worn and fraying. If the answer is yes, take it home again and get the leather into good condition so that it is easier for the craftsman to work with: old, dry, stiff leather tears and crumbles easily during handling, so the better the condition and the stronger it is, the easier it is to repair, the more comfortable it is for you to use, and the more years of use it will give you.

Wet the leather and smother it in a really good leather dressing or oil, and keep doing this until it is hardly absorbing any more oil. Between coatings, keep it in a polythene bag which will discourage its drying out.

Check it the following day and give it another coat of oil, then put it back in the bag, and keep doing this until it is supple. Don't overdo it, however – too much oil and the leather becomes slimy and too soft, and this can actually weaken it and make it almost impossible to use. Wipe off any excess oil with a damp rubber or tea-towel, wash and clean it normally, and send it for repair.

MOULD, MILDEW AND HUMIDITY

Leather suffers more in humid environments than anything else. Your tackroom should be at an even room temperature (no hotter) all year round, and dry; roughly 20°C/68°F is about right.

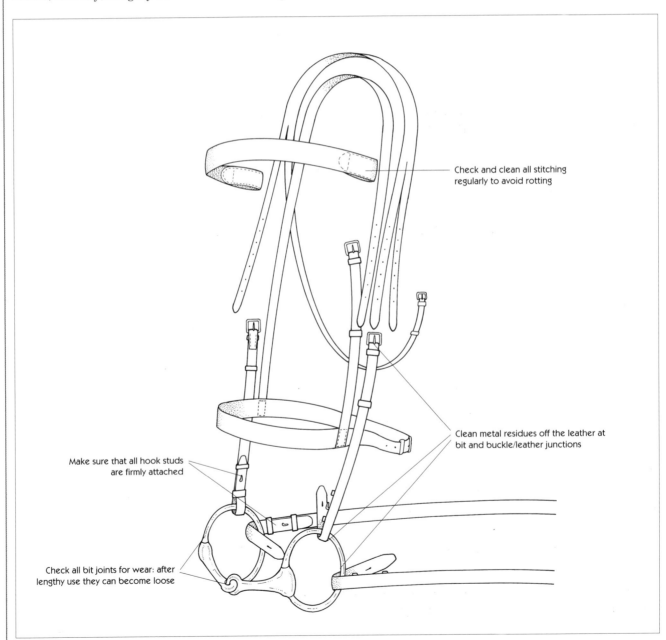

Check and clean all stitching regularly to avoid rotting

Clean metal residues off the leather at bit and buckle/leather junctions

Make sure that all hook studs are firmly attached

Check all bit joints for wear: after lengthy use they can become loose

To restore mouldy tack, you can wipe it over with a solution of one part ammonia to seven parts of water, or baby sterilising fluid, or (my favourite) Virkon equine disinfectant to kill the fungal deposits. You may need to do this more than once. Also, placing the mouldy items in sunlight outdoors will help to kill mould.

After this, wash the leather, oil it several times – because if it has been neglected it has probably dried out, too – then clean it normally and store it in a warm, dry place. If your tackroom is not warm and dry, try to find a corner of your home where you can keep it.

SYNTHETICS

The range of synthetics is so vast that it is not possible to give any specific care guidelines. All quality items, though, come with their own maintenance instructions. However, one general comment worth making is that it is particularly important to wash synthetic rugs at the recommended temperature, or on an acrylics' setting in your washing machine. Horse rugs (blankets) get very dirty, and it is tempting to wash them in too hot a temperature because of this. However, this often results in a disastrous felting, matting or even melting of synthetic fillings, and sometimes the outer covering, too, depending on type, which ruins the rug.

If you send your rugs to a laundry, preferably a specialist equine one, quiz them about temperatures and point out the recommended temperatures on your rugs. It could be as well to ask if they guarantee to replace any items which might be spoiled by incorrect laundering.

METALWORK

If you buy all stainless-steel metalwork (although stainless-steel buckles can be difficult to find) you will have little problem cleaning it – although even this sometimes needs a buff up with metal-polish wadding and a soft cloth. Of course, never let metal polish anywhere near the mouthpiece of your bit.

It is always said that you must never let metal polish touch your leather or it will rot it. However, if your leather is properly cared for anyway, and as long as you wipe off any polish with a damp sponge or cloth, then rub the spot with your soap sponge or a little oil, there shouldn't be a problem. It is almost impossible to clean buckles without getting a little polish on the leatherwork.

Nickel-plated steel, and most metals other than stainless steel, need polishing in the usual way fairly regularly with metal polish.

Washing off your bit after use is simple hygiene, and although you may get the ends of your cheekpieces and reins wet, again if the leather is well cared for, this will cause no harm.

IN STORE

If leather is not going to be used for a long time, clean it well, oil it, and cover it liberally with petroleum jelly, including all metal parts. Straps should be stored straight, and not fastened to buckles. Then wrap it in acid-free paper or old cotton sheets, and store it flat and somewhere dry with a moderate temperature.

9 STABLE and YARD EQUIPMENT

L ooking after horses has always been a labour-intensive and time-consuming task. In earlier times when labour was free or cheap and humans presumably did not have so many distractions and calls on their time, no one seemed to bother too much about this. Today, though, with our ridiculously fast pace of life, the radically changed economy, the demise of poorly paid servants whose job it was to look after the family's horses, and the vast increase in the number of leisure horses owned by 'ordinary' people who cannot afford to pay anyone to look after them, how to accomplish all these time-consuming and labour-intensive jobs has become quite a major problem.

Amongst the most time-consuming tasks, because they must be done regularly, every day, are mucking out and sweeping the yard. Exercising is also, of course, very time-consuming, but is not supposed to be a chore. So is grooming, and especially a full grooming-with-strapping, with the result that it was one of the first things to be skimped by the new post-war generation of horse owners – it is now unheard of in most private amateur stables. (It is interesting that the 'Continentals' have never strapped or wisped, and think the British are crazy for doing it.)

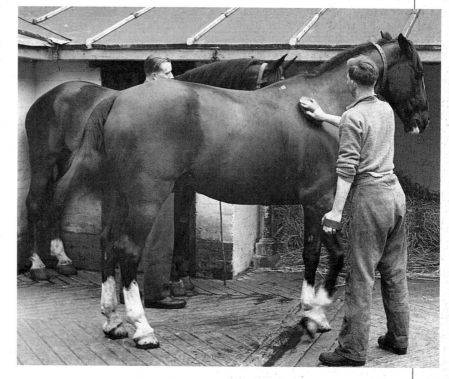

The correct way to groom a horse hasn't changed – it's still hard work!

Also abandoned was 'full' mucking-out: this involved swilling and brushing the floor, and then bedding it down and 'setting it fair', which often incorporated plaiting the straw along the back edge of the stall or in the doorway of the loose-box. Such a bed has been replaced by deep litter, or semi-deep-litter bedding, and this has certainly been a retrograde step as far as the horse's health and hygiene are concerned, unless the stabling is exceptionally well ventilated.

A glance through any horse-care book of yesteryear – even from only

177

a generation ago, but certainly pre-World War II – will show us to what extent equipment, and horse-care ideas and expectations, have changed. It is actually a real education to read a horse-care book from about a hundred years ago, and it is surprising how much you learn – and not only about what not to do, either. Stabling itself was often built to a much higher standard than it is today, particularly as regards ventilation and drainage, and the veterinary books (or as they were once called, 'farriery' books – farriers and vets being the same thing at one time) have very little reference to broken-winded horses, simply because the condition (known as 'chronic obstructive pulmonary disease' today) does not seem to have been common in the way it is today.

Yard equipment in those days was certainly made to last. Although it was often heavy, it was strong, and made with pride, skill and painstaking effort and attention to detail – even something as mundane as a yard broom or a wheelbarrow. Despite the consistent efforts of contemporary environmentalists, our society nowadays is a 'disposable' one, the prevailing attitude being that 'when it wears out/breaks I'll get another'; this philosophy applies even to synthetic saddles which are so much cheaper than traditionally made ones. The emphasis now is almost entirely on saving time and work, and equipment is often quite cheap, comparatively lightweight for 'girl grooms' (and owners) to handle, and designed, in the better items, for ease of use to save time and labour. This philosophy is not all bad, however: not all the changes have been for the better, but many have, as we shall see.

Many specialist firms now offer a wide range of stable and yard equipment; many feed merchants or more general suppliers have diversified into this field; and mail-order catalogues are readily available, offering anything from a few specialist items to a huge range, including tack, rider and horse clothing, lorinery and just about every item you could possibly think of – and many you have never heard of, but which seem like a good idea.

A flat-sided water bucket clipped to the wall for stability

STABLE FITTINGS

The safest stable is certainly one with no fittings at all, although this is not always practical. Thus the horse can have his hay or haylage fed on the ground, as on good studs (US: stud farms), his concentrates from a clean piece of fabric (sacking, or an old rug) on the ground as well, and he could be led out a few times a day to drink – though few of us would probably want to take up the last two options.

WATER CONTAINERS

This automatic drinker has been placed at a comfortable and safe height, level with the horse's elbow

A slightly smaller, more manageable bin can be used for water, although a larger-than-usual bucket which you can still carry without giving

yourself a hernia might be even better, because it is probably more likely that it will then be scrubbed out daily and filled with clean water, not just topped up by hosepipe – by which system the water is not often really clean. If necessary, buckets can be fixed to the wall with clips; with a horse that is determined to move them and tip them up, three clips will be needed, two at the sides and one at the back, and the buckets should be fixed into their corners in such a way that he cannot get at the clips and tear his lips on them during his investigations.

Automatic drinkers are a boon to busy owners, especially those with more than a couple of horses, but they should be the type with (a) a meter so you can check how much, or if, your horse is drinking, and (b) a plug in the bottom so that they, too, can be cleaned out properly every day. The usual mistake with these is to fix them too high: the top of the drinker should be fitted so it is level with a horse's elbow, and even this is really too high if the horse is to drink naturally; it could even possibly restrict his intake because of the slight discomfort involved. On the other hand, if they are too low, and also immovable, the horse could easily get a foot into them and hurt himself. Again they should be sited in a corner, and all piping, taps and other fittings covered with safe conduits, firm lids or whatever is appropriate.

Two ways to feed hay from a natural, low height from CAM Equestrian: (above) a deep, flexible hay tub, also suitable for short-chopped forage and (below) the Tufty hay manger

FEEDING FORAGE

Feeding from the ground is by far the best for your horse, as his body evolved to function this way; however, if you don't wish to feed hay or haylage loose, you can put it in a large plastic tub in a corner on the floor – if necessary, this can be clipped to the wall with one of several designs of safety clip. You could also get a good handyman – one who appreciates how strong and inquisitive horses are, and even little ponies – to safely partition off a corner with a strong, large-mesh metal grille (though not big enough for a pony's hoof to get through). Another option would be to use solid wooden boards. These, of course, cut out a little light but horses don't seem to mind, and the possibility of hooves slipping through is eliminated.

Large plastic tubs, of which there is a wide selection, are also excellent for filling with short-chopped forage feed as a replacement for, or in addition to, hay or haylage; this may be mixed in with soaked sugar-beet pulp, carrots or other roots, with the horse's concentrate ration mixed in too. This is a more natural way for the horse to get his nutrients, rather than in a separate 'human-type' meal. You could simply buy a cheap plastic dustbin (trash can) from any household store, and use the lid as a dung skep.

A home-made solution to feeding hay at low level, a corner safely partitioned off with a grille to keep hay from being scattered all over the floor

FEEDING CONCENTRATES

Provided your horse is a reasonably quiet eater, the most natural level from which he can eat his concentrates, if you feed them separately, is on the

ground. Put them in a large container on the floor at feed times, removing the container as soon as he has finished so that there is nothing lying around on the floor for him to trip over, get a foot through or throw around. For safety it should ideally have no metal parts – a large washing-up bowl is a regular choice, although in the UK there are at least two ranges of container with moulded side handles.

Fixed mangers may be needed for horses who eat over-enthusiastically and tip up containers, sling them around their boxes and so on, but they must be removable so they can be cleaned. Again, the best height is to have the top of the manger level with the horse's elbow. The large, wide, deep mangers, often of polythene these days, are good, and the corner type are safest because there is no projection on which a horse can knock himself. The reason for having roomy mangers is partly because of air flow, and partly because many horses do not like eating out of small containers: for this reason, buckets for feed should be extra wide, not the narrow, taller sort generally sold as water buckets.

A Grade A showjumper I knew years ago used to suffer regularly from flatulent colic, for no reason that anyone could trace. One night he was down with it again, but this time a new vet from the owner's usual practice turned up to attend. He treated the horse, and when he learned that these attacks occurred frequently, suggested that it would be a good idea to lower the horse's manger which was fixed rather high. He felt that because the horse had to eat at such an unnatural and uncomfortable angle, he was possibly not chewing his food properly, and so was swallowing it improperly softened and prepared, and that this was causing imperfect digestion. And so it must have been, because once the manger was lowered, the horse never suffered from colic again.

OBSERVATIONS ON HAYNETS

Haynets (US: haybags) are used in just about every yard you can name these days, except at some of the older-established studs (haynets can be very dangerous for youngstock because they can so easily get their hooves stuck in them). People say they use them because they are convenient, though in practice they are not particularly convenient at all: they are quite time-consuming to fill unless you hook them onto special holders, and they have to be tied up at horse's head height – and this is my main and significant objection to them – so they don't sag low as they empty, when a horse could get a hoof caught in them. They are useful for soaking hay because it can then be hung up to drip; then the damp hay can be tipped into a bin or other container for eating. They are also probably hard to replace for travelling, unless you have breast-bar hay-holders. On the other hand there is no need for a net to weigh hay or haylage: just pile it on a piece of sacking or old sheet, then gather up its four corners and hang

A wall-mounted corner manger is useful and practical. It should be fixed with the top about level with the horse's elbow. The rounded-off bottom edge will help prevent injury to the knees should the horse stamp whilst eating

A safe, flexible container which can be used for feeds or skepping out – but not both!

Sturdy tubs with many uses in yard, field or stable, particularly good for water and filling with short-cropped forage feed

it by these on a spring weigher; then tip it into the horse's bin. Hayracks also need to be at horse's-head height or slightly above for safety, so are just as bad as haynets from this point of view.

The reason horses should eat from ground level (or nearly so) is because it is more natural and comfortable for them, and I am sure they must digest their food better this way. Also, constantly pulling at a net or a rack for several hours a day not only develops all the 'wrong' muscles, for a riding horse (on the underside of the neck), but also puts a strain on the horse's back because it obliges it to sink downwards – which is not what you want in any horse or pony. Eating at ground level means that the horse can maintain his natural vertebral bow and conformation (see Chapter 1) because his head and neck are lowered.

A physiotherapist once traced an athletic family horse's recurrent back problems to the fact that he was fed from a haynet. The unnatural angle at which he – like all other horses fed so – was obliged to eat was constantly 'kinking' his back, and affecting his vertebrae and ligaments to the extent that he was never really sound, and was therefore often out of work. The physiotherapist recommended the following treatment: physiotherapy by machine, plus a remedial management programme which including giving the horse all his feed and water from ground level, and lungeing him in a Chambon over ground poles for a few weeks; he was not to be ridden, and no attempts were to be made to influence his head carriage. This produced a remarkable recovery. The improvement in the horse's musculature was very noticeable, as was his apparent contentment and comfort (not surprisingly), and this improvement continued when his work was resumed.

A hanging manger from CAM Equestrian which can be used in trailers, fields or stables. For comfort and good digestion, mangers should be placed with their top at the level of the horse's elbows

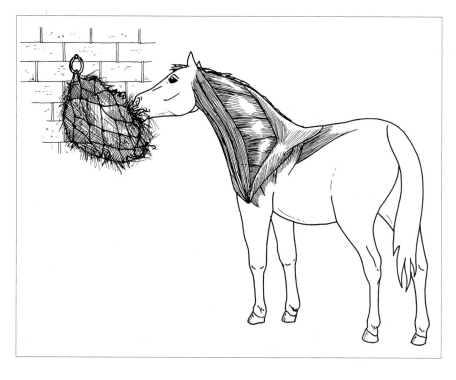

Left: Still a common way of feeding hay, nets have distinct disadvantages. Apart from being time-consuming to fill (unlike tubs), they have to be fixed high for safety, and the horse needs to make an upward and sideways movement to pull the hay out, which goes a long way towards developing the wrong 'riding' muscles in his neck

181

This anecdote is a case in point, and it certainly makes one wonder to what degree back problems, bad behaviour under saddle, and performance and schooling problems are the result of incorrect muscle development or even injury due to feeding horses from unnatural levels.

YARD EQUIPMENT

MAINTENANCE

Probably the most valuable item on any yard is a really capacious two- or four-wheeled wheelbarrow, and maybe even two – one for muck, and one for carting hay and haylage and perhaps buckets, too. The usual small, single-wheeled sort are not big enough to be really useful, and are very difficult to balance and push, particularly as the pusher has to bear much of the weight. The two-wheeled sort relieves the problem of balance, and the four-wheeled ones leave the ground to take all the weight, as they should! Some have levers and other devices to help tip the body up, which can be a major job for a small person or anyone with a handicap – even a sprained wrist or back from trying to empty an ordinary barrow.

Muck sacks are very much cheaper than barrows, but you need to be

Below: A much more useful barrow than the common little single-wheeled variety. This roomy, two-wheel barrow is easy to push and to balance, and is not being prone to tipping over like the single-wheeled sort

Below: A useful array of mucking out tools, including four-tined straw forks, shovel, shavings rakes and two-tined pitchforks used for carrying hay in the 'old days' when there was plenty of labour to sweep up after you

STABLE AND YARD EQUIPMENT

quite burly to lift them when full. Usually circular affairs made from synthetic fabric, they have a drawstring around the edge which pulls close when they are full; then you have to haul them to the muck heap – not a brilliant idea for busy female owners, at least.

Sweeping yards is a really time-wasting, thankless task, and an injurious one to anyone with an existing back weakness. Wide-headed brooms save much work and time, and the natural bristle type are far more effective than the synthetic ones which split and positively gather up bedding and other debris until they are completely clogged. It is wise to get a handle the right length for you: short handles, in particular, may cause back strain if you are anything from average to tall in height.

Strong shovels with wide blades are the most useful type to get, and those with polythene or plastic blades, or even hardened rubber, are lighter than any metal other than aluminium. A strong, sturdy sort with a T or D handle is the most practical, but it must be well made otherwise the top of the handle will probably come off, making it very difficult to use.

Depending on the bedding materials you use, you will need a shavings fork (with a large number of angled tines), a four-tined fork for straw, and – rarely seen these days – a two-tined pitchfork, used for carting large loads of hay about the yard – though this was in times when there were plenty of staff to sweep it up. Muck-scoops and short rakes are useful for clearing up droppings from paddock and yard, and for skepping out stables without having to constantly bend down. Old water buckets make good droppings holders, and are easily carried to, and tipped onto the manure heap.

A useful tub on a trolley for carrying just about anything, including skepped-out droppings from several stables

FIELD EQUIPMENT

WATER

Horses at grass obviously need a safe source of water, and most paddocks these days need to supply it, rather than rely on probably polluted streams and ponds, where these are present. Water containers can be simple dustbins tied to a fence post, and filled by hosepipe or from a bowser; they should be moved daily to prevent the ground becoming too poached in wet weather. Piped water saves a lot of time, whether it comes in a self-fill form, or via a tap. Any container should have rounded edges and corners and be fitted along a fence line, not at right-angles to it when it can form a potentially dangerous projection into the fields on both sides of the fence. Even when sited parallel to the fence line, horses from both fields can still reach it, and it is much safer.

Troughs and other containers should not be placed in the middle of a field: again, they just form obstacles with which playing or skirmishing horses can easily collide.

Muck scoops to save your back when on dung-collecting duties in the paddocks

183

Most troughs are still made of galvanised metal, but very tough synthetic ones (plastic and polythene) are now available, which are said to be guaranteed against cracking and even chewing. Many people still use old baths, but often omit to place guards around them to prevent injury – and how they get away with it is beyond me. I have seen the most appalling cuts to knees and legs, where horses have injured themselves on the corners or lips of these.

A tough, safe plastic water trough from CAM Equestrian

Left: A 'home-made' water trough. An old bath safely boarded in as a safe water container. You could also use old tyres to protect the horse from the sharp edges of the bath

FORAGE

Hay supplies in fields are most safely fed loose from the ground: however, this is usually regarded as very wasteful (though to my mind, safety is more important than economy) and generally haynets are used. It is recommended that they are tied to the tops of the fence posts or to tree branches against the trunk, for safety and ease of manipulation by the horse. Large, movable hay holders such as are used for cattle can be used for horses, but again, if placed in the middle of a field they form a potentially harmful obstacle. They can be placed along a fence line to serve two fields, but the fence each side should be solid should there be any kicking, and the corners rounded off as far as possible.

When horses are fed concentrates in the field, probably the best way is to feed them individually from buckets to ensure that they each get their proper ration, and for someone to stand with each horse to protect him against marauders. If this is not possible, the bullies, at least, should have a minder on the end of a leadrope to prevent problem, or be removed from the field at feed times. The traditional practice of feeding horses from travelling mangers, hooked at wide distances onto the fence, again works well, provided someone stays to supervise.

Haynets for outdoor animals should be tied firmly, as shown here, to fence posts and not to the rails

In my experience horses do not take well to being fed from cattle or sheep troughs left in the field: again, if there is something to trip over, horses will trip over it (unlike cattle), or gallop into it, or roll on it, or something, so it is not worth the risk. Horses are said to be intelligent, but sometimes one can't help having quite a few doubts!

Large bales of haylage can be left in the field for horses to eat from. Place new bales in a different place each time to reduce poaching. Uneaten, trampled haylage should be raked up and put on the muck heap as it will otherwise hamper the growth of grass by preventing light reaching the blades

TACK STORAGE AND SECURITY

Many people who keep their horses and equipment away from their homes, either on their own separate premises, on a rented yard or at livery, are worried about security or not only their horses but their tack and equipment. Thieves seem to get ever bolder and anything we can do to make theft difficult for them is a help.

Horses can be electronically 'chipped' in the crest of the neck' they can be freeze-marked, lip-tatooed and hoof-branded. Premises can be arranged so that all gates to fields lead on to private roads or tracks or other private land. Gates on to public highways are asking for trouble. High, thick and prickly hedges are a fair deterrent around your perimeter and your local police will be glad to assess your premises and advise

on suitable burglar alarms and other devices (chains, padlocks, mortise locks and so on) as well as simple ways of rearranging your premiss to make them more secure.

COMFORT IN THE STABLE

Although rubber mats may make life easier for owners and, in some cases, safer and more comfortable for horses, I do hate to see them with no bedding on top of them! This is a big selling point – save on bedding: don't use any – but my experience is that horses *prefer* bedding. They do not like staling on to rubber and they would definitely rather lie on bedding than wet rubber, which it nearly always is. The constant contact of skin with urine also causes skin diseases. Rubber matting is ideal for padding the walls of stables and for providing a warmer, cushioning and slip-resistant flooring – but I should always use bedding on top of it.

A stall-guard from CAM Equestrian. These make a welcome difference to stabled horses in all but the coldest weather, giving a feeling of air and freedom whilst keeping horses in their boxes

Left: Heat lamps are not expensive to buy and install and are a boon for older, wet or debilitated horses in cool weather

PULLING MANES

If you feel cruel and mean to your horse when pulling his mane (and even if you don't) a device which could make both you and your horse feel better about the process is the ManeMaster™ (see Suppliers list). This is a simple, lever-operated razor comb which gives a definite pulled appearance to mane and tail. It seems easy to use and certainly takes the distress out of trimming manes and tails.

The ManeMaster™ razor comb

SUPPLIERS

USEFUL ADDRESSES

UK

The British Equestrian Trade Association
Wothersome Grange, Bramham, Wetherby, West
Yorkshire LS23 6LY

Society of Master Saddlers (UK) Ltd
Kettles Farm, Mickfield, Stowmarket, Suffolk
IP14 6BY

Worshipful Company of Loriners (Head Office)
8 Portland Square, London E1W 9QR

British Association of Holistic Nutrition & Medicine
Borough Court, Hartley Wintney, Basingstoke,
Hants RG27 8JA

USA

Saddle, Harness and Allied Trades Association
1101-A Broad Street, Oriental, NC 28571, USA

AUSTRALIA

Australian Equestrian Trade Association
2334 Putty Road, Bulga, New South Wales 2330
Australia

SUPPLIERS

UK

Some of the products available from the following
suppliers are shown in this book.

Aerborn® Equestrian Ltd
Pegasus House, 198 Sneinton Dale, Nottingham,
England NG2 4HJ

Frank Baines Saddlery
Northcote Street, Walsall WS2 8BQ

Balance International
Westcott Venture Park, Westcott, Aylesbury,
Buckinghamshire HP18 0XB

Bucas
Togher Industrial Estate, Cork, Eire
Distributed in the UK by
Horsemaster Distribution
Ickleford Manor, Hitchin, Herts SG5 3XE

Buxactic Ltd
The Winnows, Home Farm, Sedgwick Park,
Horsham, West Sussex RH13 6QE
Supplier of Sprenger Equestrian Products

CAM EQUESTRIAN Ltd
Eardisley, Hereford HR3 6NS

Day Son & Hewitt
St George's Quay, Lancaster LA1 5QJ

Fieldhouse Riding Equipment
Birchills House Industrial Estate, Green Lane,
Walsall, West Midlands WS2 8LE

SUPPLIERS

First Thought (Equine) Ltd
Little Duskin Farm, Covet Lane, Kingston,
Canterbury, Kent CT4 6JS
Flair Saddle System

A. J. Foster Saddlemakers
22 Station Road, Walsall, West Midlands WS2 9JZ

Goldson Horseware
Lower Lambourne Farm, Tolcarne Hill, Redruth,
Cornwall TR16 5HA

Juliet Isaacs
6 Stowmarket Road, Needham Market, Suffolk IP6
8DS
Supplier of the Spanish Halter

E. Jeffries and Sons Ltd
George Street, Walsall, West Midlands WS1 1SD

Llynwon Saddlery
Llynwon, Trecastle, Brecon, Powys LD3 8RG
Pliance saddle testing system

MagnetoPulse Ltd
Unit 5, Poole House, Pool Street, Bodmin, Cornwall
PL31 2HA

ManeLine, Inc.
PO Box 887, Oxford, OX3 8YL
Supplier of the ManMaster™ Comb

Heather Moffett
East Leigh Farm, Harberton, Totnes, Devon TQ9 7SS

Prolite
The Saddlery, Fryers Road, Bloxwich, Walsall, West
Midlands W23 2XJ

Proteq
Graingers, West Ashling, Chichester, Sussex
PO18 8DN

Roe Richardson Ltd
Old Forge Yard, Swanley Village, Kent BR8 7NF
Reactorpanel saddles

Monty Roberts and Kelly Marks
'Intelligent Horsemanship'
PO Box 2035, Marlborough, Wilts SN8 2TL

Shires Equestrian Products
15 Southern Avenue, Leominster, Herefordshire
HR6 0QF

Thorowgood Ltd
The Saddlery, Fryers Road, Bloxwich, Walsall, West
Midlands W23 2XJ

Tirus Equestrian Products
PO Box 440, Norwich, Norfolk NR4 7EP

USA

Saddle Right™ Inc.
PO Box 42579, Las Vegas, Nevada 89116–0579

Mr Frank Wipfli
Western Saddlery Inc.
PO Box 11206, Pleasanton, CA 94588
Supplier of the American Spirit Bridle

Wheeler Enterprises Inc
Route 2, Box 26A, Ellendale, MN 56026
Manufacturer and distributor of The Stableizer®

INDEX

INDEX

ACKNOWLEDGEMENTS

The author and publishers would like to thank the following people for supplying photographs for this book:

Kit Houghton, pp2, 7, 8, 9top, 10, 11, 21, 26, 30, 32btm, 35, 46rt, 49, 50btm, 51, 52, 53rt, 59, 62top, 63, 66, 68, 69, 70, 72, 73, 74, 84, 86, 87btm, 90, 96, 97btm, 98, 101, 102, 106, 107, 108btm left&rt, 109, 112, 114, 124, 125, 128, 130, 131, 133, 134, 138top, 140, 141top, 142, 143top, 144, 146, 147, 152, 158, 169, 185

Sotheby's pp6&29top (*The Great Stallion, The Byerley Turk, Held By a Groom,* (1731) John Wootton; p29btm (*Over the Sticks,* George Wright); p31 (*Lord Newport with his Favourite Hunter, Rowton, 1862* by Sir Francis Grant and Claude Lorraine Ferneley; p56 (*Riders in an Extensive Landscape* by Alfred de Dreux)

Heather Moffett, pp12, 42btm, 43(all Iain Burns), 47(courtesy *Your Horse* magazine) (from her book *Enlightened Equitation* publ. by David & Charles)

Author's collection, pp27, 54, 55, 61, 77, 99, 170

Riding magazine, pp28, 171, 176, 177

Balance International, pp37, 38, 39, 44, 110

The Side Saddle Association, pp57, 58

Your Horse magazine/Angus Murray, pp62btm, 136

Robert Harding Picture Library/Ferrero-Labat, p92

Allsport, p96btm

P. Bertrand, p105top

Mary Evans Picture Library, p129 (by Frederic Remington published in the *Century* magazine)

Horse magazine, p135

Bob Langrish, p143btm

Artworks by:

Sally Alexander pp34, 35, 83, 85, 89, 93left, 94rt, 95, 97, 99, 100, 105, 110, 111, 112, 113left, 115, 116, 117top, 121, 122top, 123, 124, 126, 127, 130, 138, 141, 160, 161, 162, 163, 167, 168top, 172, 174

Paul Bale/Visual Image pp19, 145

Dianne Breeze pp42, 86, 93btm rt, 94left, 113rt, 117btm, 118, 119, 120, 122btm, 125, 137top, 154, 155, 166, 168btm, 178, 179, 184, 186left

Samatha Elmhurst pp12, 13, 14, 15, 16, 17, 18, 20, 22, 23, 24, 25, 65 (based on an illustration which first appeared in *Your Horse* magazine), 159, 181

The author and publishers are grateful to Maureen James at The Side Saddle Association for providing additional information in the section on the side saddle.

Thanks to Jane Holderness-Roddam who assisted with some of the photography and to Ross Millar, and his mount, who modelled with great patience on the same session.

A number of suppliers kindly leant photographs of their products. Contact addresses are given on pp187–8.

Fieldhouse Riding Equipment, pp33, 45btm, 46left, 50top

Thorowgood Ltd, pp40, 41

A. J. Fosters, pp48, 88

Frank Baines Saddlery, p53left

Roe Richardson Ltd, p75

First Thought (Equine) Ltd, p76

Pliance, p78

Saddle Right, p79

Proteq, p80top

Prolite, pp80btm, 81top&ctre

Aerborn® Equestrian Ltd, p81btm, p82

Sprenger, p97top&ctre, 93top, 94top, ctre &btm rt, 97ctre left, 103, 104

Shires Equestrian Products, pp108top, 126rt, 150btm, 157, 164

E. Jeffries and Sons Ltd, pp111btm, 132btm left

Tirus Equestrian Products, p132top

Day Son & Hewitt, pp132btm rt, 148top

Kelly Marks, pp135(courtesy *Horse* magazine), 139(courtesy *Horse & Rider* magazine)

Wheeler Enterprises, p137btn

Juliet Issacs, p138btm rt

Goldson Horseware, pp150top, 151top

Bucas, p151btm

MagnetoPulse Ltd, p153

CAM EQUESTRIAN, pp179top&ctre, 180, 181top, 182, 183, 184top, 186top rt

ManeLine, Inc., p186btm rt